THE VIRGINIA GUN OWNER'S Guide

Who
can bear arms?

❖

Where
are guns forbidden?

❖

When
can you shoot to kill?

by *Alan K*
and *Steve M*

illustrations by Gregg Myers and Ralph Richardson

BLOOMFIELD PRESS
Phoenix, Arizona

Copyright © 1996 Alan Korwin
All rights reserved

BLOOMFIELD PRESS

12629 N. Tatum #440
Phoenix, AZ 85032
(602) 996-4020 Offices
1-800-707-4020 Order Hotline
www.bloomfieldpress.com

ISBN: 0-9621958-7-1
Library of Congress Catalog Card Number: 96-86264

ATTENTION

Firearms Training Instructors, Clubs, Organizations,
Educators and all other interested parties:
Call us for information on quantity discounts!

To Order: For single copies or for wholesale shipments, call 1-800-707-4020, or write to us at the address above.

FOR UPDATES: Send us a self-addressed stamped envelope.

Every gun owner needs this book—
"It doesn't make sense to own a gun and not know the rules."

Printed and bound in the United States of America
at Griffin Printing of Sacramento, Calif.

10 9 8 7 6 5 4 3 2 1

TABLE OF CONTENTS

ACKNOWLEDGMENTS

This book is very much a result of the help we received, great and small, from the good people who provided their thoughts, answered our endless questions, and shared resources with us. Thank you.

Leon App, Conservation and Development Program Supervisor
Dept. of Conservation and Recreation

Ray Cahen, Legislative Director, Virginia Shooting Sports Association

Darrell Carden, Vice Commodore, Hopewell Yacht Club

Lucien J. Charette, Executive Director,
Virginia Shooting Sports Association

Barton Cooley, Mayor, Hillsville, Virginia

Harper Corder, Special Agent, United States Forest Service

Col. William Deneke, Founder, Virginia Shooting Sports Association

Thomas W. Evans

James J. Fotis, Executive Director,
Law Enforcement Alliance of America

Jeff Freeman, Virginia Legislative Liaison
National Rifle Association

Dennis Fusaro, Director, Gun Owners of America

Richard E. Gardiner, Attorney at Law

Fred Griisser

Charly Gullett, Author

Stephen P. Halbrook, Ph.D., Attorney at Law

Larry Hart, Virginia Dept. of Game and Inland Fisheries

Rich Jefferson, Coordinator of External Affairs and Marketing,
Virginia Dept. of Game and Inland Fisheries

Bruce Jones, Virginia Wildlife Federation

Cheryl and Tyler Brittany Korwin

Georgene Lockwood, Author

Larry Malinish

Leslie and Steven Blaise Maniscalco

Ted McCormack, Assistant Director, Commission on Local Gov't.

Tanya Metaksa, Executive Director, Institute for Legislative Action, National Rifle Association

Paul Moog, President, Northern Virginia Civilian Defense League

Major Justin B. Murphy, Staff Duty Officer, Fairfax County Police

Mark H. Overstreet, Researcher, National Rifle Association

Ernie Padgett, President, Virginia Shooting Sports Association

The Pensus Group, including Richard Shaw, Chris Shaw, David Maule-ffinch and Terrence Plas

Ron Pike

Erich M. Pratt, Director, Gun Owners of America

Larry Pratt, Executive Director, Gun Owners of America

Robert Saunders, Jr., Harbormaster of the City of Hopewell

Jim Snyder, Membership Director, Northern Virginia Civilian Defense League

Donna Tate, Office Manager, Virginia State Police

Easter Thompson, Vice President, Public Relations STG Marketing Communications, Inc.

Capt. R. Lewis Vass, Records Management Officer, Virginia State Police

Jeannie Whitehurst, Library Information Specialist, Virginia Beach Wahab Public Law Library

M.H. Wilkinson, Director, Commission on Local Gov't.

Gary R. Wright, Director of Administration, City of Norfolk Circuit Court

We found the Virginia State Police to be cooperative and professional during the research stages of this book, and we were impressed with their diligence in implementing the various elements of Virginia gun law.

The Dept. of Game and Inland Fisheries is a wonderful resource for the state and their cooperation in the development of this book is much appreciated.

The National Rifle Association Institute allowed the use of material in their pamphlet, "Your State Firearms Laws."

PREFACE

Virginia has strict gun laws. You have to obey the laws. There are serious penalties for breaking the rules.

Many gun owners don't know all the rules. Some have the wrong idea of what the rules are. It doesn't make sense to own a gun and not know the rules.

Here at last is a comprehensive book, in plain English, about the laws and regulations which control firearms in Virginia.

This book is published under the full protection of the
First Amendment with the expressed understanding that you,
not we, are completely responsible for your own actions.

The One-Glaring-Error theory says there's at least
one glaring error hidden in any complex piece of work.
This book is no different. Watch out for it.

FOREWORD • WARNING! • DON'T MISS THIS!

This book is not a substitute for the law. You are fully accountable under the exact wording and current interpretations of all applicable laws and regulations when you deal with firearms under any circumstances.

Many people find laws hard to understand, and gathering all the relevant ones is a lot of work. This book helps you with these chores. Collected in one volume are the principal state laws controlling gun use in Virginia.

In addition, the laws and other regulations are expressed in regular conversational terms for your convenience, and cross-referenced to the statutes. While great care has been taken to accomplish this with a high degree of accuracy, **no guarantee of accuracy is expressed or implied, and the explanatory sections of this book are not to be considered as legal advice or a restatement of law.** In explaining the general meanings of the laws, using plain English, differences inevitably arise, so **you must always check the actual laws.** The authors and publisher expressly disclaim any liability whatsoever arising out of reliance on information found in this book. New laws and regulations may be enacted at any time by the authorities. **The authors and publisher make no representation that this book includes all requirements and prohibitions which may exist. This book covers state laws—local laws are not covered.**

This book concerns the gun laws as they apply to law-abiding private residents in the state of Virginia only. It is not intended to and does not describe most situations relating to licensed gun dealers, museums or educational institutions, local or federal military personnel, American Indians, foreign nationals, the police or other peace officers, any person summoned by a peace officer to help in the performance of official duties, persons with special licenses (including collectors), non-residents, persons with special permits or authorizations, bequests or intestate succession, anyone under indictment, felons, prisoners, escapees, dangerous or repetitive offenders, criminal street gang members, delinquent, incorrigible or unsupervised juveniles, government employees, or any other people restricted or prohibited from firearm possession.

While this book discusses possible criminal consequences of improper gun use, it avoids most issues related to deliberate gun crimes. This means that certain laws are excluded, or not explained in the text. Some examples are: criminally negligent homicide and capital murder; manslaughter; concealment of stolen firearms; enhanced penalties for commission of crimes with firearms, including armed robbery, burglary, theft, kidnapping, drug offenses and assault; smuggling firearms into public aircraft; taking a weapon from a peace officer; possession of contraband; possession of a firearm in a prison by a prisoner; false application for a firearm; removal of a body after a shooting; drive by shootings; and this is only a partial list.

The main relevant parts of Virginia state laws which relate to private gun ownership and use are reproduced in Appendix D. These are formally known as *Code of Virginia*. Other state laws which may apply, such as Hunting Laws and official agency regulations, are discussed, but these laws are *not* reproduced. Key federal laws are discussed, but the laws themselves are *not* reproduced. Case law decisions, which affect the interpretation of the statutes, are generally *not* included.

FIREARMS LAWS ARE SUBJECT TO CHANGE WITHOUT NOTICE. You are strongly urged to consult with a qualified attorney and local authorities to determine the current status and applicability of the law to specific situations which you may encounter. The proper authorities are in Appendix C.

Guns are serious business and require the highest level of responsibility from you. **What the law says and what the authorities and courts do aren't always an exact match.** You must remember that each legal case is different and frequently lacks prior court precedents. A decision to prosecute a case and the charges brought may involve a degree of discretion from the authorities involved. Sometimes, there just isn't a plain, clear-cut answer you can rely upon. **ALWAYS ERR ON THE SIDE OF SAFETY.**

Note to this Historic First Edition

Never before have Virginia's gun laws been released in a single edition. As the earliest existing compiled copy of state gun laws this is guaranteed to age from the moment of its release. When future generations look back at this first edition, it will represent "the way things used to be," as it seems quite likely that new laws and court cases will change the landscape in time to come.

That will make this edition quite a conversation piece and perhaps of collectible value, but it also brings out a dilemma you should not ignore. The accuracy of this book will diminish with time, and the historical value of its contents is not a substitute for current information about gun laws.

Keep in mind that first editions, by their very nature, may have errors which are only detected after their initial release. It is the book's readers who will eventually fine tune the contents, and we encourage you to notify us about anything you feel is inaccurate, incomplete or in need of attention in any way. Despite all our efforts at completeness and accuracy, we recognize that we aren't perfect and that corrections may be needed. You must recognize this too.

> **This book will be updated periodically, and news about updates is available from the publisher, Bloomfield Press.** You are invited to send us an old-fashioned stamped self-addressed envelope which we will fill and return when news of updates is available.
>
> If you believe you have found an error or item needing adjustment, notify the publisher. A free copy of this book will be provided to any reader whose comments are used in the next edition.

Special Note on Pending Legislation

Bills have been proposed by law makers nationally who would:
- Outlaw specific or classes of firearms by name, by operating characteristics, or by appearance
- Restrict the amount of ammunition a gun can hold and the devices for feeding ammunition
- Restrict the number of firearms and the amount of ammunition a citizen may buy or own
- Require proficiency testing and periodic licensing
- Register firearms and owners nationally
- Use taxes to limit firearm and ammunition ownership
- Create new liabilities for firearm owners, manufacturers, dealers, parents and persons involved in firearms accidents
- Outlaw keeping firearms loaded or not locked away
- Censor classified ads for firearms and eliminate firearms publications and outlaw any dangerous speech or publication
- Melt down firearms that are confiscated by police
- Prohibit gun shows and abolish hunting
- Deny or criminalize civil rights for government-promised security
- Repeal the Second Amendment to the Constitution

In contrast, less attention has been paid to laws that would:
- Mandate school-based safety training
- Provide general self-defense awareness and training
- Encourage personal responsibility in resisting crime
- Protect citizens who stand up and act against crime
- Guarantee citizens' right to travel legally armed for personal safety
- Fix the conditions which generate hard-core criminals
- Assure sentencing of serious criminals, increase the percentage of sentences actually served, provide more prison space and permanently remove habitual criminals from society
- Improve rehabilitation and reduce repeat offenses
- Reduce plea bargaining and parole abuses
- Close legal loopholes and reform criminal justice malpractice
- Reform the juvenile justice system
- Improve law enforcement quality and efficiency
- Establish and strengthen victims' rights and protection
- Hold the rights of all American citizens in unassailable esteem
- Provide for the common defense and buttress the Constitution

Some experts have noted that easy-to-enact but ineffectual "feel good" laws are sometimes pursued instead of the much tougher course of laws and social changes that would reduce crime and its root causes. Many laws aim at disarming citizens while ignoring the fact that gun possession by criminals is already strictly illegal and largely unenforced. Increasing attacks on the Constitution and civil liberties are threatening freedoms Americans have always had. You are advised to become aware of any new laws which may be enacted. Contact your legislators to express your views on proposed legislation.

To our children
and the potential they hold for the future

THE RIGHT TO BEAR ARMS 1

In the United States of America, people have always had the right to bear arms. The Second Amendment to the United States Constitution is the historic foundation of this right to have and use guns. The Second Amendment is entitled The Right To Keep And Bear Arms. This is what it says:

> "A well regulated Militia, being necessary to the security of a free State, the right of the people to keep and bear Arms, shall not be infringed."

The intentions of the revolutionaries who drafted the Constitution were clear at the time. It was this right to bear arms that allowed those citizens 200 years ago to break away from British rule. An armed populace was a precondition for independence and freedom from oppressive government. The founders of the United States of America were unambiguous and unequivocal in their intent:

No free man shall be debarred the use of arms.
–Thomas Jefferson

The Constitution shall never be construed to authorize Congress to prevent the people of the United States, who are peaceable citizens, from keeping their own arms.
–Samuel Adams

Little more can reasonably be aimed at with respect to the people at large than to have them properly armed.
–Alexander Hamilton

Americans have the right and advantage of being armed.
–James Madison

> The great object is that every man be armed.
> Everyone who is able may have a gun.
> **–Patrick Henry**

Today the issue is controversial and emotionally charged. There are powerful and vocal groups on all sides of the topic of guns. Some people have taken to saying that the Second Amendment doesn't mean what it always used to mean, and there have been calls to repeal it. The Supreme Court has been mostly quiet on the subject, and its few pronouncements have been used to support all sides of the debate. Importantly, all 50 states recognize a citizen's right to act in self defense, completely apart from firearms debates.

Nothing in Virginia law may conflict with our fundamental creed, the U.S. Constitution, and so the right to bear arms is passed down to Virginians, as it is to the citizens of all the states in the union. The states, however, have passed laws to organize and control the arms which people bear within their borders. That's what this book is about.

In addition to the Second Amendment to the U.S. Constitution, the Constitution of the Commonwealth of Virginia reaffirms the right of its citizens to bear arms to protect themselves:

Virginia State Constitution

Article 1, Section 13

MILITIA; STANDING ARMIES; MILITARY SUBORDINATE TO CIVIL POWER.

That a well regulated militia, composed of the body of the people, trained to arms, is the proper, natural, and safe defense of a free state, therefore, the right of the people to keep and bear arms shall not be infringed; that standing armies, in time of peace, should be avoided as dangerous to liberty; and that in all cases the military should be under strict subordination to, and governed by, the civil power.

Introduction to the State Gun Laws

The majority of Virginia's "gun laws" can be found in a book called *Title 18.2, Crimes and Offenses Generally*, of the *Code of Virginia*. The official complete *Code of Virginia* is contained in a set of hardcover books approximately four feet across, published by the Michie Company in Charlottesville, Va. (800) 562-1197. Sets of the state law are widely available in libraries. Westlaw has a CD of state law available, but since they are not the official publishers, it lacks valuable annotations and notes.

In addition to Title 18.2, Virginia has gun laws in at least 16 other titles of the state code, including:

Alcoholic Beverage Control Code, Title 4.1
Commissions, Boards and Institutions Generally, Title 9
Counties, Cities and Towns, Title 15.1
Courts Not of Record, Title 16.1
Courts of Record, Title 17
Criminal Procedure, Title 19.2
Education, Title 22.1
Game, Inland Fisheries and Boating, Title 29.1
Institutions for the Mentally Ill, Title 37.1
Military and Emergency Laws, Title 44
Motor Vehicles, Title 46
Police (State), Title 52
Prisons and Other Methods of Correction; Title 53.1
Professions and Occupations, Title 54.1
Property and Conveyances, Title 55
Trade and Commerce, Title 59.1

You'll find the main relevant sections of all these laws printed in *The Virginia Gun Owner's Guide* in Appendix D. Many of the fine details concerning guns come from other sources, listed in Appendix C. In addition, "the law" includes many things that are not statutes passed by the legislature, and may not be covered in detail in this book, including court decisions, official regulations, common law, civil law, policies and more.

The state of Virginia has a *rule of preemption* about gun laws, in §15.1-29.15 of the state code. This prohibits local authorities from passing laws that aren't specifically allowed by state law. Power is delegated only to the state to regulate firearms, in the hope of providing uniform rules statewide, in theory at least.

However, the preemption law went into effect on January 1, 1987. Local ordinances passed *before* this date are unaffected and may be in effect where you live. Many state statutes grant certain gun-legislating power to counties and even cities, which may have their own gun laws in place. It is a difficult situation for Virginians who wish to legally bear arms, especially if they travel within the state. An act that is perfectly legal at home may be a crime a few blocks away, a different crime down the road, and then legal again as you travel further.

It is important to note that *The Virginia Gun Owner's Guide* deals primarily with laws at the state and federal levels, and not laws at the local level. For a few interesting examples of local ordinances see Chapter 4. To learn if there are laws in effect that relate to your community, you must contact the proper authorities and read any local ordinances that may exist. For a list of phone numbers and addresses for many of these authorities see Appendix C. Getting local authorities to provide copies of their local gun laws may be tougher than it sounds.

A Word About Federal Law

The Virginia Gun Owner's Guide covers federal laws that are directly related to your right to keep and bear arms. This is only a small portion of all federal gun laws.

Federal law generally does not control the day-to-day details of how you can carry a firearm in any given state, or the rules for self defense and crime resistance, or where you can go for target practice. The individual states control these things. Federal law focuses on the commercial aspects, interstate transportation, certain prohibited weapons, arming the proper authorities, crimes against the nation and other specifically defined areas.

Many people think that federal laws are "higher" than state laws, or that they somehow come first. Federal and state laws control different things. The states and the feds each have control over their respective areas.

The Dreaded "§" Section Symbol:
Code of Virginia §18.2-308

The character "§" means "section." You read it aloud (or to yourself) as "section" whenever it appears. Every individually named chunk of law in America is called a section and has a section number, so you see this symbol a lot. It's an integral part of the written name for every statute on the books. A section may be just a few words or may be extremely long, and it may be amended by new laws. Code of Virginia section eighteen point two dash three-oh-eight, the law shown above, is one of the main Virginia gun laws.

The section "§" symbol intimidates many people and as such, is valuable for keeping the law mysterious and seemingly unknowable to the general public. Don't let it scare you. Just think "section" whenever you see "§." To write a section symbol, make a capital "S" on top of another capital "S."

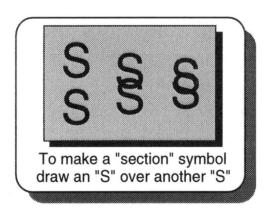

To make a "section" symbol
draw an "S" over another "S"

WHAT IS A FIREARM?

In general, §18.2-433.1 of Virginia law defines a firearm as:

"...any weapon which is designed to or may readily be converted to expel any projectile by the action of an explosive; or the frame or receiver of any such weapon."

In addition, the "brandishing" law, §18.2-282, includes pneumatic weapons and any object that looks like a gun (in essence, anything that could fool a person into thinking it is a gun) whether it can be fired or not, as firearms.

For students on school grounds, under §22.1-277.01, a starter pistol is included in the definition along with the frame or receiver of a firearm, a silencer, or any destructive device.

Antique firearms made before 1899 are not considered firearms for purposes of background checks and multiple handgun purchases (§18.2-308.2:2), but do fit the Virginia definition of a firearm for other purposes.

Guns that have been thoroughly disabled and are only for show are not regarded as guns under federal law. Questions about how to make a specific gun unserviceable can be directed to the Firearms Technology Branch of the Bureau of Alcohol, Tobacco and Firearms.

BB guns may sometimes be treated almost as if they were regular firearms by some authorities. Some types designed for hunting are quite powerful and the safest course of action is to always treat them as if they are regular firearms.

In this book, the words *gun, firearm* and *arms* are used interchangeably to refer to all handguns and long guns. When you see the terms *handgun, rifle, shotgun, long gun, semiautomatic pistol* or *semiauto,* or *revolver,* the reference is to that specific type of firearm only.

WHO CAN BEAR ARMS IN VIRGINIA?

An adult in Virginia may have a gun except:

1–A person convicted of a felony may not possess, transport or carry a firearm. This is a class 6 felony under §18.2-308.2. A convicted felon may be able to get permission to possess a gun from the circuit court with jurisdiction in which the person lives. This may be granted, sometimes for long guns only, to allow a person to hunt for food. However, removal of some or all state prohibitions may not remove the federal bans against a felon, but the state order to restore rights may be useful when working with the Bureau of Alcohol, Tobacco and Firearms in restoring federal rights.

2–Anyone serving a term of imprisonment in any correctional or detention facility may not possess firearms or ammunition. Violation is a class 6 felony, see §53.1-203.

3–A person who has been acquitted of specified crimes by reason of insanity and committed to a mental health facility may not possess or transport a firearm. Violation is a class 1 misdemeanor under §18.2-308.1:1.

4–A person who has been judged legally incompetent or mentally incapacitated may not purchase, possess or transport a firearm. A violation is a class 1 misdemeanor under §18.2-308.1:2.

5–A person who has been involuntarily committed to a mental health institution may not purchase, possess or transport a firearm. A violation is a class 1 misdemeanor under §18.2-308.1:3.

6–A person who is under a protective or restraining order may neither purchase nor transport a firearm. A violation is a class 1 misdemeanor under §18.2-308.1:4.

7–A person who has been convicted of two drug-related misdemeanors in a 3-year period may neither purchase nor transport a firearm, under §18.2-308.1:5. This inability is removed five years after the second misdemeanor if there are no further drug convictions.

8–A person under 29, who as a juvenile over 14 committed certain specified offenses that would have been felonies if the person was then an adult, may not possess or transport a firearm, or carry one concealed. Violation of this law, §18.2-308.2, is a class 6 felony.

9–Foreign nationals (aliens) may not possess, transport or carry concealed assault weapons, a class 6 felony under §18.2-308.2:01.

A court petition process exists for restoring the right to bear arms if it is lost to any of the items except number 2 above, and number 7 includes an automatic restoration of rights. The proper authorities and military forces may be exempt from some of these restrictions. See the individual statutes for specific details.

In addition, you may also be prohibited from firearm possession under federal laws designed to keep weapons out of the hands of criminals. These overriding restrictions are listed in Section 8 of the Firearms Transaction Record, Form 4473, which must be completed when you buy a gun from a federally licensed dealer. Federal law prohibits gun purchase by, or transfer to, anyone who:

- Is charged with or has been convicted of a crime which carries more than a one-year sentence (except two-year state misdemeanors);
- Is a fugitive from justice;
- Unlawfully uses or is addicted to marijuana, a depressant, a stimulant or a narcotic drug;
- Is mentally defective;
- Is mentally incompetent;
- Is committed to a mental institution;
- Has been dishonorably discharged from the armed forces;
- Has renounced U.S. citizenship;
- Is an illegal alien;
- Is under a court order restraining harassment, stalking or threatening of an intimate partner or partner's child;

- Has been convicted of a misdemeanor domestic-violence offense as described by federal law (for more on this new addition to federal law see Chapter 7).

In filling out a Firearm Transaction Record form (required for every gun purchase from a dealer) you state that you are not in any of these categories. It's a five-year felony to make false statements on a Firearms Transaction Record form, and it's illegal to knowingly provide a firearm to a prohibited possessor.

Under §18.2-308.2:1, it is a class 6 felony to transfer a handgun to a person you know has been acquitted of a crime by reason of insanity, a person under 18-years old, or to a person who has been convicted of a felony.

Landlord Rental Agreements

A landlord cannot prohibit or restrict your tenancy in any public housing for lawful possession of any firearms. Under §55-248.9, any such provision in a lease is unenforceable, and if a landlord brings suit against a tenant on such grounds the tenant may recover actual damages and attorneys fees from the landlord.

Special License Plates

Special Virginia license plates are available from the motor vehicles department, under §46.2-749.6, to supporters of the National Rifle Association. It should be noted that a resident who wishes to take advantage of transporting firearms to and from shooting ranges "unloaded and securely wrapped," as allowed by law, should be a "regularly enrolled member of a target shooting organization" under §18.2-308. The NRA qualifies as such an organization.

JUVENILES

The law sets no minimum age at which a child can have or use a firearm under adult supervision. This is a choice made by parents or legal guardians of the minor, who have a legal obligation to act in a responsible manner. Virginia prohibits anyone under the age of 18 from possessing a handgun or "assault firearm" unless accompanied by an adult, under code §18.2-308.7. Violation is a class 1 misdemeanor and a handgun used in violation must be forfeited. This does not apply in the home or on the property of the minor, the minor's parents, grandparents or legal guardian. Also exempt are minors legally hunting or enroute to hunt with an unloaded weapon, minors on someone else's property with written permission from the landowner and prior permission from a parent or guardian, and minors serving in the armed forces or national guard.

Selling or giving a handgun to a minor is a class 6 felony under §18.2-309. This does not apply to family members or for a sporting event or activity.

Toy guns that can shoot blanks or balls by means of an explosive charge are regulated under §18.2-284. It is a class 4 misdemeanor to sell, trade or give this type of toy to anyone. The law specifically exempts cap pistols from the regulation.

One of the few cases where a juvenile may be taken into immediate police custody is for possession of a weapon on school property (§16.1-246). Under §16.1-269.1, use of a firearm in a serious offense is a factor for transferring a juvenile to adult court. A juvenile can lose driving privileges or be denied a driver's license for various periods of time for certain weapon violations (§16.1-278.9). Provisions for serious juvenile offenders, which includes illegal use of firearms, are found in §16.1-285.1.

Child Safety Law
It is a class 3 misdemeanor to recklessly leave a loaded firearm unsecured and accessible to a child under 14 years of age.

It is a class 1 misdemeanor to allow a child under 12 to use a firearm except under the supervision of an adult. An adult is defined as: 1–a parent or guardian who is supervising the child, or, 2–a person over 21 years old, supervising the child with permission from the parent or guardian. See Code of Virginia §18.2-56.2 for the letter of the law.

Federal Regulation of Juveniles

Federal law generally prohibits people under 18 from having handguns or matching ammunition, or providing these to juveniles, unless they meet the following additional requirements. While carrying written consent from a parent or guardian (who must not be prohibited from possessing a firearm themselves), a minor may have a handgun:

1–in the course of employment;

2–in legitimate ranching or farming;

3–for target practice;

4–for hunting;

5–for a class in the safe and lawful use of a handgun;

6–for transport, unloaded in a locked case, directly to and from such activities.

Also excluded is a minor who uses a handgun against an intruder, at home or in another home where the minor is an invited guest. If a handgun or ammunition is legally transferred to a minor, who then commits an offense with the firearm, the firearm must be returned to its lawful owner after due process. Minors may inherit title (but not possession) of a handgun. Violation of this law carries fines and a one-year jail term.

Gun-Free School Zone Laws

Like most states, Virginia has strict prohibitions about guns and schools. For federal school zones law, see Chapter 7.

Deliberately discharging a firearm on or within 1,000 feet of school grounds is a class 4 felony, punishable by up to ten years in the state penitentiary and a $100,000 fine. See §18.2-280 for the letter of the law. This statute excludes: 1–justifiable shootings in defense of life or property; 2–lawful hunting; 3–

school-sponsored programs or 4–shooting at an established shooting range.

Merely having a gun on the premises of a public or private elementary, middle or high school is a class 6 felony under §18.2-308.1. School buses are included, as is any property used for school-sponsored functions while the function is taking place. Possession of other types of weapons such as knives, tasers, brass knuckles or blackjacks is punishable as a class 1 misdemeanor. Unloaded, cased firearms in a motor vehicle and unloaded rifles and shotguns in the firearm rack of a motor vehicle are not prohibited. Also allowed are weapons as part of a school-sanctioned program.

Under §22.1-277.01, a student who has a firearm on school property or at school sponsored activities may be expelled for one year. This statute uses an expanded definition of firearms to include the frame or receiver of a firearm, a silencer or any destructive device. Possession of a firearm as part of a school-sponsored program is allowed. Unloaded, cased firearms in a motor vehicle and unloaded rifles and shotguns in the firearm rack of a motor vehicle are also allowed.

Any county, city or town may prohibit any shooting, hunting or carrying loaded firearms while hunting, within 100 yards of a school, as a class 4 misdemeanor under §29.1-527.

Before admitting a student to a public school, the school board must require the parent or guardian to provide a sworn statement indicating whether the student has ever been expelled from a public or private school for a firearm offense. Making a false statement is a class 3 misdemeanor under §22.1-3.2. The document becomes part of the student's permanent record. In addition, the superintendent of a school division is notified by the courts when a juvenile is declared delinquent for an offense involving weapons (§16.1-305.1).

All incidents involving illegal carrying of firearms on school property must be reported to the office of the principal, under §22.1-280.1. All such reports must be submitted to the school's division superintendent. The superintendents are required to file annual firearm incident reports to the Dept. of Education.

HOW DO YOU OBTAIN FIREARMS?

Guns and ammunition may be bought or sold between private residents of this state under the same conditions as any other private sale of merchandise, provided you comply with all other laws (you can't sell prohibited weapons, or knowingly sell to prohibited possessors or to minors, the one-handgun-a-month rule applies for handguns, etc.). Temporary loan or rental of a firearm from a state resident is allowed for any lawful sporting purpose.

Sale *and delivery* of firearms by a private resident to *any non-resident* is prohibited by federal law. Such sales are allowed, but delivery must take place through licensed dealers in the two people's states—it's a violation for the non-resident to transport the firearm interstate. Additional details are found later in this chapter under *Transport and Shipping* and in *Out-of-State Purchases.*

If you are going to deal in guns (or for that matter, import, manufacture or ship firearms in interstate or foreign commerce), you need a license from the Bureau of Alcohol, Tobacco and Firearms. Federal and state authorities may exercise a degree of judgment in determining when multiple firearm sales by a private individual constitute "dealing" in firearms, which is a felony without a license. Federal regulations provide some guidance on the matter. A dealer is:

> "A person who devotes time, attention, and labor to dealing in firearms as a regular course of trade or business with the principle objective of livelihood and profit through the repetitive purchase and resale of firearms, but such a term shall not include a person who makes occasional sales, exchanges, or purchases of firearms for the enhancement of a personal collection or for a hobby, or who sells all or part of his personal collection of firearms." (CFR §178.11)

Federally licensed dealers of firearms and ammunition are spread across the state. Firearms may be paid for in the same ways as any other retail merchandise. You may sell a gun you own to any dealer in the state willing to buy it from you.

In-State Purchase

For all firearm purchases from a licensed dealer you must present government issued photo-identification that is more than 30-days old, establishing your name, address, date of birth and signature. A driver's license (or state ID card issued under §46.2-345 and §46.2-348 in place of a driver's license) is the usual form of ID expected by most dealers. Obtaining such ID under false pretenses for the purpose of obtaining firearms is a class 4 felony.

An additional second form of identification is required to establish you as a Virginia resident. Although many definitions of residency may exist, for the purpose of obtaining firearms under §18.2-308.2:2, the second ID can be a:

1–lease;

2–utility or telephone bill;

3–voter registration card;

4–bank check;

5–passport;

6–automobile registration;

7–hunting or fishing license;

8–receipt of currently paid personal property or real estate tax;

9–other document acceptable to the Dept. of Criminal Justice Services.

10–Any other form of ID acceptable by the Bureau of Alcohol, Tobacco and Firearms under ATF Rule 79-7 (allowing for a combination of documents which, when taken as a group, include the necessary detail they may lack individually).

Members of the military can establish residency by showing their military picture ID and a copy of their permanent orders.

When you buy firearms from a licensed dealer you must fill out a federal Firearms Transaction Record, form 4473. There are no duplicate copies made of this form and the original is filed by the dealer. When a dealer goes out of business, the records are sent to a federal repository. The form requires personal identification information, identification of the gun and its serial number, and your signature. By signing the form you are stating that you are not ineligible to obtain firearms under federal law. Licensed dealers keep copies of this form available.

In addition to the federal form, Virginia requires you to fill out a Virginia Firearm Transaction Record, SP-65. The Virginia form is similar to the federal form with the addition of information establishing Virginia residency and a place for indicating if you've purchased a handgun from any source in the last 30 days. A false answer is perjury, a felony, which would revoke all your rights to own, have or use firearms.

A copy of the Virginia form, without any information about the firearm purchased, is mailed to the Dept. of State Police. The State Police are prohibited from keeping the transaction record for more than 30 days but dealers are required under §54.1-4201 to keep the form for at least two years. The form is subject to local law enforcement inspection as part of a bona fide criminal investigation. In the case of multiple handgun purchases within a 30-day period, the State Police may keep the transaction record for up to 12 months.

To purchase a handgun and matching ammunition you must be at least 21 years old. Your request to purchase the handgun from a dealer is made on the SP-65 form and reported to State Police, who must conduct a criminal-history background check, required by Virginia law. A waiting period of up to fifteen days applies in some other states, but Virginia uses an instant check system, described below.

To buy a rifle or shotgun and matching ammunition you must be at least 18 years old. The Virginia instant background check, described below, is required for long guns as well as handguns. Some ammunition may be used in either a handgun or a rifle. This type of ammo can be sold to a person between the ages of 18 and 21 only if the dealer is satisfied it will be used in a rifle and not a handgun.

A standard informational notice must be posted on the premises of all licensed dealers, and a copy of the information, containing basic details on the laws governing purchase, possession and use of firearms must be made available to customers.

As long as all other laws are complied with, a non-resident may temporarily borrow or rent a firearm for any lawful sporting purposes from a dealer. A dealer must conduct a background check before the transfer, but when use is at an on-site range this is not a typical practice. You may own any number of firearms and any amount of ammunition.

Instant Background Check

Code of Virginia §52-4.4 establishes a toll-free number for conducting instant background checks. The service is available from 8 a.m. to 10 p.m. seven days a week. Dealers are required to obtain a background check before transferring any firearm to an eligible person. The request for the check must be made on the official SP-65 state form, which are serially numbered and issued in controlled batches to Virginia dealers only. A two-dollar fee for the background check is collected by the dealer and forwarded to the State Police.

The State Police are required by law to respond to background requests while the dealer is still on the phone, or by return call without delay. If it appears that the applicant has a criminal record or is otherwise ineligible, the police have until the end of the dealer's next business day to respond.

The Virginia system automatically checks six different databases to determine if you are ineligible to purchase a firearm: the National Crime Information Center (NCIC); the Virginia Central Criminal Records Exchange (CCRE); the Virginia Criminal Information Network (VCIN); the Interstate Identification Index (III); the Virginia database of mental incompetency, the protective orders database (contained in VCIN) and the Virginia calendar file on handgun purchases. Various laws require the authorities to file and to update information from these databases. For examples see Code of Virginia Title 37.1 and the Brady law. You have the right to inspect the criminal record files if you believe you are in it, and to have inaccurate information corrected, under §9-192.

If the State Police do not respond by the end of the dealer's next business day, the dealer is permitted to transfer the firearm without further delay. See Code of Virginia §18.2-308.2:2 for the letter of the law. The State Police background-check request log, containing your name as the buyer, the dealer, the date of the request and the official reference number is kept for 12 months.

If the computer system goes down the State Police must estimate the anticipated length of delay and inform the dealer. If the delay will extend past the end of the dealer's next business day then the sale may be concluded immediately.

The 30-Day Rule: Multiple Handgun Purchases

Under most circumstances, law-abiding Virginians are restricted by §18.2-308:2.2 to purchasing no more than one handgun in any 30-day period. There is no truth to the notion that Virginian's are required to purchase one handgun per month. If you want to purchase more than one handgun in any 30-day period, you must make special application to the Department of State Police who will perform an enhanced background check. This involves contacting local authorities for information that might not be reported at the state level, and any other measures the State Police deem appropriate.

Applications for multiple handgun purchases may be available at your local police or sheriff's dept. Not all local law enforcement agencies are qualified under state police regulations to provide these forms. If your local police do not have the form, the nearest state police office will. The gun dealer you are working with should know where to get the form in your area.

An application for a multiple handgun purchase lists the number and type of handguns you want to purchase and the intended use of the firearms. Typical intended uses of firearms include purchase for a collection, sporting or competitive use, and personal or business protection. When you meet the State Police requirements, a certificate valid for seven days is issued to you. You must give this certificate to the dealer at the time of purchase and the dealer keeps it on file for a minimum of two years.

Most denials for multiple handgun purchases are due to incomplete information on the request form. Of the people who have applied, 94% had valid reasons and were approved by the

State Police. If you are turned down for an incomplete application you may at any time re-apply with the information that was missing. If you are ultimately denied, you may appeal the decision by writing to the Superintendent of State Police. The appeal process requires you to prove your stated requirement for the purchase. It also requires the State Police to show proper cause for the denial.

Another exception to the one-gun-per-30-days restriction is in the case of handguns lost or stolen within 30 days of their purchase. (Replacement of other lost or stolen handguns takes place under the regular multiple-purchase routine.) In this rare case, if you feel it is "essential" to replace it, you may do so without making the special application. To do this, you must provide the gun dealer with evidence of the police report for your lost or stolen property. This is accomplished with a special Lost/Stolen Handgun Report, form SP-194, since a police criminal report is generally not releasable (some departments may allow the report itself to be used). The form is serially numbered to allow tracking and must be given over to the dealer at the time of purchase to prevent re-use. The SP-194 is submitted by the dealer to the State Police with the Virginia Firearms Transaction Record.

In addition to the Virginia regulations on multiple handgun purchases, the purchase of more than one handgun from the same dealer in a five-day period must be reported to the Bureau of Alcohol, Tobacco and Firearms and, under the Brady law, to local authorities as well, before the close of business on the day of the sale.

Out-of-State Purchases

Residents and businesses in Virginia are specifically granted permission in the state statutes, under §59.1-148.1, to buy and take delivery of long guns from licensed dealers in states adjoining Virginia. Under §59.1-148.2, licensed dealers, collectors, importers and manufacturers may sell long guns to residents of states adjoining Virginia. Such purchases must conform to the local laws of both states and federal laws. Purchase of handguns out of your home state is prohibited by federal law.

The adjoining-states language is left over from a former federal "contiguous states" rule that used to limit interstate sales to states that shared borders. That was replaced at the federal level with language allowing purchase in any state, as long as the sale involved a rifle or shotgun, took place face-to-face and, once again, if it complied with both states' laws. In such a sale, the firearm can be shipped directly to your home.

Since an out-of-state dealer cannot presently access the Virginia background check system, you may find that the system in the dealer's state, or some other procedure, will be used. Some dealers, concerned with overlapping and often conflicting state and federal gun laws, have been known to refuse sales to residents of other states.

Determining whether a Virginian meets the state's intricate eligibility requirements may be difficult without the Virginia background-check system, and only Virginia dealers can obtain the serial-numbered SP-65 forms needed for access. Law-enforcement authorities in other states presumably may gain access for official business as needed.

In any case, to purchase a firearm from an out-of-state dealer, you can always have that dealer transfer the firearm (handgun or long gun) to a Virginia dealer, from whom you can legally make the purchase and take possession with few concerns about the perplexing proprieties of interstate purchases.

Gun Shows

Gun shows are periodically sponsored by national, state and local organizations devoted to the collection, competitive use or other sporting use of firearms. Show promoters must give 30-day advance notice to the State Police before a show is held, and 72 hours before the show they must provide a list of all registered exhibitors.

The exhibitor list must be available for inspection by law-enforcement authorities during the show and a complete list must be sent to the authorities when the show concludes. The list includes the name, residence and business address of the exhibitors. Failure to comply is a class 3 misdemeanor under §54.1-4201.1.

One exemption exists to the exhibitor list requirements—it does not apply to any town that had a population of between 1,995 and 2,010 in the 1990 census. This is a roundabout way of saying Hillsville (the only one, at 2,008). Their once-a-year four-day Labor Day gun show and flea market (mostly flea market) is so large—it attracts 2,000+ dealers and 350,000 people—that the decision was made to simply exclude it.

You may buy firearms from an in-state dealer at a gun show the same as you could on their regular retail premises. Out-of-state dealers can display their wares and take orders, but cannot make deliveries to non-licensees at the show. Purchases made from an out-of-state dealer must be transferred to a licensee within this state, from the out-of-state dealer's licensed premises. Non-dealers may exhibit and sell firearms at gun shows, from their personal collection, to anyone who is not a prohibited possessor.

Transport and Shipping

You may ship and transport firearms around the country, but it's illegal to use the U.S. Postal Service to ship handguns, under one of the oldest federal firearms statutes on the books, dating from Feb. 8, 1927. (The oldest federal law still in effect—except for Constitutional provisions—appears to be a firearm forfeiture law for illegal hunting in Yellowstone National Park, passed on May 7, 1894. It's interesting to note that no federal gun laws from the country's first 128 years are still on the books. The very first federal gun laws, in the late 1700s, actually *required* gun possession.) The Post Office says to use registered mail and not identify the package as containing a firearm.

You may have a weapon shipped to a licensed dealer, manufacturer or repair shop and back. However, depending upon the reason for the shipment and the shipper being used, the weapon may have to be shipped from and back to someone with a federal firearms license. You should check with the intended recipient and you must inform the shipping agent in writing before shipping firearms or ammunition.

Any handgun purchased outside Virginia, if shipped to you in Virginia, must go from a licensed dealer where you bought it to a licensed dealer here. Many dealers in the state will act as a "receiving station" for a weapon you buy elsewhere, sometimes for a fee. Taking any gun with you from a private transfer out of state, if it's coming back to your home state, is generally prohibited by federal law.

The only times when you may directly receive an interstate shipment of a gun are: 1–the return of a gun that you sent for repairs, modification or replacement to a licensee in another state and 2–a long gun legally obtained in person from an out-of-state dealer.

Interstate Travel

Personal possession of firearms in other states is subject to the laws of each state you are in. The authorities have been known to hassle, detain or arrest people who are legally traveling with weapons, due to confusion, ignorance, personal bias and for other reasons, even when those reasons are strictly illegal.

Federal law guarantees the right to transport (not the same as carry) a gun in a private vehicle, if you are entitled to have the gun in your home state and at your destination. The gun must be unloaded and locked in the trunk, or in a locked compartment other than the glove compartment or the console, if the vehicle has no trunk. Some states have openly challenged or defied this law, creating a degree of risk for anyone transporting a firearm interstate. Carrying a firearm (armed and ready) is practically impossible unless you're willing to face misdemeanor or felony criminal charges as you pass through each state.

Article IV of the U.S. Constitution requires the states to respect the laws of all other states. In addition, the 14th Amendment to the Constitution forbids the states from denying any rights that you have as an American citizen. These fundamental requirements are unfortunately frequently ignored by some states. Your Constitutional guarantees may be little comfort when a state trooper has you spread eagled for possession of a firearm that was perfectly legal when you were at home.

The bottom line is that the civil right and historical record of law-abiding American citizens traveling with firearms for their own safety has evaporated due to laws and policies at the state level. In Virginia this is made worse by laws at the county and even city or town level.

People often have no idea what the gun laws are in any state but their own (and rarely enough that), a complete set of the relevant laws is hard to get, understanding the statutes ranges from difficult to nearly impossible, and you can be arrested for making a simple mistake.

The legal risk created by our own government for a family traveling interstate with a personal firearm may be greater than the actual risk of a criminal confrontation. Because of this, the days of traveling armed and being responsible for your own safety and protection have all but ended for people who leave their home state. The proper authorities are generally exempt from these restrictions.

Countless people have asked Bloomfield Press for a book that would cover all 50 states, to resolve the problem. This is an appealing idea, but: having such a book won't save you from arrest, as you leave one state where, say, a loaded gun in the glove box is perfectly all right (Arizona for example), to another state where such a gun counts for two crimes (loaded gun, accessible gun) as in California; the amount of labor needed for such a work is formidable to say the least; it would take time and resources on a national scale to accomplish the task; keeping the information current in such a book is a full-time job; and using a book fifty times the size of this one is, well, a joke.

The main fault with the "just write a book" fix is that it's the wrong approach. You don't fix a major national problem like this by writing a book—even though those books would be enormously valuable and ought to exist. You fix it by restoring the lost National Right to Carry, also known as the Second Amendment, to the position it always held in America until the last few decades, during which its erosion has been nearly total for interstate travelers.

Those readers who purchased this book hoping it would somehow enable or empower them to legally travel interstate with a loaded personal firearm must contact their elected representatives and begin to ask about The Lost National Right to Carry. It has quietly disappeared through incremental attrition at the local level.

Common or Contract Carriers

You may transport firearms and ammunition interstate by "common carriers" (scheduled and chartered airlines, buses, trains, ships, etc.), but you must notify them and comply with their requirements. Although federal law requires written notice from you and a signed receipt from the carrier when you pick up the firearm, verbal communication is often accepted.

Call in advance and get precise details and the names of the people you speak with—you wouldn't be the first traveler to miss a departure because of unforeseen technicalities and bureaucratic run-arounds.

For air travel, firearms must be unloaded, cased in a manner that the airline deems appropriate, and may not be possessed by or accessible to you in the "sterile" area anywhere on the gate side of the passenger security checkpoint, including on the aircraft. You may ship your firearms as baggage or you may give custody of them to the pilot, captain, conductor or operator for the duration of the trip.

Airlines must comply with firearms rules found primarily in the Code of Federal Regulations, Title 14, Sections 107 and 108, and other laws. A little-known provision of the Brady law prohibits carriers from identifying the outside of your baggage to indicate that it contains a firearm, a prime cause for theft in the past.

LOSS OF RIGHTS

The right to bear arms is not absolute. Gun control—in the true sense—means disarming criminals and is a good idea, a point on which everyone but the criminals agree. The list of people who may not bear arms at all appears earlier in this chapter. A person whose rights are whole may lose those rights, mainly for conviction of a felony.

Forfeiture of Rights

Your right to bear arms can be lost. Conviction of any felony removes your civil right to bear firearms under state and federal law. The right to bear arms is forbidden to anyone who is or becomes a prohibited possessor under federal law, as described earlier, or as defined under Code of Virginia §18.2-308.2. Recklessly handling a firearm while hunting can revoke your right to hunt with a firearm from one year to life under §18.2-56.1. A felon may possess a firearm only after petitioning the circuit court, in the district in which that person lives, for permission, and by overcoming any federal disability that may also exist. The state court uses its discretion to grant the petition or not.

Seizure and Forfeiture of Weapons

The authorities can take your weapons if they have just cause. Firearms may be seized by a peace officer during an arrest. A search warrant can be issued (§19.2-53) under which weapons may be seized, a warrant for machine guns can be issued under §18.2-296, and a warrant for sawed-off shotguns and sawed-off rifles can be issued per §18.2-306. Any firearm used in a crime, upon conviction, is forfeited to the Commonwealth (§18.2-310). A court can order a forfeited weapon destroyed, sold to a licensed dealer, turned over to the state for use by the law enforcement agency that seized it, or disposed of by court order. See §18.2-310 and §19.2-386.11 for the letter of the law.

If you had no knowledge of events that lead to the seizure, the weapon must be returned to you after due process (in other words, if someone used your firearm without your knowledge). You may petition the court for the return of your personal property provided: 1–you are not otherwise prohibited from possessing the weapon and 2–it is not a prohibited weapon.

All firearms seized, forfeited, found or otherwise held by the State Police and believed to be involved in a crime are tracked through the Dept. of State Police Criminal Firearms Clearinghouse (see §52-25.1). The information kept includes details on the firearm, how it was obtained, the person from whom it was taken if any, the original place of sale and all subsequent owners if known, and the current disposition of the firearm.

Certain weapons are contraband (or contraband if unregistered) and are subject to seizure by the authorities. Included are stolen weapons, unregistered weapons identified under the National Firearms Act (see Chapter 3), Striker-12 or similar shotguns, defaced weapons and prohibited weapons under state law.

Personal property, including firearms and ammunition, may be seized by the Bureau of Alcohol, Tobacco and Firearms when used or intended to be used or involved in violation of any U.S. laws which ATF agents are empowered to enforce. Acquittal or dismissal of charges allows you to regain any confiscated property, but this may be more difficult than it sounds.

Many state laws specifically require that firearms be seized, forfeited, turned over to the authorities or destroyed if they are involved in a violation.

Grounds for Forfeiture

§4.1-318	While involved in and within 100 yards of illegal alcohol manufacture, transport or sale.
§4.1-336	In the immediate vicinity of an illegal alcohol manufacturing operation, with proceeds from the sale of any forfeited firearms going to the Literary Fund.
§15.1-133.01:1	Firearms unclaimed after more than 60 days
§18.2-283.1	Illegal possession of a weapon in a courthouse

§18.2-295	Failure to show state papers for a machine gun to law enforcement on request
§18.2-308	Any weapon carried illegally concealed
§18.2-308.1	Any weapon illegally on school grounds
§18.2-308.1:1	Possession or transportation by any person who has been acquitted of a crime by reason of insanity
§18.2-308.1:2	Possession or transportation by a person judged mentally incompetent or incapacitated
§18.2-308.1:3	Possession or transportation by a person involuntarily committed to a mental institution
§18.2-308.1:4	Purchase or transportation by a person under a restraining or protective order
§18.2-308.1:5	Purchase or transportation by a person convicted of two specified misdemeanor drug offenses in a specified time period, with the disability automatically lifted after five years
§18.2-308.2	Possession, transportation or carry by certain former juvenile offenders or convicted felons
§18.2-308.2:01	Certain firearms possessed, transported or carried by foreign nationals (aliens)
§18.2-308.2:1	Firearms possessed with the intention of providing them to prohibited possessors
§18.2-308.5	Firearms with less than 3.7 ounces of metal
§18.2-308.7	Handguns or certain other weapons possessed by juveniles
§29.1-208	Firearms seized related to hunting violations
§29.1-521.2	Firearms fired in or across a road while hunting
§29.1-524	Firearms used for hunting deer after dark
§29.1-549	Firearms used for hunting deer from a water craft
§29.1-556	Hunting with any weapon not specifically permitted by law
§52-25.1	Sets up a clearinghouse for forfeited guns

Restoration of Rights

A person with a truly compelling reason, and sufficient time, money and luck, can conceivably pursue a relief from federal firearms prohibition through the federal courts. Successful examples of this are exceedingly rare.

Federal law (18 USC §925) also provides a method for restoring a person's right to bear arms if it has been lost. This has been useful to some citizens who are responsible community members and whose restrictions were based on decades-old convictions of youth, or other circumstances that pose little threat. The Treasury Dept., responsible for implementing this law, has claimed for several years that they have no budget with which to accomplish this work, and the restoration of rights process has effectively ground to a halt for anyone whose disability is based on federal charges.

However, BATF has reportedly recognized the restoration of firearms rights to individuals in Virginia, if the state has already granted a complete restoration of civil rights to the person, and the disability was based solely upon a prior state-level restriction.

WHAT DOES IT ALL MEAN?

Virginia law divides crimes into two categories to help match the punishment to the crime. Felonies are extremely serious; misdemeanors are less serious.

Felonies are divided into *classes* (see Code of Virginia §18.2-10), starting with the most serious, Class 1, through Class 6. Generally, a felony conviction revokes your civil rights, including your right to bear arms, to hold public office and your right to vote, and may include limits on your right to travel, associate with designated people and other conditions at court discretion.

Misdemeanors are also grouped into classes (see §18.2-11). Class 1 is the most serious charge, diminishing in severity to Class 4.

Punishments are matched to the seriousness of the crime. This runs from a Class 1 felony, which can be punishable by death or life imprisonment, to a Class 4 misdemeanor, which carries a fine of under $250 and no jail sentence. See the Crime and Punishment Chart in Appendix B for the basic penalties for each type of crime.

WHAT DO YOU NEED TO GET A FIREARM FROM A FEDERALLY LICENSED DEALER?

- You must be at least 18 years old for a long gun, 21 years old for a handgun, and not be a "prohibited possessor" under state or federal law;

- You need a government-issued photo ID which establishes your name, address, date of birth and signature, and was issued at least 30 days previously. You need a second ID to verify your place of residence;

- You must file forms with the dealer and pass an instant background check for any disqualifying factors before taking delivery of a firearm;

- If the firearm is a handgun you may not buy it within 30 days of your last handgun purchase if any (a few exceptions exist);

- If you are in a county with a population exceeding 1,000 people per square mile (apparently includes only Arlington and Fairfax) you need prior permission at the discretion of the chief of police of the county;

- And if you are not a Virginia resident:

  –It must be legal to have the weapon in your home state, and the transaction must comply with your state's laws;

  –The State Police have up to 10 days to conduct the background check if the request is made by mail (same for a resident but virtually all requests are now made under the instant phone system);

  –You may take possession of a long gun over the counter if you could in your home state;

  –You may not purchase a handgun out of your home state (federal law) but you may have a licensed dealer ship a handgun to your home state for purchase there, if dealers in both states are willing to arrange such a transaction;

- You must be able to pay for your purchase.

CARRYING FIREARMS 2

Open Carry

Virginians generally have the right to bear arms openly. Unless special conditions apply (and there are quite a few, discussed in this chapter and Chapter 4), it is generally legal to carry a loaded or unloaded gun if it is not concealed from plain sight.

Certain cities or counties may have laws that severely restrict carrying firearms in public. The city of Chesapeake is an example where it is generally illegal to carry a loaded firearm on any city street or property. The maximum fine is $100. Virginians must know their local laws, in addition to the state laws covered in *The Virginia Gun Owner's Guide*, in order to avoid violating any firearms requirements.

Concealed Weapons

Carrying a concealed firearm (or any other concealed weapon) on yourself without a state-issued permit is generally illegal in Virginia. The law here makes no distinction between loaded or unloaded firearms. See §18.2-308 for the letter of the law. A first offense is a class 1 misdemeanor, a second offense is a class 6 felony. The third and all subsequent offenses are class 5 felonies.

A weapon is considered concealed when it is "hidden from common observation," or when it is disguised to prevent it from being recognized as a weapon. For the concealed weapon to be a violation of the law, the weapon must also be "about your person," which means near enough to be readily accessible, and is a condition that may be open to a degree of interpretation. If you are arrested for a minor infraction you can be strip searched if the authorities believe you have a concealed weapon (§19.2-59.1).

Court cases have reached decisions that indicate it is illegal to carry in a handbag (Schaff 1979), in a gym bag (Hall 1990), under a car floormat (Watson 1993), in a car console (Leith 1994), and in a pocket covered by a duffel bag (Main 1995).

A person may carry a concealed weapon without a permit under the following circumstances:

1–In your own home or the courtyard surrounding your home (technically known as *curtilage*) if any;

2–When a regular member of a target shooting club is transporting a weapon to or from an established shooting range, if the weapon is unloaded and securely wrapped;

3–When a regular member of a collector's club is transporting a weapon to a bona fide weapons exhibition, if the weapon is unloaded and securely wrapped;

4–When carrying a firearm between your abode and a place of purchase or repair, if the weapon is unloaded and securely wrapped;

5–When engaged in lawful hunting under weather conditions that make temporary protection of the weapon necessary.

A firearm contained in a case designed for firearms will generally satisfy the requirement for *securely wrapped*. By requiring club membership for the carry privileges in state law, the state of Virginia encourages its law-abiding citizens to join organizations where training is readily available.

The *securely wrapped* language is a remnant from the Uniform Pistol and Revolver Act promoted by the American Bar Association and others after WWI. At the time there were no high-tech polymer cases that came with firearms. A merchant would simply wrap your new firearm in brown paper and secure it with a string. This was considered a proper and normal way to transport a firearm, and the language simply stuck.

In addition, State Police officers honorably retired after at least 15 years of service may carry concealed, while carrying written proof of need, issued by the Superintendent of State Police. Other state-law exceptions include U.S. mail carriers, prison guards, conservators of the peace (with a few exceptions), employees of the Dept. of Corrections, law enforcement agents of the armed forces or Naval Criminal Investigative Service, federal agents, and the Harbormaster of the City of Hopewell (one of four original east coast ports, where jurisdiction over international arrivals may fall outside regular police domain; it is believed to also include city marina property operated by the private Hopewell Yacht Club; the authority is rarely exercised).

Guns In Cars

The same rules that apply to carrying a handgun on yourself apply to carrying a handgun in a car. If no attempt is made to conceal the handgun you can have it in your car with few restrictions (mostly related to where you drive to, including schools and other areas that may be restricted). A loaded handgun resting on the seat next to you or on your dashboard is legal, as long as the firearm is not "hidden from common observation." To have a loaded handgun (or unloaded for that matter) hidden from plain sight you must have a concealed-carry permit, described in Chapter 2 and §18.2-308.

A securely wrapped and unloaded firearm may be carried in a car under the same conditions as it may be carried on your person, as described above (club members to ranges or exhibits, or between your abode and a place of purchase or repair). To avoid any confusion about how securely wrapped a firearm may be, always use quality cases designed for firearms.

Federal law guarantees all citizens the right to transport a firearm unloaded in the trunk of a car, as long as it is legal where you start and at your destination. Chapter 7 has details.

A common question regarding firearms in cars is whether or not you can carry a loaded handgun in your glove compartment without a permit. The short answer is no. The police generally consider a handgun in your glove compartment to be "about your person" (readily accessible) and "hidden from common observation" (concealed). This leaves you subject to arrest, though no specific court case or statute is definitive on the subject. See §18.2-308 for the letter of the law.

There's an irony to the concealed-weapons laws for citizens in Virginia. In one case you may have a loaded handgun in your car within arms reach and be perfectly legal. The same handgun moved further away and in a closed or even locked glove box, even if unloaded, may get you arrested. No one ever said that all the laws make sense, just that they are the laws.

Special Category Firearms

It is a class 1 misdemeanor to carry certain loaded firearms in certain places open to the public. The firearms affected by §18.2-287.4 include any:

> "semi-automatic center-fire rifle or pistol which expels a projectile by action of an explosion and is equipped at the time of the offense with a magazine which will hold more than twenty rounds of ammunition or is designed by the manufacturer to accommodate a silencer or equipped with a folding stock, or;" a

> "shotgun with a magazine which will hold more than seven rounds of the longest ammunition for which it is chambered."

This law only applies to: 1–cities with populations of 160,000 or more (includes at least Virginia Beach, Chesapeake, Norfolk and Richmond); 2–counties with an Urban-County-Executive form of government (Fairfax only) or those counties or cities surrounded by or adjacent to such a county (Arlington, Loudon and Prince William counties), or any county having a County-Manager-Form form of government (Henrico only). As always it's best to play it safe, but you can see how difficult it has become to know if you are in compliance in Virginia. It should also be noted that this law is written in a way that often confuses people into believing that carrying *any* firearm is prohibited—and with a few minor changes, the law would indeed completely outlaw carrying firearms—making it something to watch very closely.

The prohibition against carrying those loaded firearms does not apply to: 1–law-enforcement officers or licensed security guards; 2–anyone engaged in lawful hunting; or 3–recreational shooting at established ranges or shooting contests.

THE CONCEALED HANDGUN PERMIT

Carrying a concealed handgun is an awesome responsibility. The legislative battles to establish the concealed-carry permit law were long and hard-fought, and the law is not perfect. It is now up to the citizens to demonstrate intelligent use of this law, to exhibit restraint in all but the most life-threatening situations, and to work hard to make Virginia a better place to live.

Obtaining a permit to carry a concealed handgun used to involve the often arbitrary decisions of government workers, who required you to prove a need for the permit. Personal safety, crime deterrence and Constitutional guarantees were not enough. In May of 1995, §18.2-308 was amended so that any citizen who met basic standards would qualify and could receive a permit.

Where the previous law called for a discretionary *proven need*, the new law says the government *shall issue* a permit to any qualified applicant. In the first twelve months following the change in the law, approximately 40,000 concealed handgun permits were issued. The permit is valid for two years and may be renewed for additional two year periods.

A license to carry a concealed handgun in Virginia is usually referred to as a concealed-carry permit. In many parts of the country it is referred to as a permit to carry a concealed weapon, or CCW.

It is important to note that the Virginia concealed-carry permit is by law a concealed *handgun* permit. Handguns are the only weapons that can be legally carried with the permit. The following are examples of weapons specifically prohibited from concealed carry under Virginia law:

1–bowie knives;

2–switchblades;

3–ballistic knives;

4–razors;

5–slingshots;

6–spring sticks;

7–metal knuckles;

8–blackjacks;

9–nun chucka;

10–shuriken;

11–fighting chains;

12–any multi-pointed throwing discs or dart;

13–any weapon similar to those listed.

The concealed-carry permit contains your name, address, date of birth, sex, social security number, height, weight, color of hair and eyes, and your signature. It is signed by the judge issuing the permit or by the judge's clerk, and includes the issue and expiration dates. You must possess the permit at all times while carrying a concealed handgun and present it with photo-identification to any law enforcement officer when asked.

The statutory court clerk fee for handling an application is $10, your local authorities may charge up to $35 for conducting a background check, and the State Police may charge up to $5 for processing the application. You may encounter lower fees or other fees that are not required by law; these are the maximum fees established by law.

Your permit has limits:

1–You cannot carry a concealed handgun into any business or special event where alcohol is sold or served, except that the owner or event sponsor, or their employees, while on duty there, may carry if they have permits;

2–You cannot carry a concealed handgun on to private property if it is prohibited by the owner;

3–Your concealed-carry permit does not entitle you to carry a handgun in a place where handguns are prohibited by law. The permit doesn't extend your range of carry, it merely allows you to be discreet where you would otherwise have to carry openly (or unloaded and securely wrapped). See the information in *Prohibited Places* at the end of this chapter.

4–It is a class 1 misdemeanor for a permit holder to carry while intoxicated or on illegal drugs.

Although the statute says concealed carry is prohibited where alcohol is "sold or served" it appears that the intent was to restrict carry where alcohol is served, in what most people think of as bars, as opposed to convenience stores, supermarkets or other package stores. The safest course of action is to avoid carry in any place with a liquor license—ball parks, race tracks, even a "banquet" license that a block party might have—whether the liquor is sold or provided free of charge.

Qualifications for a Concealed-Carry Permit

The circuit courts are required by law to issue your concealed-carry permit if you:

1–Are a legal resident of Virginia;

2–Are at least 21 years of age;

3–Can provide proof of demonstrated competence with a handgun by any of the following means:

• Completion of any hunter education or safety course approved by the Dept. of Game and Inland Fisheries (or similar agency of any other state);

• Completion of any National Rifle Association firearms safety or training course;

• Completion of any firearms safety or training course offered to the public by a law enforcement agency, junior college, college, or private or public organization;

• Completion of any firearms safety or training course at a firearms training school using instructors certified by the NRA or the Dept. of Criminal Justice Services;

- Completion of a law-enforcement firearms safety or training course for security guards, investigators or special deputies;

- Showing evidence of experience with a firearm through participation in organized shooting competition or military service;

- Having been previously licensed to carry a firearm in Virginia, unless the license was revoked for cause; and

- Completion of any firearms safety or training course by a state-certified or NRA certified firearms instructor;

- Completion of any other training the court deems adequate.

Disqualification

The disqualifying factors for a concealed-carry permit are listed in §18.2-308. Each of the disqualifying factors also serve as cause to revoke a permit after it is issued.

1–Acquittal of a crime by reason of insanity, see §18.2-308.1:3;

2–Being deemed legally incompetent or mentally incapacitated, see §18.2-308.1:2;

3–Being involuntarily committed for mental-health reasons, see §18.2-308.1:3;

4–Being placed under a restraining or protective order, see §18.2-308.1:4.

5–Receiving mental-health or substance-abuse treatment in a residential setting within a five-year period prior to the application, see §18.2-308;

6–Having a felony conviction or pending felony charge, see §18.2-308.2;

7–Having two or more misdemeanor convictions within a three-year period prior to the application (not including traffic violations); if one of the misdemeanors is a class 1 offense denial is automatic, if not, it's at the discretion of the judge;

8–Having a stalking conviction or pending stalking charge;

9–Being dishonorably discharged from any of the Armed Forces of the United States;

10–Being addicted to or a user or distributor of illegal drugs;

11–Being a habitual drunkard, convicted of drunk driving, or convicted of public drunkenness within the last three years;

12–An alien not lawfully admitted to permanent residence in the United States;

13–Being a fugitive from justice;

14–Having been convicted of any assault, assault and battery, sexual battery, unlawful discharge of a firearm in public or from a vehicle, or brandishing a firearm in the last three years;

15–Being convicted of an offense as a juvenile, if the offense would be a felony for an adult.

A person who has been discharged from the restrictions of incompetency, involuntary commitment or an insanity acquittal must wait five years before applying for a permit.

In addition, any Sheriff, Chief of Police or Attorney for the Commonwealth can disqualify you by swearing that you are likely to use a weapon unlawfully or negligently and endanger others. The statement must be based on the official's personal knowledge or on the sworn statement of "a competent person having personal knowledge."

Concealed-Carry Permit Application

The application requires your name, address, date of birth, sex, social security number, height, weight, color of hair and eyes, signature, a list of your residences for the last five years, and must be signed by a notary or other official witness. You also must agree to be fingerprinted. Making a false statement on the application is considered perjury and is punishable as a class 5 felony.

You give the application, along with a certificate of training-course completion, to the circuit court of the city or county where you live. The court consults with local law enforcement and runs a background check through the Virginia Central Criminal Records Exchange. Unless you are disqualified, the permit must be issued within 45 days of application (a 90-day period was in effect in the first year).

Once issued, the court provides the State Police and local law enforcement agencies with a copy of the order issuing a permit to you. Your application is stored by the court for at least ten years, when it may be destroyed under §17-47.4.

Application Denials

If you are denied a permit you have a right of appeal, described in §18.2-308.L and §17-116.05:1. Appeal is made to the Court of Appeals or to any judge on the court within 30 days of the denial. The petition of appeal must include a copy of the original application and the circuit court order denying the permit. The decision of the court of appeal is final. If you appeal and win, the taxable cost of the appeal is paid by the Commonwealth.

Anyone who believes they have a criminal history record in the Central Criminal Records Exchange has a right to inspect a copy of the record (§9-192), and a process exists for getting the record changed if it is incomplete or inaccurate.

Record Keeping

When you've been officially approved as law-abiding, trained and qualified for a concealed-carry permit, the State Police put your name and description in the Virginia Criminal Information Network for access by law enforcement officials for investigative purposes. The chilling effect of being cataloged in the state crime computer, for obtaining a government-authorized permit to bear arms, has deterred many gun-owning residents from applying for the permit.

A WORD TO THE WISE

You should **expect changes** to the recently issued policies surrounding the new concealed-carry permit. Anticipate a shakedown period while everything comes up to speed, with new regs possible, and old ones adjusted, eliminated or interpreted differently. Everyone may not agree on everything, and **elements of this book will undoubtedly change**. Remember that you may face serious repercussions for what may be seemingly minor infractions. _The VIRGINIA Gun Owner's Guide is just one tool for helping you on a long road to knowledge, and the road is not perfect._ That road has many turns and pitfalls—you should not rely on a single vehicle for such a complicated route, and be extremely cautious as you travel its course. Take steps to stay current.

Bloomfield Press will be preparing **updates** periodically. To receive free news about updates send us a stamped, self-addressed envelope. The address is on page two.

PROHIBITED PLACES

In days long gone people would check their firearms before entering where guns were not allowed, such as a place of worship or a courthouse. Today, prohibited places make it necessary to leave your firearm in your car, as risky as that might be, or at home, which also carries some risk.

Some of the restrictions on possession of firearms are found in the *Code of Virginia*. Other prohibitions are found in federal statutes and regulations, agency regulations and codes, and local laws, and the list that follows may not include all of these. A concealed-carry permit does not excuse a person from these restrictions and in fact, a person legally carrying a concealed handgun by permit is under some restrictions that other people are not.

1–*Places of worship.* It is a class 4 misdemeanor to carry any dangerous weapon into a place of worship, without good cause, while a religious meeting is under way, see §18.2-283.

2–*Courthouse.* It is a class 1 misdemeanor to carry weapons or ammunition into a courthouse. Firearm frames, receivers and silencers are also prohibited, see §18.2-283.1.

3–*Schools.* It is a class 6 felony to have a firearm on any public, private or parochial elementary, middle or high school, or its grounds, or school bus, or site of any school event, unless it is either part of an activity sanctioned by the school, or if it is unloaded and properly carried in a motor vehicle, see §18.2-308.1.

4–*Where alcohol is served.* Concealed-carry permitees are prohibited from carrying a concealed firearm into any place or event where alcoholic beverages are served or sold, with an exception for the boss and employees, see §18.2-308.

5–*Private property.* Concealed-carry permitees are prohibited from carrying where forbidden by private property owners, see §18.2-308.

6–*Federal facilities.* Guns are generally prohibited in federal facilities. Knowingly having a gun or other dangerous weapon (except a pocket knife with a blade under 2-1/2 inches) in a federal facility is punishable by a fine and up to one year imprisonment. Exceptions include authorities performing their duties, possession while hunting, or possession for other lawful purpose. You cannot be convicted of this offense unless notice of the law is posted at each public entrance or if you had actual notice of the law (which, it could be argued, you now do). A federal facility is a building (or part), federally leased or owned, where federal employees regularly work.

7–*Airports.* Firearm possession is prohibited by federal law on the gate side of airport-passenger security checkpoints. You are allowed to check firearms as baggage if you do it in accordance with federal rules (see Common and Contract Carriers in Chapter 1).

8–*Military bases.* Possession of firearms on any military base is subject to control by the commanding officer.

9-*Chesapeake.* The town of Chesapeake has a municipal ordinance prohibiting loaded firearms. Other localities may also have firearm restrictions, and it is important to remember that *The Virginia Gun Owner's Guide* generally does not cover local ordinances.

10–*Certain firearms.* Certain high-capacity firearms (21-round magazine capacity or greater in a handgun or long gun, or a firearm designed by the manufacturer for a silencer or for a folding stock, or a shotgun with an eight-round or greater capacity) cannot be carried loaded in cities with more than 160,000 population, and other conditions apply, see §18.2-287.4

11–*Certain hunting grounds.* The Dept. of Game and Inland Fisheries has regulations prohibiting carrying firearms in certain hunting areas except during hunting season. The authority to prohibit other people from having firearms, except as it pertains to wildlife management, is not clear (see Chapter 6).

UPDATE

CHANGES TO THE FIRST EDITION
This update released: November 3, 1997

**The information in this pamphlet brings the first edition of
The Virginia Gun Owner's Guide (VGOG) up to date through
the close of the 1997 Virginia legislative session.**

The basic rules for gun ownership, possession and use remained the same,
but numerous subtle changes were made during the last legislature, as you
can see from the information below.

To determine which edition of the book you have, look at the bottom of the
second page. The series of backwards numbers you'll find there is known as
the *print code line*. The lowest number in that line is the edition number.
At the time of this update, there is only one edition in print; your book will
have a number "1" at the end of the line. Scheduled for 1998 release, the
second edition will have a "2," and may include changes not shown here.

VGOG Statutes affected in 1997 legislature: §15.1-29.15; §18.2-51.1;
§18.2-287.2; §29.1-301; §18.2-308; 18.2-308.2:2; §29.1-300.1; §37.1-129

**VGOG
PAGE**

32 The Dept. of State Police is not required to respond to dealer
background checks on Dec. 25th, and that day will not be counted in
determining the "dealer's next business day."

51 Unlicensed concealed carry for "the proper authorities" is expanded to
include retired local law-enforcement officers who have served at least
15 years of duty, and local and state police officers who are retired for a
service-related disability.

53 New concealed-handgun permits, and permit renewals, are valid for five
years (formerly two years).

54 Tax limits for permits: The government may not charge you more than
$50 for a total application. You may be charged up to $35.00 for the
background check, which includes fees charged by the FBI.

602-996-4020 • 1-800-707-402 • www.bloomfieldpress.com

In order to curb abuses, courts are now required to accept the same payment methods used for all other fees and penalties. The tax, called a "fee," must be accepted in one payment by the person accepting the application. The tax cannot be required until the entire application is accepted.

Serious problems with concealed carry in liquor-licensed facilities have been corrected. The restriction on carry in *any* liquor-licensed business or special event has been changed: it is illegal to carry a concealed handgun into a restaurant or club licensed to sell *and* serve alcohol for on-premises consumption. A *club* is defined as a private non-profit organization operated for a national, social, patriotic, political, athletic or similar purpose. The owner, event sponsor, or their employees may carry while on duty if they have a concealed-handgun permit.

56 Circuit Courts are required to consult with law enforcement authorities and receive a report from the Central Criminal Records Exchange in order to issue a permit; the Central Criminal Records Exchange is required to notify the court that issued your permit if you become ineligible because of any disqualifying factor.

In item 7 (disqualifying misdemeanors), the three-year period has been increased to five years.

57 No form other than the one provided by the State Police can be used for a concealed-handgun permit, making the application uniform statewide.

Fingerprinting for a concealed-handgun permit is not required by state law, though many localities took it upon themselves to make such a requirement. Now, §18.2-308 authorizes counties or cities to pass an ordinance requiring fingerprinting for a concealed-handgun permit if they wish. If fingerprints are required, you must submit them along with a physical description for use by the FBI through the Central Criminal Records Exchange.

After the record check, the State Police must return the fingerprint card to the local agency. The local agency must promptly notify you that you have 21 days to request the return of your card. Cards not claimed within 21 days must be destroyed, as a gesture to prevent the authorities from compiling records on people' who have not committed crimes. Fingerprints taken under this program may not be copied, held or used for any other purpose. It's not clear whether this state requirement is binding on federal authorities.

A concealed-handgun permit shall be issued within 45 days of the application, even if the record check is not complete. The court must revoke the permit if the record check later shows the applicant is disqualified.

58 **Reciprocity**. Virginia has joined the national movement to establish rights for its residents when they travel outside the state, and to grant rights to others who visit the state, by adopting a state-by-state reciprocal-agreement scheme. Concealed-carry permits from other

states will be valid in Virginia if: 1–There is a way to instantly verify the validity of the permit 24 hours a day; 2–Qualifications for the permit are "substantially similar to or exceed" the Virginia requirements, as determined at the discretion of the authorities; 3–The other state has entered into an agreement to grant reciprocity to people with a Virginia concealed-handgun permit.

The State Police are required to work with the Attorney General to determine if any states qualify for reciprocity. The State Police will maintain the list of states they deem qualified and make it available as part of the Virginia Criminal Information Network.

It is already well known that many states will not qualify. Studying the laws of your home state (a common permit requirement) hardly prepares you for, and is typically quite different from, the laws of any other state. In such cases the authorities will have to ignore the "substantially similar" requirement to declare matches. The "meets or exceeds" requirement sounds good but is a virtual roadblock with any state that exceeds Virginia requirements, because they would meet our terms but we would not meet theirs. Texas, for example, requires a 50-shot marksmanship test, with every shot timed, and a 175 score out of a possible 250. (Virginia has no specific shooting-test requirement).

A total of 49 "agreements" between the states would be required to allow Virginians to exercise their rights nationwide. To link all states to all other states under this plan would require 1,225 deals, but that number would be reduced by the number of states that have no government registration system for concealed-carry permit holders, eliminating them from possibly qualifying.

Federal legislation has been introduced to grant some relief, but the idea of federally "allowed" right-to-carry, for government license holders only, has a chilling effect; and unlicensed people would have no rights under such plans. The cleanest approach may be a return to the fundamental rights, nearly forgotten, that if you have a gun, you're not a criminal, and the gun isn't illegal, then that is not a crime and there are no grounds for arrest or harassment. This has been proposed as the American Historical Rights Protection Act (contact Bloomfield Press for a copy).

61 Item #4—Concealed-handgun permit holders are prohibited from carrying a concealed handgun into any club or restaurant where alcohol is sold and served for consumption on premises.

62 Item #9 (Chesapeake)—Changes have been made to the preemption statute, §15.1-29.15, to protect honest people from prosecution or conviction for transporting firearms through Chesapeake and other localities with highly restrictive laws (see below). Despite these changes, you may still be subject to arrest and have to prove your innocence at a later time. Caution is advised in such areas that do not maintain a high regard for personal rights, civil liberties and constitutional guarantees.

75 (And also on page 81) A careful analysis by Beretta Product Manager Gabriele de Plano reveals that the USAS-12 shotgun is not prohibited under Virginia law.

83 One of the more important acts of the 1997 legislative session was to strengthen the provisions of §15.1-29.15, the preemption law. While local laws may remain in place under the revised statute, such laws have had their teeth pulled. Under the new version of §15.1-29.15, a person may not be prosecuted or convicted under any local law that regulates transportation of a firearm if: 1–The person lawfully possesses the firearm and has a valid concealed-handgun permit or; 2–the person is otherwise transporting the firearm legally. In other words, the authorities only have domain over the criminals, not the honest people.

This change to the law restores your ability to legally transport a firearm in the state by eliminating various Second Amendment "infringement traps" arbitrarily set up and run by local officials. Unfortunately, the broad protection from *prosecution* or *conviction* is no guarantee that you won't be *arrested* or *detained* for violation of a local law by local law-enforcement street patrols.

120 Item #7–No license is needed for anyone aiding a disabled person who is properly licensed and hunting.

NOTES:
- Copies of the updated statutes will be printed in Edition 2 of *The Virginia Gun Owner's Guide*, or visit our website for a copy.
- It is legal to own and wear bullet-resistant garments, but wearing such during the commission of specified crimes increases the penalties.
- Other statute changes include: Extra penalty for attack of a peace officer now includes attack of a firefighter; a junior lifetime hunting license is now available; mental health reporting requirement under §37.1-129 has been repealed.
- Changed area codes in Appendix C will appear in the next edition of the book.
- Send us a stamped self addressed envelope for future news about updates.

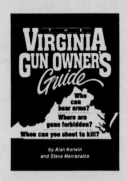
BLOOMFIELD PRESS • 12629 N. Tatum #440 • Phoenix, AZ 85032

12–*Illegal still.* It's illegal to have a firearm anywhere near you while you're involved with an illegal alcohol still or its products, see §4.1-318 & 336.

The prohibited places listed may not apply to the proper authorities in the performance of their duties—peace officers, licensed security guards and bodyguards, members of the military, prison guards, special exempt agents of the government and many more. The federal list alone includes more than 50 different statutes that exempt special people from gun laws.

HOW CAN YOU CARRY A GUN?

HOW CAN YOU CARRY A GUN?

In each of these illustrations the legality depends on where the person is at the moment, and if the person has a government-issued concealed-carry permit.

In the top two examples, the handguns are being carried concealed. Unless you are in your own home or on your courtyard property (known as *curtilage*), it is generally illegal to carry a concealed handgun in Virginia without a valid government permit. Even with a permit, you may not carry a firearm into a prohibited place. Prohibited places may include entire cities that have made it illegal to carry a loaded firearm in public.

In the bottom two pictures, the handguns are being carried openly. It is generally perfectly legal to openly carry a firearm, but open carry is an uncommon practice in Virginia, it may make you the subject of a lot of attention, and the prohibited places list still applies. Many counties and cities have passed laws that outlaw bearing arms depending on the type, time of day, time of year, place and whether or not a firearm is loaded.

As you can see, the right to keep and bear arms has become significantly (infringed, restricted, encumbered, limited, hampered, diminished, gray, outlawed, pick one) under state law. Many small laws have combined that now supplant the original intention and operation of the Second Amendment in modern-day Virginia.

Much of this has been done in the name of stopping crime. Other efforts appear directed at disarming the public. While efforts at stopping crime have had questionable results, the effect of the gun laws on the law abiding in the state has become acute. The new concealed-carry law has eased the restrictions somewhat, but less than 1% of Virginians have been willing to register with the government for a right-to-carry license.

WHEN CAN YOU CONCEAL A FIREARM?

WHEN CAN YOU CONCEAL A HANDGUN?

- In your home or on your property immediately around your home (known as *curtilage*);
- If you are a member of a shooting club you may carry a firearm to and from an established range as long as the weapon is unloaded and securely wrapped;
- If you are a member of a collector's club you may carry a firearm to and from a firearm exhibition as long as the weapon is unloaded and securely wrapped;
- When going to and from your home and a place of purchase or repair as long as the weapon is unloaded and securely wrapped;
- When you are hunting in bad weather and it is necessary to protect the weapon;
- With a valid Virginia concealed-carry permit in any places that aren't prohibited by law.

TYPES OF WEAPONS 3

There are weapons and there are weapons. Guns are only one kind of weapon. If a gun is modified in certain ways, it may become a prohibited weapon, which may make it a crime to own or possess. Certain weapons, defined by name or by operating characteristics and appearance, may only be owned if they were made before Sept. 13, 1994.

A responsible gun owner needs an understanding of the different types of firearms, their methods of operation, selections for personal defense, holstering options, ammunition types, loading and unloading, cleaning and maintenance, accessories, safe storage and more. Many fine books cover these areas. This chapter of *The Virginia Gun Owner's Guide* only covers weapons from the standpoint of those which are illegal, restricted or otherwise specially regulated.

PROHIBITED WEAPONS

In 1934, responding to mob violence spawned by Prohibition, Congress passed the National Firearms Act (NFA), the first major federal law concerning guns since the Constitution. This was an attempt to control what Congress called "gangster-type weapons." Items like machine guns, silencers, short rifles and sawed-off shotguns were put under strict government control and registration. These became known as "NFA weapons."

This gave authorities an edge in the fight against crime. Criminals never registered their weapons, and now simple possession of an unregistered "gangster gun" was a federal offense. Failure to pay the required transfer tax on the weapon compounded the charge. Other types of personal firearms were completely unaffected.

Political assassinations in the 1960s led to a public outcry for greater gun controls. In 1968, the federal Gun Control Act was passed, which absorbed the provisions of earlier statutes and added bombs and other destructive devices to the list of strictly controlled weapons. It is generally illegal to make, have, transport, sell or transfer any prohibited weapon without prior government approval and registration. Violation of this is a class 6 felony under state law, and carries federal penalties of up to 10 years in jail and up to a $10,000 fine.

Defaced Deadly Weapons

Removing, altering or destroying the manufacturer's serial number on a gun is a federal felony. Knowingly having a defaced gun is a federal felony. Virginia Code §18.2-311.1 makes it a class 1 misdemeanor to intentionally deface, alter or in any way destroy the serial number, the model number, the name of the maker or any other ID mark of any firearm.

State Prohibited-Weapons List

Under Virginia law certain types of weapons are restricted and must be registered with the Bureau of Alcohol Tobacco and Firearms. Machine guns must also be registered with the Dept.

of State Police. Possession of some other weapons or devices is completely prohibited. The following restrictions and requirements are in addition to federal law.

1–*Explosive materials, devices or firebombs* (§18.2-85): Having, making, transporting, distributing or using is a class 5 felony. Exceptions include use by the military, law enforcement, fire fighters, for scientific research, for educational purposes and for any other lawful purpose.

2–*Hoax bombs* (§18.2-85): Making, placing, sending or using a device in a way that causes another person to believe it is a real bomb, is a class 6 felony.

3–*Machine guns* (§18.2-288 to §18.2-298): The special requirements of Virginia's Uniform Machine Gun Act are discussed in detail, along with the federal requirements for machine gun owners, later in this chapter.

4–*Sawed-off shotguns and rifles* (§18.2-300): Possession or use in a crime is a class 2 felony; other possession or use is a class 4 felony. Exceptions apply to the military, law enforcement or by private persons in compliance with federal NFA weapons laws. Under §18.2-299, firearms less than .225 caliber are excluded.

5–*Plastic firearms* (§18.2-308.5): Firearms designed to evade detection by X-ray machines and metal detectors are illegal. If a firearm does not contain at least 3.7 ounces of metal, its possession, importation, sale, transfer or manufacture would be a class 5 felony. The lightweight Austrian-made Glock, with its polymer frame, created the commotion that lead to passage of this law. A model 21 (.45 cal) Glock uses about 18 ounces of metal, or nearly five times more than is required.

6–*Silencers* (§18.2-308.6): Possession is a class 6 felony. Silencers possessed in compliance with federal NFA weapons laws are not prohibited.

7–*Striker-12 or "Street Sweeper" shotguns* (§18.2-308.8): It is a class 6 felony to possess, sell, transfer or import this type of shotgun. See §18.2-308.8 for a description of Striker-12-type prohibited weapons.

8–*Blackjacks* (§18.2-311): Selling, bartering, having or giving away blackjacks, metal knuckles, throwing stars, switchblade knives or ballistic knives or similar weapons is a class 4 misdemeanor. Possession of any of these is considered evidence of intent to sell.

9–*Restricted ammunition* (§18.2-308.3): This is ammo designed to defeat bullet-proof vests. See §18.2-308.3 for technical definitions. Use in a crime or attempted crime is a class 5 felony.

A list of weapons which may not be carried concealed, even with a concealed-carry permit, appears in Chapter 2.

ILLEGAL GUNS

(Also called NFA weapons or prohibited weapons)

These weapons and destructive devices are among those that are legal only if they are pre-registered with the Bureau of Alcohol, Tobacco and Firearms.

1–A rifle with a barrel less than 16 inches long;

2–A shotgun with a barrel less than 18 inches long;

3–A modified rifle or shotgun less than 26 inches overall;

4–Machine guns (state registration also required);

5–Silencers of any kind;

6–Firearms over .50 caliber;

7–Street Sweeper, Striker-12 and USAS-12 shotguns
   (not legal in Virginia even if BATF-registered).

Guns with a bore of greater than one-half inch are technically known as destructive devices. Some antique and black powder firearms have such large bores but are not prohibited, as determined on a case-by-case basis by the Bureau of Alcohol, Tobacco and Firearms.

AFFECTED WEAPONS

The federal Public Safety and Recreational Firearms Use Protection Act (sometimes called the Crime Bill or the assault-weapons ban, set to expire on Sept. 13, 2004), allows citizens to possess certain firearms and accessories only if they were made before Sep. 13, 1994. New products must have a date stamp and are off-limits for the public. If you have an affected weapon or accessory that has no date stamp, there is a legal presumption that the item is *not* affected (that is, it is a pre-crime-bill version) and is OK. Affected weapons (there are about 200) include all firearms, copies or duplicates, in any caliber, known as:

Norinco, Mitchell, and Poly Technologies (Avtomat Kalashnikovs, all models); Action Arms Israeli Military Industries Uzi and Galil; Beretta AR-70 (SC-70); Colt AR-15; Fabrique National FN/FAL, FN/LAR, and FNC; SWD M-10, -11, -11/9, and -12; Steyr AUG; Intratec TEC-9, -DC9, and -22; and revolving cylinder shotguns, such as (or similar to) the Street Sweeper and Striker 12, and, any **rifle** that can accept a detachable magazine and has at least 2 of these features: a folding or telescoping stock; a pistol grip that protrudes conspicuously beneath the action; a bayonet mount; a flash suppresser or threaded barrel for one; and a grenade launcher, and, any **semiautomatic pistol** that can accept a detachable magazine and has at least 2 of these features: a magazine that attaches outside of the pistol grip; a threaded barrel that can accept a barrel extender, flash suppresser, forward handgrip, or silencer; a shroud that is attached to, or partially or completely encircles, the barrel and permits the shooter to hold the firearm with the non-trigger hand without being burned; a manufactured weight of 50 ounces (3-1/8 lbs.) or more when unloaded; and a semiautomatic version of an automatic firearm, and, any **semiautomatic shotgun** that has at least 2 of these features: a folding or telescoping stock; a pistol grip that protrudes conspicuously beneath the action; a fixed magazine capacity in excess of 5 rounds; and an ability to accept a detachable magazine, and, any **magazines,** belts, drums, feed strips and similar devices if they can accept more than 10 rounds of ammunition (fixed tubular devices for .22 caliber rim fire ammo are not included).

MACHINE GUNS

Under strictly regulated conditions, federal law allows private citizens to have weapons that would otherwise be prohibited. An example is the machine gun.

Unlike normal firearm possession, the cloak of privacy afforded gun ownership is removed in the case of so-called "NFA weapons"—those which were originally restricted by the National Firearms Act of 1934. The list has grown since that time, through subsequent legislation. As a law-abiding private citizen, if you want to have an NFA weapon you must meet special federal conditions, in addition to Virginia requirements covered earlier in this chapter. These requirements are designed to keep the weapons out of criminal hands or to prosecute criminals for possession.

1–You must register the weapon itself in the National Firearms Registry and Transfer Records of the Treasury Dept. This list of arms includes about 193,000 machine guns.

2–You must obtain permission in advance to transfer the weapon by filing "ATF Form 4 (5320.4)" available from the Bureau of Alcohol, Tobacco and Firearms.

3–An FBI check of your background is performed to locate any criminal record that would disqualify you from possessing the weapon. This is done with the help of a recent 2" x 2" photograph of yourself and your fingerprints on an FBI form FD-258 Fingerprint Card, which must be submitted with the application.

4–The transfer of the weapon from its lawful owner to you must be federally registered. In other words, a central record is kept of every NFA weapon and its current owner.

5–You must pay a $200 transfer tax. For some NFA weapons, the transfer tax is $5.

A properly licensed dealer can sell a registered machine gun to a qualified private buyer, and help you through the federal and state procedures.

You may apply for approval to make NFA weapons, such as short rifles or sawed-off shotguns. The application process is similar to the process for buying such weapons. Unregistered NFA weapons are contraband and are subject to seizure. Having the unassembled parts needed to make an NFA weapon counts as having one.

The authorities are generally exempt from these provisions. Virginia law allows open trade in automatic weapons between manufacturers and dealers, and includes state and city police, prisons, the state and federal military, the national guard, museums, educational institutions, and people with special licenses and permits.

The official trade in machine guns is specifically prohibited from becoming a source of commercial supply. Only those machine guns (and other NFA weapons) which were in the

National Firearms Registry and Transfer Records as of May 19, 1986, may be privately held. This includes about 5,000 machine guns in Virginia. The number available nationally will likely drop, since no new full-autos are being added to the registry, and the existing supply will decrease through attrition. Virginians own about 9,000 NFA weapons in total.

State Controls on Machine Guns

Failing to register a machine gun with the State Police within 24 hours of acquiring it is a class 3 misdemeanor (§18.2-295). The registration is good as long as you own the firearm, the certificate must be kept with the weapon, and it is a class 3 misdemeanor to not have the certificate available for inspection by the proper authorities upon request. A machine gun can be confiscated for failure to show the registration certificate and may be forfeited to the Commonwealth. Failure to notify the State Police when transferring a machine gun is a class 3 misdemeanor. Registration data may not be viewed by the general public.

Under §18.2-290, having a machine gun for an aggressive or offensive purpose is a class 4 felony. Any machine gun is considered to be possessed for aggressive or offensive purposes if: a–it is not registered with the state; b–it is possessed by a criminal; c–it is not at the home or business of its registered owner; or d–if any ammunition or empty shells for it are nearby. If a machine gun is in a room it is presumed to be possessed by each person in the room (§18.2-292).

In contrast however, the law does allow, under §18.2-293.1, "the possession of a machine gun for a purpose manifestly not aggressive or offensive," that covers the sporting and private uses for which law-abiding citizens might own a fully automatic firearm. It is also legal to have a machine gun for scientific purposes or to have one that is non-functional as a momento, provided in either case that the item is registered with the state. Dealers are required to keep a state register (in addition to federal records) of all machine guns they handle, and information on each buyer, under §18.2-294. Having or using a machine gun for a crime of violence is a class 2 felony (§18.2-289).

These Virginia state requirements for machine gun owners are in addition to the federal requirements.

CURIOS, RELICS AND ANTIQUES

Curios and relics are guns that have special value as antiquities, for historical purposes, or other reasons that make it unlikely they will be used currently as weapons. The Curio and Relic List is a 60-page document available from the Bureau of Alcohol, Tobacco and Firearms. They can also tell you how to apply to obtain curio or relic status for a particular weapon.

Antique firearms, defined as firearms with matchlock, flintlock, percussion cap or similar ignition systems, manufactured in or before 1898, and replicas meeting specific guidelines are exempt from certain federal laws. For complete details contact the Bureau of Alcohol, Tobacco and Firearms. Remember, though, if it can fire or readily be made to fire it is a firearm under Virginia state law. However, state law does exempt antiques from background checks and the one-handgun-per-30-day program.

NEW LEGISLATION

Congress and state legislatures nationwide have been considering a variety of selective and categorical firearms bans. Citizens are advised to follow developments and remain keenly aware of any firearms or accessories that were formerly legal and then declared illegal. One such example is the Striker-12 shotgun, described earlier.

WHAT'S WRONG WITH THIS PICTURE?

It is a federal felony to have these weapons and destructive devices unless they are pre-registered with the Bureau of Alcohol, Tobacco and Firearms.

- A rifle with a barrel less than 16 inches long
- A shotgun with a barrel less than 18 inches long
- A modified rifle or shotgun less than 26 inches overall
- Street Sweeper, Striker-12 or USAS-12 shotguns (not legal in Virginia even if BATF-registered)
- Fully automatic firearms (machine guns, which must also be registered with the State Police)
- Silencers of any kind
- Firearms using fixed ammunition over .50 caliber
- Armor-piercing ammunition
- Explosive, incendiary or poison gas bombs
- Explosive, incendiary or poison gas grenades
- Explosive, incendiary or poison gas mines
- Explosive, incendiary or poison gas rockets with more than 4 ounces of propellant (includes bazooka)
- Missiles with an explosive or incendiary charge greater than 1/4 ounce
- Mortars

Keep in mind that additional weapons may be added to this list in the future.

THERE'S NOTHING WRONG WITH THIS PICTURE!

THERE'S NOTHING WRONG WITH THIS PICTURE!

Practicing the shooting sports outdoors is a natural and wholesome pursuit as long as you comply with the laws.

- The shooters are at a remote location, on private land with the landowner's permission, or at an established shooting range.
- The remote location is outside city limits, violates no county ordinances, and does not cause a noise problem for neighbors.
- The target has a backstop which prevents bullets from causing a potential hazard.
- No wildlife or protected plants are in the line of fire.
- The shooters are using eye and ear protection.

LOCAL LAWS 4

The Preemption Law

On Jan. 1, 1987, state law prohibited local authorities from passing firearms laws. This is called *preemption*, and is found in Code of Virginia §15.1-29.15. Preemption is supposed to provide uniform statutes for residents statewide.

However, the preemption law has a huge exception—it allows local authorities to pass their own laws, at any time, if expressly allowed under other state statutes. Such statutes do exist and make broad grants of gun-legislating power to counties and cities, as described below. In addition, any county or city ordinances that came before the preemption law are still valid.

This has lead to a motley patchwork of local laws that affect Virginians as they travel within the state. So although Virginia has a preemption statute, it does not have true preemption or the benefits of equal treatment under the law.

You may also find some localities have enacted laws *after* preemption was established, which may appear to conflict with state law. Remember that even if you are arrested wrongfully, you are still arrested and can face severe risks while in the throes of the legal system.

Enabling Laws

The laws that authorize local lawmaking are known as *enabling laws*. Within stated limits, local governments have been granted powers to pass certain laws regulating firearms.

- §15.1-29.20. Prohibits holding a shooting range to noise control standards more restrictive than the ones in place when construction of the range was approved. The effect of this statute is to protect ranges from being "zoned" out of business by changing noise ordinances.

- §15.1-518. Allows a county's board of supervisors to prohibit shooting firearms, including guns that are air or gas operated, anywhere they believe is too populated for safety.

- §15.1-518.1. Allows the governing body of a county to prohibit hunting within one-half mile of any area the county believes is too heavily populated for safety. Such areas must be precisely described and posted.

- §15.1-523. Allows the governing body of any county to impose a license tax of up to 25 dollars on a handgun dealer.

- §15.1-524. Allows counties to require sellers of handguns to report the sale to the clerk of the circuit court. The report may require the name and address of the buyer, the date of purchase, and the number, make and caliber of the handgun. The county may require the report within ten days of the sale, and the court clerk must keep a record of the reports.

- §15.1-525. Continues in effect the law known as *Chapter 297 of Acts of 1944* that requires permits to sell or buy handguns in any county with a population density of more than 1,000 people per square mile. Currently, this appears to affect only Arlington and Fairfax counties.

  Any person or firm in such a county who seeks to go into the business of selling handguns at retail must register with the chief of police and obtain a permit to sell. The chief issues the permit, "...upon his being satisfied with the fitness of the dealer..." Fitness is not defined. The permit is good for one year.

Any person seeking to buy a handgun in such a county must first get a permit to purchase from the chief of police. The chief may require any information to determine your "...fitness to own and possess..." a handgun. At the chief's discretion, the permit may be issued, refused or deferred until an independent investigation is made of the applicant. In no case may a permit be granted unless the chief is satisfied that you are a "proper person" to own and keep a handgun.

A person who is granted a permit by the police chief must give it to the dealer when the transaction is made. On the permit, the dealer records the date of delivery, your name and address, and the number, make and caliber of the firearm. This paperwork must then be returned to the chief by the end of the next day. The chief is required by this law to record all permits issued, including date and name of purchaser, creating a government registry of everyone who buys a handgun in the county.

It is a misdemeanor for anyone to violate any part of this law. This procedure is in addition to the regular state and federal paperwork and tracking systems, and in actual practice the process may be different than this description, which is based on the statute itself.

As an effort to keep firearms out of the hands of criminals, this statute was enacted 50 years ago. Today, it is redundant with the broader, more stringent and uniform requirements of the Brady law and the Virginia instant background check. Since the new statutes make requirements by law instead of individual discretion, they also reduce any potential for abuse.

- §15.1-865. Allows municipal corporations to regulate or prohibit: 1–any dangerous, offensive or unhealthful business, trade or enterprise (these and other terms of this law are not specifically defined); 2–transportation of any offensive substance; 3–the manufacture, storage, transportation or possession and use of any explosive or inflammable substance; 4–the use and exhibition of fireworks; and 5–the discharge of firearms. Also allows such cities to require safety devices on storage equipment for such items.

- §18.2-287 allows the governing body of a county to adopt laws prohibiting a person from carrying firearms while on public highways in the county, including a fine of up to $100. Laws passed under this statute do not apply when:

  - You are in a moving vehicle;

  - You are acting in defense of people or property;

  - You are authorized to hunt on private property on both sides of the highway you are on.

- §18.2-287.1 allows the governing body of a county or city to adopt laws making it illegal to transport, possess or carry a loaded shotgun or rifle in any vehicle on any public road or highway within the county or city. Laws enacted under this statute may carry a fine of up to $100, the Dept. of Game and Inland Fisheries must be notified of any such law for it to be enforceable, and the law does not apply when:

  - Law enforcement or military members are performing their duties, or

  - You reasonably believe the loaded shotgun or rifle is needed for your safety during the conduct of your business or employment. Determining what you "reasonably believe" may depend upon what the police, a judge or a jury thinks is the truth.

Other restrictions may occur indirectly as a result of zoning ordinances or other laws. In addition, Title 29.1, *Game, Inland Fisheries and Boating*, grant numerous powers to localities for regulating hunting which affect firearms possession and use.

Where Can You Go Shooting

The population density of Virginia makes it difficult to safely shoot outdoors in many areas. In addition, local ordinances may be in effect restricting shooting outdoors, and state prohibitions apply as well. Shooting is not prohibited on private land provided the shots pose no risk to life or property, and the location is sufficiently remote to avoid complaints about noise.

For many residents, shooting takes place at established indoor or outdoor shooting ranges which are run by the armed forces, national guard, commercial operators, private clubs and others.

COUNTY AND CITY LAWS

Many county or city firearms laws simply duplicate existing state statutes. Duplicate laws are in place primarily to allow a crime to be prosecuted on a local level. Other county or city laws may be of the type authorized by enabling statutes.

Laws in place before state preemption are the most diverse. They include waiting periods, permits for purchasing firearms, and background checks, among others. As a result, Virginia gun owners are faced with the confusing prospect of needing to know the laws peculiar to their county and city as well as the state laws.

Local police or the sheriff's dept. are often the first place a person contacts for gun-law information. However, the police are generally not legal experts, and you have no way to evaluate the quality and correctness of the information you receive—which depends entirely upon who answers the phone. Most important, if you inadvertently violate a law, "the police told me I could do it," may not be much of a defense.

Read the law yourself. Many laws are surprisingly easy to understand. Copies of state and local laws are available at public libraries throughout the Commonwealth. If you do not have easy access to a library, call your local seat of government. Counties and cities generally maintain dedicated law libraries. Just ask one of these for any local firearms-related laws. There may be a small fee to gather, copy and mail the laws to you.

If for any reason you are unsure about the law, don't take any chances. Contact a lawyer. The National Rifle Association Attorney Referral Program can recommend a local lawyer knowledgeable in firearms law.

A FEW EXAMPLES OF LOCAL LAW

No two towns or counties are likely to handle the same type of situation in exactly the same way. Richmond's purchase-permit law bears little resemblance to the purchase-permit law in Fairfax County. Virginia Beach approaches the law in yet another way.

A portion of the laws for Fairfax County, the City of Richmond and the City of Virginia Beach are included here as examples. The full text of the laws paraphrased below are available from the respective county or city law libraries listed in Appendix C.

Fairfax County

The Fairfax County Code contains several laws that when taken together, create a waiting period with a background check before you can purchase a handgun:

- Fairfax §6-3-6; *Application for acquisition of pistol; procedure:* To satisfy §6-3-6 you must apply to the chief of police before buying, borrowing or renting a pistol from a firearms dealer. Dealers are required to provide the application to you and to forward them to the chief of police. The net effect is a three-day waiting period and background check, in addition to the state procedure.

- Fairfax §6-3-7; *Waiting period required prior to delivery of pistol to purchaser:* The chief of police must mail a post card to the dealer stating the time and date the above application (§6-3-6) was received. No dealer may deliver a handgun until seventy-two hours after the time the application was received by the chief of police.

- Fairfax §6-3-8; *Prohibiting delivery of pistol from dealer to applicant; grounds; notices:* The chief of police may inform the dealer, within seventy-two hours of receiving the application, that the applicant is not eligible to possess a handgun because of; age, mental illness, drug addiction, previous conviction of a violent crime or habitual drunkenness. It is illegal to transfer the handgun in any of these cases.

- Fairfax §6-3-9: *Applicant may appeal refusal to deliver pistol; procedure:* If you are denied your request to purchase a handgun, you may apply (within 10 days) to the County Circuit Court for a review of the denial.

The above sections do not apply to:

1–Law enforcement personnel;

2–Licensed dealers;

3–Rental of pistols while used on a supervised range;

4–Returning a pistol to it's rightful owner if it was left on consignment or for repairs.

Other firearms related sections of the Fairfax County Code include:

- Fairfax §6-1-2 prohibits: 1–Hunting or discharging firearms in areas of high population; 2–hunting or shooting on or within 100 yards of any public school grounds or public park; 3–hunting or shooting with a shotgun loaded with slugs; 4–hunting with firearms larger than .224 caliber (shotguns loaded with shot not included);

- Fairfax §6-1-2.1 defines areas where shooting BB-guns, air rifles and pellet guns are prohibited;

- Fairfax §6-1-5 prohibits transferring guns to minors, with exceptions;

- Fairfax §6-1-6 prohibits minors from carrying and discharging guns, with exceptions.

The Fairfax County Police Dept. Public Information Division will answer specific firearms questions by residents. Remember though, such oral answers may not be binding in court. See Appendix C for contact information.

City of Richmond

In the Code of the City of Richmond, §20-160 prohibits transporting loaded shotguns or rifles. This section was enacted under State statute §18.2-287.1 and includes all of the provisions of that statute. Other sections of the Code of the City of Richmond mirror state laws concerning carrying concealed weapons, furnishing firearms to minors and discharging firearms in public places.

Laws regulating the purchase or sale of ammunition and firearms include:

- Richmond §20-149; *Sale or Exchange:* This law requires any person selling or exchanging certain weapons and ammunition to obtain a seller's permit from the chief of police prior to the sale. The items listed are: pistols, dirks, Bowie knives, sling shots, switchblade knives or any similar weapon. Also included are pistol or rifle ammunition. The permit must be shown to the person buying the weapon or ammunition.

  It is important to note this law does applies not only to dealers. Private citizens are also affected.

- Richmond §20-150; *Purchase Permit:* The law requires a purchase permit be obtained from the chief of police by any person wishing to buy or otherwise procure, for ownership or temporary use, the same weapon types and ammunition covered in the seller's permit above. However, low power, .22 caliber rifles and ammunition "commonly used for target practice" are not included.

Richmond §20-153; *Records and Reports of Dealers:* All firearms dealers are required to keep a register of firearms sales. The register includes the type and number of the weapon purchased, the name of the purchaser and the date of sale. The register may be inspected by any city police officer, and is given to the chief of police monthly, creating a government registration system for every person who buys a gun in the city.

- Richmond §20-151; Waiting period for pistols, handguns and ammunition (15 days).

- Richmond §20-152; Waiting period for ammunition designed to defeat bullet proof vests. (15 days) It should be noted that such ammunition is already forbidden under federal law and is not commercially available.

- Richmond §20-159; *Negligent storage of loaded firearms:* This law provides punishment for the parents of children who gain access to a loaded firearm if the gun is fired and death or injury results.
- Richmond §20-171; *Establishment of Training Program.* As of July 1, 1985, the chief of police is required to set up a program to offer training to Richmond citizens in the safe handling of firearms.

Law-abiding residents of Richmond who wish to avoid their city's cumbersome purchase-permit requirements may take advantage of the simple instant-check system in surrounding Chesterfield or Henrico counties.

Virginia Beach

Virginia Beach Code §38-8 prohibits transporting loaded shotguns or rifles, and was enacted under state statute §18.287.1. Most sections of the Virginia Beach Code mirror state laws concerning carrying concealed weapons, discharging firearms in public places and selling switchblades and metal knuckles.

In addition, Virginia Beach regulates the sale of handguns by requiring a purchase permit:

- Virginia Beach §38-6; *Permit prerequisite to purchase of certain weapons:* This law requires anyone who wants to buy a handgun to first obtain a permit from the chief of police. To qualify for a purchase permit you must be: 1–at least 21 years old; 2–a resident of Virginia Beach for at least 30 days and 3–not be prohibited from firearms ownership by state or federal law. The permit fee is $10. Permits are available at the Virginia Beach First Police Precinct. See Appendix C for contact information.

The purchase-permit requirement does not apply to:

1–Sales between private individuals;

2–Sales between licensed dealers, manufactures or importers;

3–Sales or trade-ins of handguns to licensed dealers;

4–Rental of handguns for use on the premises of the dealer.

LOCAL ORDINANCE SAMPLER

The hurdles gun owners are subjected to by laws at the local level are made abundantly clear by the following partial list of such statutes. The partial list of cities and counties affected by local ordinances gives you an idea of the complexity which has replaced the original concept that the right to keep and bear arms shall not be infringed. The idea that Virginia is a state with the benefit of a preemption law is more of a theory than a practical reality. A similar situation regarding hunting laws can be found in chapter 6.

This is a *partial* list of local laws. No one has ever determined exactly how many cities, towns and counties have passed gun laws or how many laws that might be. After the list of laws you will find a list of localities where the laws apply.

1–It is unlawful to transport, possess or carry a loaded rifle in any vehicle while on the road from Oct. 1 through Feb. 15.

2–It is unlawful to transport or possess a loaded shotgun or loaded rifle in any vehicle on the road from 1/2 hour after sunset to 1/2 hour before sunrise.

3–It is unlawful to transport or possess a loaded shotgun or loaded rifle on the road from Oct. 1 through Feb. 15.

4–It is unlawful to possess a loaded firearm on the road except when permission to hunt is obtained from landowners on each side.

5–It is unlawful to transport or possess a loaded shotgun or loaded rifle on the road from sundown to sunrise.

6–It is unlawful to transport or possess a loaded firearm on the road in a vehicle.

7–It is unlawful to transport or possess a loaded firearm on the road during deer season.

8–It is unlawful to discharge a firearm from or across any sidewalk, highway or on public land.

9–Minors are restricted as to where and when they may possess firearms.

10–It is unlawful to transport, possess or carry a loaded rifle or shotgun in any vehicle on any public street, road or highway within the boundaries of the road.

11–A permit is required to sell or exchange handguns or ammunition.

12–A permit is required to purchase handguns.

13–A waiting period is required to purchase handguns.

14–A permit is required to purchase ammunition.

15–A waiting period is required to purchase ammunition.

16–It is unlawful to carry a concealed weapon without a permit.

17–It is unlawful to furnish firearms or other weapons to minors.

18–Negligent storage of loaded firearms is unlawful if a minor gets the firearm and an accident results in death or injury.

19–It is unlawful to point or brandish a firearm or anything that looks like a firearm.

20–Sale of handguns to minors, drug addicts, habitual drunkards, persons of unsound mind and fugitives from justice is prohibited.

City or County	Ordinance numbers that apply
Albermarle	10
Bath	2
Chesapeake	6, 10
Chesterfield	4
Culpepper	4, 6, 10
Danville	10
Fairfax	9, 12, 13, 17, 20
Fauquier	4, 6, 8, 9, 10
Goochland	5, 9
Greensville	3, 4
James City	10
King George	4, 6
Loudoun	4, 10
Louisa	9
Madison	4, 6, 10
Nelson	4
New Kent	10
Northumberland	9, 10
Orange	4, 7
Petersburg	10
Prince George	9
Prince William	9
Richmond (county)	9
Richmond (city)	9, 10, 11, 12, 13, 14, 15, 16, 17, 18
Roanoke	10
Rockbridge	10
Southampton	1
Stafford	6
Surry	10
Virginia Beach	9, 10, 12 , 16, 19
Warren	10
Williamsburg	10

WHAT'S WRONG WITH THIS PICTURE?

1–Shooting within city limits is normally prohibited.

2–Shooting in that part of the county might be against the law if the specific county involved has passed such a law.

3–It's illegal to deface signs.

4–Trespassing is illegal.

5–You can't use targets which leave debris.

6–Shooting at wildlife requires a permit or license.

7–The target doesn't have a backstop. The shooter is not controlling the entire trajectory of the bullet.

8–If the shot crosses the road it is illegal.

9–The shooter isn't wearing eye or ear protection.

10–There are no saguaro cacti in Virginia.

DEADLY FORCE and SELF DEFENSE 5

"I got my questionnaire baby,
You know I'm headed off for war,
Well now I'm gonna kill somebody
Don't have to break no kind of law."

- from a traditional blues song

Virginia is one of a handful of states with no statutory laws to define when you can use deadly force in self defense. Although the lack of clearly defined law complicates the issue, the rights of self defense are well established through previous court cases that set *precedents*. A shooting committed in self defense may be viewed as *justifiable* or *excusable* by the courts. The differences are discussed in detail in this chapter. It is the specific circumstances of a shooting that determine whether the shooting is justified or excusable, and if not, which crime has been committed.

Whenever a shooting occurs, a crime has been committed. Either the shooting is legal as a defense against a crime or attempted crime, or else the shooting is neither justified nor excusable, in which case the shooting itself is the crime.

Your civil liability (getting sued) in a shooting case can be a greater risk than the criminal charges which this book covers. You can be charged with both, and your legal protections are less vigorous in civil cases than in criminal ones. With very narrow exceptions, overcoming criminal charges does not protect you from a civil lawsuit—you can be tried more than once.

USE OF DEADLY PHYSICAL FORCE

A reasonable person hopes it will never be necessary to raise a weapon in self defense. It's smart to always avoid such confrontations. In the unlikely event that you must resort to force to defend yourself, **you are generally required to use as little force as necessary to control a situation. Deadly force can only be used in the most narrowly defined circumstances, and it is highly unlikely that you will ever encounter such circumstances in your life.** You have probably never been near such an event in your life so far. Your own life is permanently changed if you ever kill a person, intentionally or otherwise.

When can you "shoot to kill" and not be convicted of a crime? When the authorities or a jury, after the fact, determine that your actions were justifiable. *You never know beforehand.* And as a strategic matter, experts teach students to "shoot to stop." Your intent should be to protect, not to kill.

No matter how well you understand the law, or how justified you may feel you are in a shooting incident, your fate will probably be determined much later, in a court of law. Establishing all the facts precisely is basically an impossible task and adds to your legal risks.

What were the exact circumstances during the moments of greatest stress, as best you remember them? Were there witnesses, who are they, what will they remember and what will they say to the authorities—each time they're asked—and in a courtroom? What was your relationship to the deceased person? How did you feel at the moment you fired? Did you have any options besides pulling the trigger? Can you look at it differently after the fact? Has there been even one case recently affecting how the law is now interpreted? Was a new law put into place yesterday? How good is your lawyer? How tough is the prosecutor? How convincing are you? Are the police on your side? Does the judge like your face? What will the jury think?

Be smart and never shoot at anyone if there is any way at all to avoid it. Avoiding the use of deadly force is usually a much safer course of action, at least from a legal point of view. You could be on much safer ground if you use a gun to protect yourself *without* actually firing a shot. Even though it's highly unlikely you'll ever need to draw a gun in self defense, the number of crimes prevented by the presence of a citizen's gun— *that isn't fired*—are estimated to be in the millions. And yet, just pulling a gun can subject you to serious penalties. Think of it in reverse—if someone pulled a gun on you, would you want to press charges because they threatened you and put your life in danger? You must be careful about opening yourself up to such charges.

Still, the law recognizes your right to protect yourself, your loved ones and other people from certain severe criminal acts. In the most extreme incident you may decide it is immediately necessary to use lethal force to survive and deal with the repercussions later. Read some of the case law cited in this book to get a deeper understanding of the ramifications of using deadly force—and dealing with the legal system after the fact.

The Virginia Gun Owner's Guide is intended to help you on a long journey to competence. Do not rely solely on the information in this book or on any other single source, and recognize that by deciding to prepare to use deadly physical force if it ever becomes necessary you are accepting substantial degrees of risk.

Even with a good understanding of the rules, there may be more to it than meets the eye. As an example, shooting a criminal who is fleeing a crime is very different than shooting a criminal who's committing a crime. You may be justified in shooting at someone in a specific situation, and you might miss and only wound, but if you ever shoot to intentionally wound you'll have an uphill battle in court. The law is strict, complex and not something to take chances with in the heat of the moment if you don't have to.

It's natural to want to know, beforehand, just when it's OK to shoot and be able to claim self defense later. Unfortunately, you will never know for sure until *after* a situation arises. You make your moves whatever they are, and the authorities or a jury decides. The laws and legal precedents don't physically control what you can or can't do—they give the authorities guidelines on how to evaluate what you did after it occurs. **There are extreme legal risks when you choose to use force of any kind.**

Because cases of murder outnumber cases of justifiable homicide, the authorities have a distinct tendency to think of the person holding a smoking gun as the perpetrator, later as the suspect, and finally as the defendant, while the person who gets shot, or was merely threatened with a gun, is the victim and in need of protection. If you ever come close to pulling the trigger, remember there is a possibility you will face a murder charge when it's all over. The effects of the shot last long after the ringing in your ears stops.

DEADLY FORCE PRECEDENTS

Virginia courts have, over the years, established the guidelines that control how a self-defense shooting is interpreted by the authorities. If a court finds that you are in compliance with these principles, you will be acquitted, a free person. If the court finds you in violation, *even if you are not or believe you are not*, you face the penalties of murder. You may languish in jail while the system decides your fate. The legal risk to you in a self-defense shooting can be enormous.

Homicide (the taking of a human life) falls into two categories. The criminal type, which carries severe penalties, includes capital murder, first degree murder, second degree murder and manslaughter. Non-criminal homicides involve cases of self defense and crime prevention, and are called *excusable* homicide and *justifiable* homicide. There is a third type known as civil justification, which covers sanctioned lethal activities such execution and war.

Normally, *The Virginia Gun Owner's Guide* includes the text of the law so you can read it for yourself. Since there is no "text of the law" on self defense in Virginia, we have included quotations from court decisions that impact this crucial subject. Many more court cases exist than the few selected here as examples, and an effort was made to pick representative or clearly stated cases. Court precedents may change and can be subject to different interpretations. The interpretation that matters the most is the one that takes place when it is you who is on trial for your life. Unfortunately for the average person, court precedents are much harder to keep up with than changes to the statutes (which is not exactly an easy feat in itself).

THE TWELVE PRINCIPLES OF DEADLY FORCE AND SELF DEFENSE

1. *Whenever one person is criminally charged with killing another person Virginia courts presume it is second-degree murder.* Second-degree murder is punishable by 5–20 years in jail and a $100,000 fine. This means the State must only prove that you committed the homicide to make the case for second-degree murder. To increase the charge the prosecutor must prove beyond a reasonable doubt that the special conditions (willful, deliberate, premeditated or other actions) of a first-degree murder were committed.

It is up to the defendant (often referred to as the prisoner or the accused in a self-defense case) to prove that a lesser homicide was committed. The lesser charges are manslaughter, which is still a crime, punishable by 1–10 years in jail and a $2,500 fine, or justifiable or excusable homicide, which are not crimes. This may seem like "guilty until proven innocent" but is a long established standard in Virginia courts.

> When the Commonwealth has proved the commission of a homicide, and has pointed out the accused as the criminal agent, then it may rest its case, and unless the accused shows circumstances of justification, alleviation or excuse, a verdict of murder in the second degree will be warranted. (Boone v. Commonwealth, 1954)

> ...the burden is upon the accused, if he would reduce the offense below murder in the second degree, to show the absence of malice and the other mitigating circumstances necessary for the purpose. (McDaniels v. Commonwealth, 1883)

2. In claiming self defense you are admitting that you committed the homicide. Your claim that your actions were necessary in protecting yourself includes the admission that you committed what the courts will view as a second degree murder charge until shown otherwise. "I shot in self defense," begins with "I shot."

> Self-defense is an affirmative defense,... and in making such a plea defendant implicitly admits that killing was intentional and assumes the burden of introducing evidence of justification or excuse that raises a reasonable doubt in the minds of the jurors. (McGhee v. Commonwealth, 1978)

> If the evidence so offered by the accused is shown to be false, and is insufficient to cause the jury to have a reasonable doubt as to his guilt, the case so made by the Commonwealth is not overcome, and a verdict of second-degree murder is still warranted. (Johnson v. Commonwealth, 1949)

3. For a shooting to be a justifiable homicide you must be completely free from fault to the tiniest detail. This is self defense in the truest sense. You are minding your own business and not violating any laws when the unprovoked attack of a stranger compels you to defend yourself (or an innocent third person) with lethal results. The evidence and testimony you present in your defense must raise a "reasonable doubt" in the minds of the jury that your actions were not criminal.

> Justifiable homicide in self-defense occurs where a person, without any fault in provoking or bringing on difficulty, kills another under reasonable apprehension of death or great bodily harm to himself. (Bailey v. Commonwealth, 1958).

> In these several kinds of justifiable homicide, it may be observed, that the slayer is in no kind of fault whatsoever, not even in the minutest degree; and is therefore to be totally acquitted and discharged, with commendation rather than blame. (Dodson v. Commonwealth, 1933)

4. If you have any fault in the event but tried to retreat until there was nowhere left to go, and only then defended yourself against a perceived deadly threat, it is excusable homicide.

> Excusable homicide in self-defense occurs where accused, although in some fault in first instance in provoking or bringing on difficulty, retreats as far as possible, when attacked, announces his desire for peace, and kills adversary from a reasonably apparent necessity to

preserve his own life or save himself from great bodily harm. (Bailey v. Commonwealth, 1958)

...if the difficulty is brought about by the accused and he finds that it is necessary to kill his assailant in order to save his own life, such killing is not in the eye of the law excusable. A man cannot go a-gunning for an adversary and kill him on the first appearance of resistance, and rely upon the necessity of the killing as an excuse therefor. (Bell v. Commonwealth, 1986)

But if a sudden fight is brought on, without malice or intention, the accused, if in fault, must retreat as far as he safely can, but, having done so and in good faith abandoned the fight, may kill his adversary, if he cannot in any other way preserve his life or save himself from great bodily harm. (Emphasis retained from the original. Dodson v. Commonwealth, 1933)

5. *You may only respond with the same level of force that is being used against you.* Until a threat reaches truly lethal proportions, responding with a firearm may well be seen as over reaction. Mere physical force, if not likely to cause serious bodily injury, may only be met with physical force, not with deadly force. Whether the threat of deadly force is justifiable (that is, presenting a gun without firing) will depend on the exact circumstances. The entire case may rest on the balance between the illegal force you reasonably believed you faced and the amount of force you responded with in defense.

A person who reasonably apprehends bodily harm by another is privileged to exercise reasonable force to repel the assault. However, the amount of force used to defend oneself must not be excessive and must be reasonable in relation to the perceived threat. (Diffendal v. Commonwealth, 1989)

6. *You may only use deadly force in your defense (or the defense of an innocent third party) during the moment in which there is an illegal threat to your life or limb.* The attacker must have made an overt act that lead you to reasonably believe death or serious bodily harm was immediately imminent. Words and threats alone are never enough. Fear that an attack will come, no matter how great, is never sufficient cause without the overt act of the other person. Once the attack has stopped the justification to shoot evaporates, and shots fired

after this point may make you the aggressor and can be interpreted as murder.

> ...bare fear of injury at the hands of another, in the absence of some overt act indicative of imminent danger at that time, will not justify the taking of human life. (Stoneman v. Commonwealth, 1874)

> Words alone are not sufficient provocation to excuse a murder. (Painter v. Commonwealth, 1969)

7. *The judgment of whether you believed that the threat was real must be made from your perspective at the time of the incident.* Your belief in the danger must be real, and you must have grounds for your belief, even if turns out later that the danger was not real. In some states the perspective must be that of a reasonable third person, which switches the judgment to the jury. But the jury in Virginia still must be convinced that you truly believed you were under mortal jeopardy at the moment you acted, leaving you at risk to what they believe.

> ...where the defendant claims self-defense that it is not necessary that he be actually in danger of his life or of great bodily harm, or that it so appear to the jury, but that the test is whether it reasonably appeared to the defendant at the time that his life was in danger or he was in danger of great bodily harm. (Harper v. Commonwealth, 1955)

> ...whether danger is reasonably apparent is always to be determined from the viewpoint of the defendant at the time he acted, and it is not essential to the right of self-defense that the danger should in fact exist. (McGhee v. Commonwealth, 1978)

8. *When two people set out to kill each other they commit mutual combat, and neither can claim self defense.* Entering a fight voluntarily is illegal, and defending yourself once in it is not a valid excuse later. Being provoked into a fight is not a defense. The law is watchful for a person who in any way instigates a fight and uses it as an excuse to kill an enemy.

> To be mutual it must have been voluntarily and mutually entered into. If this were not so, every fight would be mutual combat without regard to the manner in which it began... One who is assaulted may and

usually does defend himself, but the ensuing struggle cannot be accurately described as mutual combat. (Harper v. Commonwealth, 1936)

The general rule is that one cannot provoke an attack, bring on a combat, and then slay his assailant, and claim exemption from the consequences on the ground of self defense... He who provokes a personal encounter, in any case, thereby disables himself from relying on the plea of self defense in justification of a blow which he struck during the encounter. (Sims v. Commonwealth, 1922)

9. *If an innocent third party is killed by a stray shot during mutual combat, each person engaged in the combat is equally guilty.*

The following instruction was given to the jury in a case that was later upheld in the Virginia Supreme Court:

If you believe from the evidence that two or more men were shooting guns in mutual combat with the intent to kill and as a result of these shootings the deceased, an innocent bystander, was killed, then each is responsible for the death the same as if he had killed the person he intended to kill, unless he was acting in self-defense. (Riddick v. Commonwealth, 1983)

In that case it was never determined who actually fired the fatal shot. It didn't matter who pulled the trigger, everyone engaged in the mutual combat was equally at fault.

In stark contrast to this, in the case of a legitimate self-defense shooting, the person acting in self defense is not *criminally* responsible for an injury or death from a stray bullet. This is no guarantee that you will not be pursued in civil court, even if you are found not guilty.

If the person committing the homicide acted in self-defense, then he would not be responsible for the death. (Riddick v. Commonwealth, 1983)

10. *If you are not at fault, there is no duty to retreat.* In cases of self defense, where you are not in the smallest part at fault, you are not required to retreat from an attacker. However, defense experts generally agree that if you can leave you should.

Avoiding an attack by leaving the scene, if you can safely do so, may be your best course of action.

> If the accused is in no fault whatever, but in discharge of a lawful act, *he need not retreat,* but may repel force by force, *if need be,* to the extent of slaying his adversary. This is *justifiable* homicide in self defense. (Emphasis retained from the original. Dodson v. Commonwealth, 1933)

> Justifiable self-defense arises when the defendant is completely without fault. In such a case, the defendant need not retreat, but is permitted to stand his ground and repel the attack by force, including deadly force, if it is necessary. (Foote v. Commonwealth, 1990; quoting Perkins case, 1947 and McCoy case, 1919)

11. *Deadly force may be used when immediate action is necessary and no other options exist to prevent the commission of violent felonies.* Although the law clearly allows a citizen to act to prevent a crime, this does not make you a freelance police officer. Because the legal risks are so high, acting to prevent a violent felony must be looked upon as a last resort only. Review the sample scenarios in Chapter 8 for an idea of how complicated crime response can be.

> A distinction is made between such felonies as are attended with force, or any extraordinary degree of atrocity, which in their nature betoken such urgent necessity as will not allow of any delay, and others of a different kind and unaccompanied by violence on the part of the felon. Those only which come within the former description may be prevented by homicide. (Dodson v. Commonwealth, 1933)

12. *Deadly force may be used in the defense of an innocent third person.* You must reasonably believe that the other person is truly innocent, even if it turns out later that this was not true, and all the other conditions of self defense must be met. Force can be used only to the extent that the person being defended could have legally used force. The law is more specific about defense of a person related to you, but encompasses strangers as well.

> And the same justification extends to homicide committed in the mutual and reciprocal defense of such as stand in the relations of

husband and wife, parent and child, master and servant... (Dodson v. Commonwealth, 1933)

The Supreme Court has clearly recognized that one is privileged to use force in defense of family members. <Newbury case, 1950; Green case, 1918; Hodges case, 1892.> We find no Virginia cases, nor have any been cited to us, determining whether and when a person can use force to protect or defend a third person. Generally, however, this privilege is not limited to family members and extends to anyone, even a stranger who is entitled to claim self defense. <citing U.S. Supreme Court and cases from five other states> ...In a majority of jurisdictions, a person asserting a claim of defense of others may do so only where the person to whose aid he or she went would have been legally entitled to defend himself or herself. ...The amount of force which may be used must be reasonable in relation to the harm threatened. (Foster v. Commonwealth 1991)

... the jury has a right to consider it, together with the other evidence in the case, to determine whether or not the accused used more drastic measures than were reasonably necessary to protect his mother from death or serious bodily injury. (Nelson v. Commonwealth 1937)

RELATED LAWS

Brandishing firearms

It is a class 1 misdemeanor to hold, point or brandish a firearm, or anything that looks like a firearm, or a BB gun, if it is intentionally done in a way that causes someone to fear they may be shot or injured. This is the typical charge for illegally pointing a gun at a person. If you brandish a firearm on or within 1,000 ft. of school property, the penalty is raised to a class 6 felony (see §18.2-282). This law does not apply to using a firearm for legitimate self defense.

Recklessly Handling Firearms

It is a class 1 misdemeanor to recklessly handle a gun in a way that endangers any person or property (see §18.2-56.1). Reckless handling while hunting includes an additional penalty, at the court's discretion, of revoking the privilege of possessing a firearm while hunting for a period ranging from one year to life. The Dept. of Game and Inland Fisheries keeps a list of anyone restricted under this law, and anyone caught hunting and in possession of a firearm while prohibited is subject to a class 1 misdemeanor and an additional five-year restriction on hunting while armed.

Discharging Firearms In Public Places

Willfully firing a gun in any street in any city or town or in any public place is a class 1 misdemeanor. Willfully firing a gun on school property or on public property within 1,000 feet of school property is a class 4 felony (see §18.2-280). Legally justifiable or excusable shooting in defense of life or property is excluded. With regard to school zones, hunting is allowed if it is otherwise lawful, along with programs approved by the school or at established shooting ranges.

Firing a gun in or at any occupied building in a way that endangers life is a class 4 felony (see §18.2-279).

Shooting In Streets

Shooting a gun, bow or crossbow in or across any road or in the street of any city or town is a class 4 misdemeanor (see §18.2-286). Authorized shooting ranges and the military are exempt from this requirement.

Shooting a gun from a vehicle, creating the risk of death or injury, or causing someone to think they may be killed or injured is a class 5 felony (see §18.2-286.1).

Warning Shots

A warning shot is a bad idea for any number of reasons. It is a violation of several laws and can land you—believing yourself to be innocent—in jail. If there is no justification to shoot in self defense, then there is probably no justification for shooting at all. The shot itself poses a risk to any neighbors within range. A fatality could bring a murder charge against you. Expending a cartridge that may be needed in mortal combat if the situation turns deadly is a questionable strategic move. It also may draw more attention to the shooter than the suspects, who will flee, leaving the "innocent" (or even heroic) shooter to explain to the police what all the commotion was about. A firearm used in such an incident would likely be seized, along with other repercussions to the person firing the shot.

Wounding a Person Without Justification

A shot fired or actions taken in self defense are only justified if the authorities or a jury, after the fact, say that it was justified. In the event a person's actions are not justified, the possible charges could include:

§18.2-51. Shooting, stabbing, etc. Shooting, stabbing, cutting, wounding or otherwise causing bodily harm to a person with the intent to harm them is illegal. If done with malice it is a class 3 felony. If done without malice it is a class 6 felony.

§18.2-51.2 Aggravated Malicious Wounding. Maliciously shooting, stabbing, cutting, wounding or otherwise causing bodily harm to a person with the intent to harm them, and actually severely harming them, is a class 2 felony.

In the event of a fatality, a charge of murder or manslaughter is possible. The enormous consequences of shooting at a person emphasize the wisdom in holding your fire unless your own life is absolutely on the line.

Reporting Wounds

Anyone who treats or gives medical aid for a wound he knows or suspects was inflicted by a weapon, unless the wound was self-inflicted, must report the incident to the local Sheriff or Chief of Police. Failure to report the incident is a class 3 misdemeanor (see §54.1-2967).

Booby Traps

Setting a gun or other deadly weapon to be fired by a trip wire or any other remote method is a class 6 felony (see §18.2-281).

Threat of Force to Deter Trespass

The issue of stopping trespass is not covered by Virginia statutes. Common law requires that any use of force be reasonable to the situation in which it is used. Deadly force may not be used to stop a criminal trespass therefor, unless the other life-threatening circumstances of self defense or violent-crime prevention exist. Whether the *threat* of deadly force is justified—the presenting of a gun without firing or even without pointing it—is a matter for the authorities or a court to decide, depending on the exact circumstances of the event.

Riot and Unlawful Assembly

A riot occurs, for legal purposes, when three or more people acting together become involved in forceful or violent activities that jeopardize public safety, peace or order. Possession of a firearm during such an event is a class 5 felony. See §18.2-405 for the letter of the law.

Unlawful assembly occurs when three or more people get together with common intent to do something involving illegal force or violence that may seriously jeopardize public safety, peace or order, if it is enough to make reasonable people fear that threat. Taking part in an unlawful assembly is a class 1 misdemeanor unless you're in possession of a firearm, which makes it a class 5 felony (§18.2-406).

If you are legally bearing arms when a disturbance takes place it could be wise to withdraw from the scene. Involvement, as noted by these two laws, carries an increased legal risk for an armed civilian who might choose to join or who becomes entangled in a melee.

Larceny

Stealing a person's firearm when they're not around is grand larceny regardless of the value of the gun, punishable by up to 20 years in state prison, a fine up to $2,500, or both (§18.2-95).

Exemptions From Paramilitary Activity

It is a class 5 felony to participate in illegal paramilitary activity (§18.2-433.2). This involves training in firearms, explosives and causing injury or death for purposes of civil disorder, as described in §18.2-433.1. Legal activities involving firearms and training are specifically excluded (§18.2-433.3) from any paramilitary restrictions:

• Teaching self defense
• Practicing self defense
• Self defense
• Firearms instruction and training intended to teach the safe handling and use of firearms
• Any lawful sports involving firearms
• Any individual recreational use of firearms
• Any individual possession of firearms
• Hunting
• Target shooting
• Collecting
• Karate clubs
• Self-defense clinics
• Any other lawful sports or activities

In addition, individuals or groups involved in any with the lawful use or display of firearms are exempt from this law.

IF YOU SHOOT A CROOK OUTSIDE YOUR HOUSE DO YOU HAVE TO DRAG HIM INSIDE?

IF YOU SHOOT A CROOK OUTSIDE YOUR HOUSE DO YOU HAVE TO DRAG HIM INSIDE?

No! Acting on this wide-spread myth is a completely terrible idea. You're talking about tampering with evidence, obstructing justice, interfering with public duties, false reporting and more. If you're involved in a shooting, leave everything at the scene just as it is and call for the police and an ambulance.

Don't think for a minute that modern forensics won't detect an altered scene of a crime. At any shooting a crime has been committed. Either the shooting is justified, which means you were in your rights and the victim was acting illegally, or you exceeded your rights in the shooting, regardless of the victim's circumstance. The situation will be investigated to determine the facts, and believe it, the facts will come out. Police tell time-worn jokes about finding "black heel marks on the linoleum." And once you're caught in a lie, your credibility is shot.

If you tamper with the evidence, you have to lie to all the authorities to back it up. Then you have to commit perjury to follow through. Can you pull it off?

If the guy with the mask was shot from the front, armed as he is, the homeowner has a good case for self defense. If the thief was leaving, hands full of loot, there may not have been justification to shoot at all, and this homeowner is in trouble. Either way, he's better off leaving the body where it falls.

Suppose you shoot an armed intruder coming through your window, and the body falls outside the house. You'll have a better time convincing a jury that you were scared to death, than trying to explain how the dead crook in your living room got blood stains on your lawn.

The reason this fable gets so much play is because there is a big difference between a homeowner shooting a crook in the kitchen, and one person shooting another outdoors. Shooting at a stranger outside your house can be murder.

CAN YOU POINT A GUN AT SOMEONE?

CAN YOU POINT A GUN AT SOMEONE?

No matter how many aces a person is holding, you can't settle the matter with a gun. This also shows how the law can be interpreted in more than one way.

Unless you have solid legal grounds for doing so (and the character here does not), using a gun to put a person in reasonable fear of imminent physical injury is *brandishing a firearm*—a class 1 misdemeanor. *Reckless handling* of a gun in a way that endangers anyone is also a class 1 misdemeanor.

When you go to court, it could be argued that this is actually *attempted murder*, a felony. And if the guy with the gun is angry enough to take back his money, it could become *armed robbery*, a felony punishable by five years to life imprisonment.

By drawing your gun, the other guy may be able to shoot you dead and legally claim self defense. You may never pull a gun to leverage an argument. Merely reaching for a gun is the threat of deadly force and may have legal repercussions.

If someone pointed a gun at you, would you get angry and want to see them arrested? Consider how someone would feel if roles were reversed and it was you who pulled the gun out of some passion other than the will to survive, when it wasn't absolutely necessary to prevent a life-threatening situation.

Despite all this, the law recognizes your right to defend yourself, your loved ones, and other people. These cases, when you *can* point a gun at another person, are described in this chapter.

HUNTING REGULATIONS 6

Virginia hunting regulations are complex and highly-detailed. There are more than 180 statewide Game and Inland Fisheries laws. A number of those laws delegate the right to regulate various aspects of hunting to the counties. This chapter is intended to point you in the right direction.

The main Virginia hunting laws concerning firearms appear in Appendix D. Complete hunting laws are found in Title 29.1 of the Code of Virginia. The laws grant considerable, but not unlimited, regulatory powers to the Dept. of Game and Inland Fisheries, and their regulations have the force of law.

Hunters need far more information than just the firearms details provided here. For complete hunting regulations and procedures, contact the Virginia Game and Inland Fisheries Dept. at one of the numbers provided in Appendix C. Game and Inland Fisheries is required by law to publish an annual summary of statewide hunting regulations. Called *Hunting & Trapping in Virginia,* it provides all the details on hunting seasons and regulations. A useful overview of County Firearms Ordinances is included. This valuable publication is free of charge from the department.

Hunting licenses are sold by some circuit court clerks and by over 600 authorized agents at sporting goods retailers, hunting shops and bait and tackle stores. A hunting license is required for any person, of any age, who hunts in the state of Virginia with the following exceptions:

1–Landowners on their own land, including their spouses, children and minor grandchildren whether residents or not;

2–Tenants on the land they rent while carrying the landowner's written permission to hunt;

3–Residents 65 years old and over on private property in their county of residence;

4–A stockholder with a 50% or greater interest in a domestic corporation, on that corporation's land, or the stockholder's spouse, children or minor grandchildren whether residents or not;

5–Indians on a reservation with a written statement from their chief indicating that they are residents of the reservation;

6–A resident under 12 years of age if accompanied and directly supervised by a licensed Virginia hunter.

The Virginia Game and Inland Fisheries Department requires mandatory hunter education before receiving a hunting license for:

1–Anyone 12 to 15 years old;

2–Anyone 16 years or older who never had a hunting license.

The Hunter Education Course is free of charge and provides excellent training for all concerned citizens. Virginia accepts all other state and country hunting licenses, and their certifications of hunter education credentials, as compliance with the Virginia hunter education requirement. For more information on a course near you, contact the Virginia Game and Inland Fisheries Dept. in Richmond, or the regional office nearest you. See Appendix C for contact information.

The Hunter Education Program is conducted by over 1,300 volunteers. Instructors follow a uniform outline developed by *Game and Inland Fisheries*. The course must cover at least:

• The safe handling and use of firearms and archery equipment;

• Wildlife conservation and management;

• Hunting laws and applicable rules and regulations;

• Hunting safety ethics and sportsmanship;

- History of hunting and firearms;
- Basic first aid;
- Survival skills.

A certificate is issued by the department upon completion of the course. You must present this certificate, or show that you are not required to take the course, to receive a hunting license.

A Virginia hunting license is valid from July 1st or the date it is issued, whichever comes later, to June 30th of the following year, and must be renewed each year. To be considered a resident, you must: 1–have lived in the county or city in which you are applying for a license for six months immediately before applying for your license; 2–be a registered voter in your city or county, or 3–be an active duty member of the U.S. armed forces.

PUBLIC LANDS

The Virginia Dept. of Game and Inland Fisheries annually publishes the *Virginia Hunting Guide.* The guide provides the extensive information on where and when you can hunt in Virginia. Contact addresses and phone numbers for hunting information on public and private lands are included The guide also contains hunting forecasts for many game species in every area of the state. The *Virginia Hunting Guide* along with *Hunting and Trapping in Virginia,* are publications too useful to be without. They are free and available for the asking.

National Parks
Hunting is generally prohibited in all National Parks in Virginia.

Federal Refuges
Limited hunting is available on the Chincoteague, Presqile, Dismal Swamp, Back Bay and Eastern Shore Federal Refuges. Contact the respective Refuge Manager listed in Appendix C for complete information.

National Forests

In addition to your state hunting license, you need a special permit to hunt in the National Forests. Permits are available where state hunting licenses are sold. Appendix C contains contact addresses and phone numbers for the Forest headquarters and ranger districts in Virginia.

At the federal level, possession of firearms is not prohibited in National Forests and discharge may only be restricted in narrow circumstances. However, state and county hunting laws are enforced in the National Forests. The Dept. of Game and Inland Fisheries has regulations/policies in place which may conflict with basic federal policies, for the stated purpose of wildlife management. For example, the Dept. has a rule against *any* loaded firearms in a motor vehicle at *any* time in the National Forests (not required federally). The Dept. also has a rule prohibiting loaded firearms in National Forests altogether, except while hunting during designated hunting seasons (not required federally).

The basis for this prohibition is Game and Inland Fisheries regulation 325-02-1 §6, which says in part, "It shall be unlawful to have in possession a bow or gun which is not unloaded and cased or dismantled, in the National Forests and on Department-owned lands and on lands managed by the Department under cooperative agreement except during the period when it is lawful to take..." and it goes on to list game animals. The ability to pass a blanket prohibition against firearms does not appear to be granted in the law (§29.1-501). The law only allows the Dept. Board to make regulations "pertaining to the hunting, taking, capture, killing, possession, sale, purchase and transportation of any wild bird, wild animal or inland water fish."

This point is of concern to concealed-carry permit holders, and any other persons in Virginia, who are not hunting but have or desire to carry personal firearms while hiking, camping, driving through or otherwise using the National Forests and department-managed lands. Although the regulation does not appear to have a basis, while it remains in place a violator could face legal sanctions.

State Forests

State Forests are owned and managed by the Virginia Dept. of Forestry. With the Dept. of Game and Inland Fisheries they cooperatively manage 250,000 acres of forest land for hunting and fishing. In addition to your state hunting license, you need a special permit to hunt in State Forests. Permits are available from state hunting license agents in the areas surrounding the State Forests. Permits can also be purchased by mail from the State Forest offices listed in Appendix C. State and county hunting laws are enforced in the State Forests.

State Parks

State Parks are controlled by the Dept. of Conservation and Recreation. Hunting areas within the State Parks are cooperatively managed with the Dept. of Game and Inland Fisheries. The parks that will be open to hunting is decided yearly. The list of parks open for hunting is available by contacting the Dept. of Conservation and Recreation at the address located in Appendix C. State Park hunting information is also published in the *Virginia Hunting Guide* mentioned earlier.

State and county hunting laws are enforced in the State Parks. The Dept. of Conservation and Recreation has a regulation in place that says loaded firearms are not allowed in State Parks outside of designated hunting areas. This situation, similar to the one described above for National Forests, is of concern to concealed-carry permit holders and other individuals, since the department's authority to regulate lawful carry for non-hunting purposes is unclear.

Wildlife Management Areas

The Dept. of Game and Inland Fisheries owns about 176,000 acres of land grouped into 29 Wildlife Management Areas

(WMAs). The land tracts were purchased with proceeds from hunting licenses and are open to public hunting. Hunting seasons and laws generally match those of the surrounding county. There is no additional licensing fee for hunting on WMAs. The *Guide to Hunting in Virginia* contains hunting forecasts and contact points for each WMA. Contact a Game and Inland Fisheries office listed in Appendix C for more WMA information.

Military Areas

Military installations open to civilian hunting include Marine Base MCCDC Quantico, Fort A. P. Hill Military Reservation, the Radford Army Ammunition Plant, and the Fort Pickett Military Reservation. Hunting rules for military installations vary and availability is subject to restrictions due to military operations. Contact the installation in advance at the address listed in Appendix C.

Army Corps of Engineers Land

The U. S. Army Corps of Engineers manages certain lands around the state. Portions of this land are cooperatively managed by the Dept. of Game and Inland Fisheries and are available for hunting. No special permits other than regular hunting licenses are necessary. State and county hunting laws and seasons are observed. The *Virginia Hunting Guide* contains information on Corps of Engineers land. See Appendix C for points of contact.

Corporate Lands

Many Virginia corporations open their lands to public hunting. The *Virginia Hunting Guide* lists about 300,000 acres owned by power and timber companies available to individuals and for lease by clubs. Many, but not all, require the hunter to purchase permits (about $15–$25) from the company. Points of contact are listed in Appendix C.

SOME KEY STATE HUNTING REGULATIONS

Below you'll find the main general rules about the use of firearms while hunting. Remember, hunting regulations are not limited to guns and include archery, falconry, trapping and more. Unless a penalty is specified, hunting violations are class 3 misdemeanors.

- If you are required to have a hunting license, you must carry it with you when you hunt.

- Every hunter or person in a hunting party, in every county designated by the board of Game and Inland Fisheries (and they have designated all counties), must wear a blaze orange hat or blaze orange upper body clothing or display at least 100 square inches of blaze orange material, visible from all around, within arms reach. The blaze orange requirement does not apply: to waterfowl hunters, during special muzzle-loading deer season, and for fox hunters on horseback without firearms, and certain other hunters.

- Hunting is not allowed on Sundays. Exceptions are hunting on licensed shooting preserves, and hunting raccoon until 2:00 a.m. on Sunday morning.

- It is illegal to:

    –Intentionally interfere with lawful hunting;

    –Destroy or take down "posted" signs;

    –Destroy, damage or take down any "no hunting" or similar sign;

    –Handle any firearm in a reckless manner and endanger the life, limb or property of another person;

    –Kill or cripple any non-migratory game bird or game animal without making a reasonable effort to retrieve the animal;

    –Discharge a firearm, crossbow or bow and arrow across or within the right-of-way of any road;

    –Shine a light on places that may be used by deer at anytime while in possession of a rifle, shotgun, pistol, crossbow, bow and arrow, or speargun; if this occurs, everyone in the vehicle is considered in violation;

–Hunt deer after dark;

–Hunt under age 12 without supervision by a licensed parent, guardian or person designated by a parent or guardian;

–Shoot a rifle or pistol at birds and animals over state inland waters;

–Carry a loaded rifle or pistol on a boat on inland waters for hunting;

–Shoot waterfowl from a boat propelled by a motor;

–Hunt or trap on private land without the landowner's permission;

–Hunt while under the influence of drugs or alcohol;

–Hunt during a forest fire;

–Shoot or attempt to take any wild bird or animal from any vehicle, except as provided by law (which includes a permit for disabled hunters);

–Use an aircraft to hunt or pursue any animal for hunting;

–Hunt with a fully automatic firearm.

Many hunting regulations concerning the types of firearms allowed, which depends on the game and the season, can be found in §29.1-526 and -528. Hunting with the wrong type of firearm is a class 3 misdemeanor. Some examples are listed below:

• Only shotguns 10 gauge or smaller with barrels at least 18 inches long are allowed.

• Shotguns must be plugged to accept no more than 3 shells.

• Shotguns with rifled barrels are permitted in counties where slugs may be used.

• There are no restrictions on shot size except for spring gobbler season when shot may be no larger than number 2 fine shot.

• Rifles may be used for wild animals and birds (except migratory birds and waterfowl) and except where prohibited.

- Rifles used for deer or bear must be .23 caliber or larger.
- Rifles, pistols and revolvers may be used for hunting crows except where prohibited by local laws.
- Pistol and revolver ammunition used for hunting deer and bear must be .23 caliber or larger and have a manufacturer rating of 350 foot-pounds of energy or more.
- Pistols and revolvers firing .22 caliber rim fire ammunition and muzzle-loading pistols may be used where .22 caliber rifles are permitted.
- Muzzle-loading shotguns may be used during the general firearms season.
- Muzzle-loading rifles may be used to hunt during the general firearms season except where prohibited by local law.
- All game birds and animals except deer may be hunted with shotguns from boats.

County Firearm-Hunting Ordinances

Counties and cities have broad power to regulate hunting within their borders. The Dept. of Game and Inland Fisheries pamphlet, *Hunting & Trapping in Virginia* lists 52 ordinances in fifty-five counties or cities. These examples are included to show the type of laws you will encounter on a local level, and is *not* a complete list.

1–Rifles up to .25 caliber may be used to hunt groundhogs from March 1 to September 1 with written permission from the landowner (Halifax county).

2–It shall be unlawful to use a rifle larger than .22 rim fire except that groundhogs may be hunted with a rifle of larger caliber (Appomattox county).

3–It is unlawful to hunt with firearms from the road and within ten feet of the ditch bank (Amelia county).

4–It is against the law to hunt deer with muzzleloading rifles from stands ten feet above the ground. (Buckingham, Dinwiddie, Isle of Wight, Lancaster, New Kent and Prince William counties)

5–You cannot shoot a rifle larger than .22 caliber, a muzzleloader larger than .36 caliber, or a shotgun loaded with slugs except from stands at least ten feet above the ground, except for groundhogs in certain areas between March 1 and August 31. (James City County)

6–All rifles, pistols, or shotguns loaded with slugs prohibited for any hunting. (Fairfax County)

7–Rifles are not allowed for deer hunting. (Chesterfield, Essex, Halifax, Northampton, Prince George, Richmond, and Surry counties)

A Hunter's Pledge

Responsible hunting provides unique challenges and rewards. However, the future of the sport depends on each hunter's behavior and ethics. Therefore, as a hunter, I pledge to:

- Respect the environment and wildlife;
- Respect property and landowners;
- Show consideration for non hunters;
- Hunt safely;
- Know and obey the law;
- Support wildlife and habitat conservation;
- Pass on an ethical hunting tradition;
- Strive to improve my outdoor skills and understanding of wildlife;
- Hunt only with ethical hunters.

By following these principles of conduct each time I go afield, I will give my best to the sport, the public, the environment and myself. The responsibility to hunt ethically is mine; the future of hunting depends on me.

The Hunter's Pledge was created cooperatively by:

International Association of Fish and Wildlife Agencies
Izaak Walton League of America
National Rifle Association
Rocky Mountain Elk Foundation
Tread Lightly! Inc.
Sport Fishing Institute
Times Mirror Magazines Conservation Council
U.S. Dept. of Agriculture Extension Service
Wildlife Management Institute

NOTES ON FEDERAL LAW 7

Although federal laws regulate firearms to a great degree, the same laws prohibit the federal and local governments from encroaching on the right to bear arms. This is seen in the 2nd, 4th 9th and 14th Amendments to the Constitution, and in federal statutory laws, which number about 230.

Dealers of firearms must be licensed by the Bureau of Alcohol, Tobacco and Firearms (ATF). Federal law requires licensed dealers to keep records of each sale, but prohibits using this information in any sort of national registration plan. The information is permanently saved by the dealer and is not centrally recorded by the federal authorities. If a dealer goes out of business the records are sent to a central federal depository for storage (or a state site if approved by the Treasury Dept.). Although federal law prohibits using these records to establish a national firearms registration system, several federal attempts to do so have apparently been made.

Paperwork required by the Brady Law is collected by local authorities, but must be destroyed shortly after it is used to conduct background checks, and by law, no records of the checks may be kept. Local authorities are required to certify their compliance with record destruction to the U.S. Attorney General every six months. (The Justice Department reports that compliance with this requirement has been quite low.)

This means there's no central place for anyone to go and see if a given person owns a firearm (except perhaps in the case of those people who have registered for concealed carry, if you assume they all own guns). Firearm ownership in America is traditionally a private matter. For someone to find out if you have a gun they would have to check all the records of all the dealers in the country, a daunting task. Only ATF is authorized to check the records of manufacture, importation and sale of firearms nationally. Local authorities occasionally ask to see a dealer's records, and dealers may feel it's in their best interests to cooperate.

The dealer's records allow guns to be *traced*, a very different and important matter. When a gun is involved in a crime, ATF can find out, from the manufacturer's serial number, which licensed dealer originally received the gun. The dealer can then look through the records and see who purchased the weapon. It's a one-way street—a gun can be linked to a purchaser but owners can't be traced to their guns. One study of successful traces showed that four out of five were of some value to law enforcement authorities.

When President Reagan was shot by John Hinckley Jr., the weapon was traced and in fourteen minutes time, a retail sale to Hinckley was confirmed.

Buying, selling, having, making, transferring and transporting guns is in many cases regulated by federal laws. These regulations are covered in *The Virginia Gun Owner's Guide*, but for the most part, only state penalties are noted. There may be federal penalties as well.

Under the Assimilative Crimes Act, state law controls if there is no federal law covering a situation. It is important to recognize that there can be a question of jurisdiction in some cases. Additional federal requirements may be found in the Code of Federal Regulations and the United States Code.

A long history of federal regulation exists with regard to firearms and other weapons. The main laws include:

- Second Amendment to the Constitution (1791)
- Ninth Amendment to the Constitution (1791)
- Fourteenth Amendment to the Constitution (1868)
- National Firearms Act (1934)
- Federal Firearms Act (1938)
- Omnibus Crime Control and Safe Streets Act (1968)
- Gun Control Act (1968)
- Organized Crime Control Act (1970)
- Omnibus Crime Control Act (1986)
- Firearm Owner's Protection Act (1986)
- Brady Handgun Violence Prevention Act (1993)
- Public Safety and Recreational Firearms Use Protection Act (The Crime Bill) (1994)
- Promotion of Rifle Practice and Firearms Safety Act (1996)
- Antiterrorism and Effective Death Penalty Act (1996)
- Dept. of Defense Appropriation Act for 1997

FEDERAL FIREARMS TRANSPORTATION GUARANTEE

Passed on July 8, 1986 as part of the Firearm Owner's Protection Act, federal law guarantees that a person may legally transport a firearm from one place where its possession is legal to another place where possession is legal, provided it is unloaded and the firearm and ammunition is not readily accessible from the passenger compartment of the vehicle. The law doesn't say it in so many words, but the only non-accessible spot in the average passenger car is the trunk. If a vehicle has no separate compartment for storage, the firearm and ammunition may be in a locked container other than the glove compartment or console.

There have been cases, especially in Eastern states, where local authorities have not complied with this law, creating a degree of risk for people otherwise legally transporting firearms. To avoid any confusion, the text of the federal guarantee is printed here word for word:

Federal Law Number 18 USC § 926A
Interstate transportation of firearms

Notwithstanding any other provision of any law or any rule or regulation of a State or any political subdivision thereof, any person who is not otherwise prohibited by this chapter from transporting, shipping, or receiving a firearm shall be entitled to transport a firearm for any lawful purpose from any place where he may lawfully possess and carry such firearm to any other place where he may lawfully possess and carry such firearm if, during such transportation the firearm is unloaded, and neither the firearm nor any ammunition being transported is readily accessible or is directly accessible from the passenger compartment of such transporting vehicle: Provided, That in the case of a vehicle without a compartment separate from the driver's compartment the firearm or ammunition shall be contained in a locked container other than the glove compartment or console.

Anyone interested in a complete copy of the federal gun laws, with plain English summaries of every law, can get a copy of *Gun Laws of America*, published by Bloomfield Press. See the back section of this book for details.

The Brady Law

The Brady Handgun Violence Prevention Act was signed into law on Nov. 30, 1993. Its provisions for common carriers, reporting multiple handgun sales and license fee increases are among the rules affecting private citizens which took effect immediately. The waiting-period provisions took effect on Feb. 28, 1994, and were set to expire on Feb. 27, 1999.

In addition to the regulation of private citizens described below, the Brady Law: places special requirements on dealers, sets timetables and budgets for the U.S. Attorney General to implement the law, provides funding, sets basic computer system requirements, mandates criminal-history record sharing among authorities, enhances penalties for gun thieves and more. Your federal legislators can send you the full 12-page Brady Law.

The Brady Law refers to a "chief law enforcement officer," defined as the chief of police, the sheriff, an equivalent officer or their designee. The description below refers to such persons as "the authorities." Where the law refers to an individual who is unlicensed under §923 of USC Title 18, this description says "private citizen" or "you." Federally licensed dealers, manufacturers and importers are referred to as "dealers." The act of selling, delivering or transferring is called "transferring." The law defines *handgun* as, "a firearm which has a short stock and is designed to be held and fired by the use of a single hand." A combination of parts which can be assembled into a handgun counts as a handgun.

Under the Brady Law, to legally obtain a handgun from a dealer you must provide:

• A valid picture ID for the dealer to examine;

• A written statement with only the date the statement was made, notice of your intent to obtain a handgun from the dealer, your name, address, date of birth, the type of ID you used and a statement that you are not: 1–under indictment and haven't been convicted of a crime which carries a prison term of more than one year, 2–a fugitive from justice, 3–an unlawful user of or addicted to any controlled substance, 4–

an adjudicated mental defective, 5–a person who has been committed to a mental institution, 6–an illegal alien, 7–dishonorably discharged from the armed forces, 8–a person who has renounced U.S. citizenship.

Then, before transferring the handgun to you, the dealer must:

- Within one day, provide notice of the content and send a copy of the statement to the authorities where you live;

- Keep a copy of your statement and evidence that it was sent to the authorities;

- Wait five days during which state offices are open, from the day the dealer gave the authorities notice, and during that time,

- Receive no information from the authorities that your possession of the handgun would violate federal, state or local laws.

The waiting period ends early if the authorities notify the dealer early that you're eligible. The authorities "shall make a reasonable effort" to check your background in local, state and federal records. Long guns are unaffected by the Brady Law until the National Instant Check described below comes on line.

You are excluded from the Brady waiting-period process:

1–If you have a written statement from the authorities, valid for 10 days, that you need a handgun because of a threat to your life or a member of your household's life; or

2–With a handgun permit, in the state which issued it, if the permit is less than five years old and required a background check. The Virginia handgun permit qualifies under the Brady law.

3–In states which have their own handgun background check (Virginia has an instant check, making all Virginia residents exempt from the Brady delay); or

4–If the transfer is already regulated by the National Firearms Act of 1934, as with Class III weapons; or

5–If the dealer has been certified as being in an extremely remote location of a sparsely populated state and there are no telecommunications near the dealer's business premises (written for Alaska, but other localities may qualify).

If a dealer is notified after a transfer that your possession of the handgun is illegal, the dealer must, within one business day, provide any information they have about you to the authorities at the dealer's place of business and at your residence. The information a dealer receives may only be communicated to you, the authorities or by court order. If you are denied a handgun, you may ask the authorities why, and they are required to provide the reason in writing within 20 business days of your request.

Unless the authorities determine that the handgun transfer to you would be illegal, they must, within 20 days of the date of your statement, destroy all records of the process. The authorities are expressly forbidden to convey or use the information in your statement for anything other than what's needed to carry out the Brady process.

The authorities may not be held liable for damages for either allowing an illegal handgun transfer or preventing a legal one. If you are denied a firearm unjustly, you may sue the political entity responsible and get the information corrected or have the transfer approved, and you may collect reasonable attorney's fees.

National Instant Check: The Brady Law requires the U.S. Attorney General (AG) to establish a National Instant Criminal Background Check system (NICBC) before Nov. 30, 1998. Once this is in effect, the previous waiting process is eliminated. In order to transfer any firearm, not just handguns, when the NICBC system is in place, a dealer must:

- verify your identity from a valid photo-ID card, contact the system, identify you and receive a unique transfer number, or

- wait three days during which state offices are open and the system provides no notice that the transfer would violate relevant laws.

The NICBC system is required to issue the transfer number if the transfer would violate no relevant laws, and it destroys all records of approved inquiries except for the identifying number and the date it was issued. If the transfer is legal, the dealer includes the transfer number in the record of the transaction. The NICBC system is bypassed under conditions similar to 2, 4 and 5 listed above as exceptions to the waiting period (with number 2 broadened to include "firearms" permit).

Whoever violates these requirements is subject to a fine of up to $1,000 and a jail term of up to 1 year.

If you are denied a firearm under the NICBC, you may request the reason and the system must present you with a written answer within five business days. You may also request the reason from the AG, who must respond immediately. You may provide information to fix any errors in the system, and the AG must immediately consider the information, investigate further, correct any erroneous federal records and notify any federal or state agency that was the source of the errors.

Multiple sales of handguns (two or more from the same dealer in a five day period) have long been reported to the Bureau of Alcohol, Tobacco and Firearms, and must now be reported to local authorities as well. Local authorities may not disclose the information, must destroy the records within 20 days from receipt if the transfer is not illegal and must certify every six months to the AG that they are complying with these provisions.

Common or contract carriers (airlines, buses, trains, etc.) may not label your luggage or packages to indicate that they contain firearms. The long-time labeling practice had been responsible for the frequent theft of luggage containing firearms. Federal law requires you to notify the carrier in writing if you are transporting firearms or ammunition, but in actual practice verbal notification is frequently accepted.

Licensing fees for obtaining a new federal firearms license are increased to $200 for three years. The fee for renewing a currently valid license is $90 for three years.

Brady Law Note

While the Brady Law is new it would be prudent to anticipate a degree of confusion, inconsistent policies and enforcement, conflicting regulations and jurisdictions, regulations which do not match the letter of the law, denials of responsibility, and court cases to clarify the intent, practicalities and legality of the law. With the law being challenged in federal courts, changes to it, repeal or partial repeal are possible.

Public Safety and Recreational Firearms Use Protection Act

This law, popularized as the 1994 Crime Bill and sometimes referred to as the assault-weapons ban, affected three areas of existing firearms law: 1–Possession and use of firearms by juveniles; 2–Purchase of firearms by people under domestic violence restraining orders; and 3–It created a new class of regulated firearms and accessories. The information on juveniles is found in Chapter 1 since it relates to who can bear arms. The new class of prohibited purchasers (for domestic violence cases) is also in Chapter 1, as part of the list for federal form 4473—the form dealers use with all sales.

The portion of the law that creates the legal *assault-weapons* category, has been poorly reported and many people have an inaccurate notion of what this law accomplished. Nothing is actually banned—Americans may still buy, own, sell, trade, have and use any of the millions of affected firearms and accessories.

What the law actually did was to prohibit *manufacturers and importers* from selling newly made goods of that type to the public (and it's a crime for the public to get them). Maybe that is a ban, but not in the sense that's been popularized. Contrary to news reports, the law did nothing about the very real problem of getting armed criminals off the street. The list of affected weapons is in Chapter 3.

The net effect of the law was to motivate manufacturers to create stockpiles before the law took affect, then to introduce new products that are not affected and to step up marketing efforts overseas for affected products. In addition, demand and prices skyrocketed for the now fixed supply of goods domestically, and then adjusted downward when it became obvious that supplies were still available. None of this applies after the law expires in 2004. If this is all news to you, it's time to question your source of news.

Rifle Practice and Firearms Safety Act (1996)

The Civilian Marksmanship Program, run by the U.S. Army, has served as the federal government's official firearms training, supply and competitions program for U.S. citizens, since 1956. Its history traces back to the late 1800s, when programs were first established to help ensure that the populace could shoot straight, in the event an army had to be raised to defend the country. The program is privatized by this act.

The federal government transfers the responsibility and facilities for training civilians in the use of small arms to a 501(c)(3) non-profit corporation created for this purpose. All law-abiding citizens are eligible to participate, and priority is given to reaching and training youth in the safe, lawful and accurate use of firearms.

Functions formerly performed for this program by the Army are now the responsibility of this new corporation. The Army is required to provide direct support and to take whatever action is necessary to make the program work in its privatized form. The stated program goals are:

1–Teaching marksmanship to U.S. citizens

2–Promoting practice and safety in the use of firearms

3–Conducting matches and competitions

4–Awarding trophies and prizes

5–Procuring supplies and services needed for the program

6–Securing and accounting for all firearms, ammunition and supplies used in the program

7–Giving, lending or selling firearms, ammunition and supplies under the program. Priority must be given to training youths, and reaching as many youths as possible.

Any person who is not a felon, hasn't violated the main federal gun laws, and does not belong to a group that advocates violent overthrow of the U.S. government, may participate in the Civilian Marksmanship Program.

Antiterrorism Act of 1996

A wide variety of gun-law changes were introduced in this 48,728-word act. Eight sections introduce new law, and other sections make 17 amendments to existing federal law. Much of it deals with intentional criminal acts, and so falls outside the scope of *The Virginia Gun Owner's Guide*. Other sections could give rise to unexpected results and are included.

Section 702. Using a firearm in an assault on any person in the U.S. is a federal crime if: 1–the assault involves "conduct transcending national boundaries" (described below) and 2–if any of the following also exist: A–any perpetrator uses the mail or interstate or foreign commerce in committing the crime; B–the offense in any way affects interstate or foreign commerce; C–the victim is anyone in the federal government or the military; D–any structure or property damaged is owned in any part by the federal government, or E–the offense occurs in special U.S. territorial jurisdictions. The maximum penalty in a non-lethal assault with a firearm is 30 years.

Causing a serious risk of injury to anyone, by damaging any structure or property in the U.S., is a federal crime if the conditions described in 1 and 2 above exist. The maximum penalty is 25 years.

Threatening, attempting or conspiring to commit the above acts is a crime, and various penalties are defined.

The phrase "conduct transcending national boundaries" means "conduct occurring outside of the United States in addition to the conduct occurring in the United States." It is not clear what this might include.

The Attorney General is in charge of investigating "federal crimes of terrorism." Such crimes occur when any of a long list of felonies is committed to influence the government by intimidation or coercion, or to retaliate against government actions. An assault involving conduct transcending national boundaries, described in the first part of this law, is one of the felonies.

Section 727. Using or attempting to use deadly force against anyone in the federal government or the military, if the attack is because of the person's government role, is a federal crime (in addition to existing assault and homicide laws). All former personnel are included. Federal penalties for an attack on anyone in this protected class are defined. In the case of such an assault, a gun is considered a gun, even if it jams due to a defective part.

Dept. of Defense Appropriation Act, 1997

Section 657, Gun-Free School Zone. Congress was stopped in its attempt to exercise police powers at the state level by the U.S. Supreme Court, when the court declared the 1991 Gun-Free School Zone law unconstitutional, in 1995. That law was reenacted, to the surprise of many observers, as an unnoticed add-on to a 2,000-page federal spending bill, in a form essentially identical to the one the Supreme Court overturned.

The law makes it a federal crime to knowingly have a firearm within 1,000 feet of any school. An exemption is granted to anyone willing to register with the government for a specified license to carry the firearm, and the prohibition does not apply to: 1–Firearms while on private property that is not part of the school grounds; 2–Any firearm that is unloaded and in a locked container; 3–Any firearm unloaded and locked in a firearms rack on a motor vehicle; 4–Possession of a firearm for use in an approved school program; 5–Possession under a contract with the school; 6–Possessed by law enforcement officers in an official capacity; and 7–An unloaded firearm, while crossing school premises to public or private land open to hunting, if crossing the grounds is authorized by the school.

It is also illegal to fire a gun (or attempt to fire a gun), knowingly or with reckless disregard for safety, in a place you know is a school zone, with the following exceptions: 1–On private property that is not part of the school grounds; 2–As part of a program approved by the school; 3–Under contract with the school; 4–By law enforcement acting in an official capacity. Self defense is not mentioned. States are not prohibited from passing their own laws.

America had 121,855 public and private schools as of 1994. In effect, this law criminalizes the actions of nearly anyone who travels in a populated area with a legally possessed firearm. As with its overturned predecessor, its affect on the very real problem of youth violence is unclear, and of course, any firearm used illegally in America, whether it is near a school or not, is already a serious crime with penalties.

Section 658. Misdemeanor Gun Ban for Domestic Violence Offense. Anyone convicted of a state or federal misdemeanor involving the use or attempted use of physical force, or the threatened use of a deadly weapon, among family members (spouse, parent, guardian, cohabiter, co-parent or similar) is prohibited from possessing a firearm under federal law. This marks the first time that a misdemeanor offense serves as grounds for denial of the constitutional right to keep and bear arms. The number of people affected is unknown, and no provision is made for the firearms such men and women might already possess. Firearms possession by a prohibited possessor is a five-year federal felony.

A number of narrow conditions may exempt a person from this law, including whether they were represented by an attorney, the type of trial and plea, an expungement or set aside, or a pardon or other restoration of civil rights.

The Changing Federal Landscape
Court challenges are actively underway with regard to the Brady law and other federal firearms issues. Despite pronouncements about a moratorium on new gun laws, federal gun law grew by over 10% in the first six months of 1996 alone. **New laws may be passed at any time, and it is your responsibility to be fully up-to-date when handling firearms under all circumstances. The information contained in this book is guaranteed to age.**

Failure to comply with new laws and regulations can have serious consequences to you personally, even if you believe your Constitutional rights have been compromised. In fact, many experts have noted that increasing latitudes are being taken by some governmental authorities with respect to Constitutional guarantees. Legislative and regulatory changes present serious risks to currently law-abiding citizens, since what is legal today may not be tomorrow. The entire body of U.S. law is growing at a significant rate and it represents some potential for threats to freedoms Americans have always enjoyed. It is prudent to take whatever steps you feel are reasonable to minimize any risks.

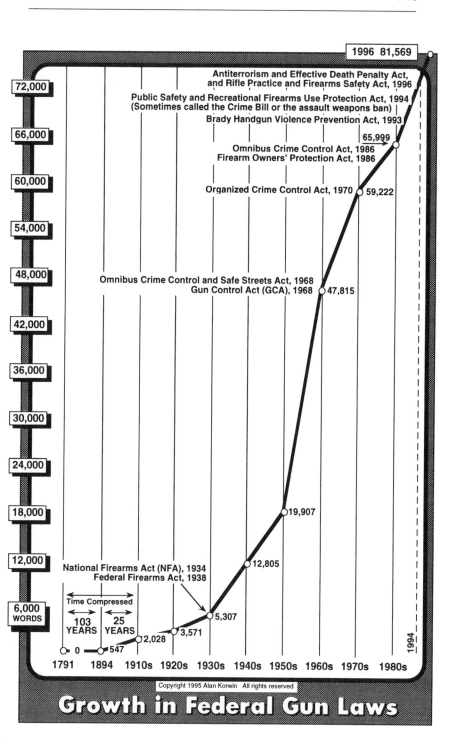

1996 81,569

72,000

Antiterrorism and Effective Death Penalty Act,
and Rifle Practice and Firearms Safety Act, 1996
Public Safety and Recreational Firearms Use Protection Act, 1994
(Sometimes called the Crime Bill or the assault weapons ban)
Brady Handgun Violence Prevention Act, 1993

66,000

65,999

Omnibus Crime Control Act, 1986
Firearm Owners' Protection Act, 1986

60,000

Organized Crime Control Act, 1970   59,222

54,000

48,000

Omnibus Crime Control and Safe Streets Act, 1968
Gun Control Act (GCA), 1968   47,815

42,000

36,000

30,000

24,000

18,000

19,907

12,000

12,805

National Firearms Act (NFA), 1934
Federal Firearms Act, 1938

6,000
WORDS

Time Compressed

103
YEARS

25
YEARS

5,307

3,571

2,028

547

0

1791   1894   1910s   1920s   1930s   1940s   1950s   1960s   1970s   1980s

1994

Growth in Federal Gun Laws

GUN SAFETY and Self-Defense Training 8

Many fine books and classes exist which teach the current wisdom on gun safety and use. In Virginia, some of the best public classes are given by the Dept. of Game and Inland Fisheries and the National Rifle Association. Advanced firearms and tactical training classes are available from private instructors and schools.

When studying firearm safety (and every gun owner should), you will likely come across the Ten Commandments of Gun Safety. These well-intentioned lists have serious drawbacks— no two lists are ever the same and there are many more than ten rules to follow for safe gun use. In addition, hunters must learn many rules which don't apply to other shooters. For instance, a hunter should never openly carry game—it makes you an unwitting target of other hunters.

The Commandments of Safety are actually a way of saying, "Here's how people have accidents with guns." Each rule implies a kind of mishap. It's good exercise to look at each rule and read between the lines to find its counterpart—the potential disaster the rule will help you avoid. For example, Rule 1 translates into, "People have accidents with guns which they think are empty." Always keep in mind the prime directive: Take time to be safe instead of forever being sorry.

THE GUN OWNER'S COMMANDMENTS OF SAFETY

1–Treat every gun as if it is loaded until you have personally proven otherwise.

2–Always keep a gun pointed in a safe direction.

3–Don't touch the trigger until you're ready to fire.

4–Be certain of your target and what is beyond it before pulling the trigger.

5–Keep a gun you carry discretely holstered or otherwise concealed unless you're ready to use it.

6–Use but never rely on the safety.

7–Never load a gun until ready to use. Unload a gun immediately after use.

8–Only use ammunition which exactly matches the markings on your gun.

9–Always read and follow manufacturers' instructions carefully.

10–At a shooting range, always keep a gun pointed downrange.

11–Always obey a range officer's commands immediately.

12–Always wear adequate eye and ear protection when shooting.

13–If a gun fails to fire: a) keep it pointed in a safe direction; b) wait thirty seconds in case of a delayed firing; c) unload the gun carefully, avoiding exposure to the breech.

14–Don't climb fences or trees, or jump logs or ditches with a chambered round.

15–Be able to control the direction of the muzzle even if you stumble.

16–Keep the barrel and action clear of obstructions.

17–Avoid carrying ammunition which doesn't match the gun you are carrying.

18–Be aware that customized guns may require ammunition which doesn't match the gun's original markings.

19–Store guns with the action open.

20–Store ammunition and guns separately, and out of reach of children and careless adults.

21–Never pull a gun toward you by the muzzle.

22–Never horseplay with a firearm.

23–Never shoot at a hard flat surface, or at water, to prevent ricochets.

24–Be sure you have an adequate backstop for target shooting.

25–On open terrain with other people present, keep guns pointed upwards, or downwards and away from the people.

26–Never handle a gun you are not familiar with.

27–Learn to operate a gun empty before attempting to load and shoot it.

28–Be cautious transporting a loaded firearm in a vehicle.

29–Never lean a firearm where it may slip and fall.

30–Do not use alcohol or mood-altering drugs when you are handling firearms.

31–When loading or unloading a firearm, always keep the muzzle pointed in a safe direction.

32–Never use a rifle scope instead of a pair of binoculars.

33–Always remember that removing the magazine (sometimes called the clip) from semi-automatic and automatic weapons may still leave a live round, ready to fire, in the chamber.

34–Never rely on one empty cylinder next to the barrel of a revolver as a guarantee of safety, since different revolvers rotate in opposite directions.

35–Never step into a boat holding a loaded firearm.

36–It's difficult to use a gun safely until you become a marksman.

37–It's difficult to handle a gun safely if you need corrective lenses and are not wearing them.

38–Know the effective range and the maximum range of a firearm and the ammunition you are using.

39–Be sure that anyone with access to a firearm kept in a home understands its safe use.

40–Don't fire a large caliber weapon if you cannot control the recoil.

41–Never put your finger in the trigger guard when drawing a gun from a holster.

42–Never put your hand in front of the cylinder of a revolver when firing.

43–Never put your hand in back of the slide of a semi-automatic pistol when firing.

44–Always leave the hammer of a revolver resting over an empty chamber.

45–Never leave ammunition around when cleaning a gun.

46–Clean firearms after they have been used. A dirty gun is not as safe as a clean one.

47–Never fire a blank round directly at a person. Blanks can blind, maim, and at close range, they can kill.

48–Only use firearms in good working condition, and ammunition which is fresh.

49–Accidents don't happen, they are caused, and it's up to you and you alone to prevent them in all cases. Every "accident" which ever happened could have been avoided. Where there are firearms there is a need for caution.

50–Always think first and shoot second.

It is the responsibility of every American to prevent firearms from being instruments of tragedy.

TEACH YOUR CHILDREN WELL

Keeping Children Safe

Choosing to own a firearm—or choosing not to—has serious implications for the safety of your children and family. Your ability to respond in an emergency or not, and a child's dangerous access to a loaded firearm without your approval, should motivate you to take serious precautions for safety where firearms are concerned.

Firearms are dangerous; they're supposed to be dangerous; they wouldn't be very valuable if they weren't dangerous. The same as with power tools, automobiles, medicines, kitchen knives, balconies, swimming pools, electricity and everything else, it is up to responsible adults and their actions to help ensure the safety of those they love and the rest of the community.

In Virginia these are not just good ideas, it's the law. A firearm owner has a direct responsibility to control a child's access to a loaded firearm under Code of Virginia §18.2-56.2.

It is your responsibility to see that your own children, children who might visit you and careless adults are prevented from unauthorized access to any firearms you possess.

A delicate balance exists between keeping a gun immediately ready for response in an emergency, and protecting it from careless adults and children. This is the paradox of home-defense firearms. The more out-of-reach a gun is for safety's sake, the less accessible it is for self defense (also for safety's sake).

Secured Storage

Leaving a loaded gun out *in the open* where careless adults or children could get at it is not being responsible and subjects you to criminal charges if an accident occurs.

Putting a loaded gun in *a hard-to-find spot* may fool some kids (and it's better than doing nothing), but remember how easily you found your folks' stuff when you were a kid.

Putting a gun in *a hard-to-get-to spot* (like the top of a closet) has advantages over hard-to-find spots when small children (like toddlers) are involved. Remember that kids reach an age where they like to climb. And you really have no idea what goes on when the baby-sitter is around.

Hinged *false picture frames*, when done well, provide a readily available firearm that most people will simply never notice. The frame must be in a spot that can't be bumped, and if ever the frame is detected its value is completely and immediately compromised.

Trigger guards warn that a gun is loaded, but they provide a low level of child-proofing since they are typically designed to be removed easily.

Gun locks can be effective in preventing accidents but are completely compromised if a child can get at the key. The location of the key then becomes the paradox factor in keeping the gun at-the-ready yet safe. The closer together you keep the gun and its key the less safety the lock provides.

Combination gun locks eliminate the key problem, but mustn't be forgotten. If written down somewhere handy they too may be discovered. Many are difficult or impossible to operate in the dark. A number of push-button lock designs have been introduced which are made to fit directly into a handgun's mechanism.

Gun safes used properly can prevent accidents and provide reasonable access to personal firearms, but it is an expensive option. Many people with gun collections keep their firearms in a floor-standing safe, for theft and fire protection, simultaneously providing a high degree of accident proofing. Single-gun handgun safes are made for floor or wall mounting and use finger touch buttons that can be operated quickly in the dark. This is an excellent option for keeping a gun available yet highly protected from unauthorized use. Be sure to never let the batteries run down in the electronic models.

A home that doesn't have many visitors and never has kids around has a different challenge than a home with four kids growing up, when it comes to staying safe. Be sure that your home is safe for your kids—safe from those who would do you harm, and safe from the potential for harm your own home holds.

Disabling

Disabling a gun provides a safety margin. The more disabled a gun is the greater the safety, but the more difficult it becomes to bring the gun to bear if it should be needed.

The least disabled condition, and hence the least safe (though better than nothing), is a *safety lever engaged* on a semi-automatic or an appropriate empty cylinder on a revolver.

An *unloaded* firearm is disabled in a sense, and incapable of firing, though that reverses completely upon the presence of ammunition. The margin of safety here, for both preventing accidents and providing defense, is as wide as the distance between the gun and its ammunition, very similar to the key and lock relationship.

Removing a firing pin or otherwise disassembling a firearm represents a high degree of disabling, essentially lowering chances of accidents to zero, and removing the possibility of putting the weapon to use in an emergency.

Keeping *no firearm at home* eliminates the ability to respond for safety if necessary, and still leaves a child at risk when visiting friends or when friends visit (especially if the child is not firearms aware).

The bottom line is that there are no perfect solutions, and that life has risks. You trade some for others, and make personal choices that affect everything you do. Be sure you make the hard choices necessary to keep your family safe in your own home.

One Man's Approach

Internationally recognized firearms instructor and author Massad Ayoob believes it's wiser to educate your children than attempting to childproof your gun. For a detailed discussion of this approach to guns and child safety, read his booklet, *Gun-Proof Your Children*, available from Bloomfield Press.

The Eddie Eagle Program

If you look behind all the hot political rhetoric, you'll notice that the main provider of firearms safety training in America is the National Rifle Association, fulfilling a century-old historic tradition that is actually embodied in federal law. Handgun Control, Inc., and the NRA agree that child accidents are tragic and that responsible citizens must take steps to protect youngsters. In response to this well perceived need, the NRA developed its highly acclaimed and widely used Eddie Eagle Safety Program. For teacher lesson plans, class materials, parent kits, video tapes, coloring books, posters and more, contact the NRA, listed in the Appendix.

THE EDDIE EAGLE SAFETY RULES FOR KIDS —

If you find a gun:

STOP!

Don't touch.

Leave the area.

Tell an adult.

HOW WELL DO YOU KNOW YOUR GUN?

Safe and effective use of firearms demands that you understand your weapon thoroughly. This knowledge is best gained through a combination of reading, classes and practice with a qualified instructor. The simple test below will help tell you if you are properly trained in the use of firearms. If you're not sure what all the terms mean, can you be absolutely sure that you're qualified to handle firearms safely?

☐ Action	☐ Forearm	☐ Receiver
☐ Ammunition	☐ Fouling	☐ Repeater
☐ Automatic	☐ Frame	☐ Revolver rifle
☐ Ballistics	☐ Gauge	☐ Rifling
☐ Barrel	☐ Grip	☐ Rimfire
☐ Black powder	☐ Grip panels	☐ Safety
☐ Bolt	☐ Grooves	☐ Sear
☐ Bore	☐ Gunpowder	☐ Semi-automatic
☐ Break action	☐ Half cock	☐ Shell
☐ Breech	☐ Hammer	☐ Shooting positions
☐ Buckshot	☐ Handgun	☐ Shot
☐ Bullet	☐ Hangfire	☐ Shotgun
☐ Butt	☐ Hunter orange	☐ Sights
☐ Caliber	☐ Ignition	☐ Sighting-in
☐ Cartridge	☐ Kneeling	☐ Sitting
☐ Case	☐ Lands	☐ Smokeless powder
☐ Casing	☐ Lever action	☐ Smoothbore
☐ Centerfire	☐ Magazine	☐ Standing
☐ Chamber	☐ Mainspring	☐ Stock
☐ Checkering	☐ Maximum range	☐ Trigger
☐ Choke	☐ Misfire	☐ Trigger guard
☐ Clip	☐ Muzzle	☐ Unplugged shotgun
☐ Cock	☐ Muzzleloader	
☐ Comb	☐ Pattern	
☐ Cylinder	☐ Pistol	
☐ Discharge	☐ Powder	
☐ Dominant eye	☐ Primer	
☐ Effective range	☐ Projectile	
☐ Firearm	☐ Prone	
☐ Firing Pin	☐ Pump action	
☐ Firing Line	☐ Pyrodex	

CONCEALED-HANDGUN TRAINING

Virginia requires its law-abiding citizens, under §18.2-308, to show the circuit court issuing a handgun-carry permit proof that you have "demonstrated competence" with a handgun. This is described in Chapter 2, and the degree of training is left in large measure up to you.

Even though you can make do with less, it makes sense for you personally to get a high degree of training. Many states expect two full days of training or more to obtain a carry license. Most experts consider this a bare minimum if you're serious about bearing arms.

Some people buy a handgun, a box of ammo, load it up and put it in the night stand. Some will go so far as to run a few rounds through the gun to make sure it works, and then put it in the night stand. This does not constitute a commitment to firearms proficiency. Commitment is an essential element to responsible firearms ownership.

Take the time to get training. The NRA offers firearms training for all levels of experience. Contact them at the phone number in Appendix C and attend one of their excellent courses. The Virginia Dept. of Game and Inland Fisheries' hunter safety course is another good place to start. Their numbers are also in Appendix C. Qualified private trainers are spread all across the state. Whatever training you receive, look at it as a beginning. You must practice frequently throughout your life to keep the needed skills.

Mistakes made with firearms can be tragic. The effect on your life and your loved ones can be devastating. And every mistake made is fuel for the fire of those who seek to deny gun rights. As a gun owner you must rise to a higher level of responsibility.

Here are some sample questions that concealed-carry permit applicants—and all responsible gun owners—probably should know:

Areas of Study:

1–Where are firearms prohibited in Virginia?
(At least seven places in addition to those prohibited by local laws, study chapters 2 and 4)

2–What are the possible penalties for improper display of a weapon in Virginia?
(At least three possible charges could be brought, study chapter 5)

3–What risks exist in drawing a firearm in public?
(Could be used to justify a self-defense claim by another party, accidental discharge, discharge in prohibited area, more, study chapter 5)

4–When does state law justify the use of deadly force?
(Legal precedents set by case law describe justifiable and excusable use of deadly force, study chapter 5)

5–What factors affect the strict legal definitions for justifiable or excusable use of deadly force?
(This is a complex issue frequently subject to debate and interpretation, fact-intensive and specific to the circumstances, study chapter 5 and 8, and other books, such as In The Gravest Extreme, *by Massad Ayoob)*

6–What responsibility does a person have for firing shots that miss the intended target?
(Severe liabilities and penalties may result from the effect of stray bullets, study chapters 4 and 5)

7–Can you bring a firearm into a bar?
(Special requirements apply to people with concealed-carry permits, study chapter 2)

8–What types of weapons are illegal?
(For federal- and state-law restrictions, study chapter 3)

9–Who can legally bear arms in Virginia?
(Age, background, mental condition and more are taken into account, study chapter 1)

10–Under what circumstances can minors bear arms?
(Study chapters 1 and 4)

11–How can firearms be carried throughout the state?
(Different rules apply for carrying on yourself, in vehicles, while hunting, for minors, in school zones, local ordinances may apply, especially on roads, and more, study chapters 1, 2 and 4)

12–What are the requirements for getting a concealed-carry permit?
(Personal background and demonstrated competency with a handgun are involved, study chapter 2)

13–What do you have to do to ship firearms or carry them with you on a train, plane, or as you travel by car?
(Federal regulations control interstate transit, study chapter 1 and 7)

14–How remote do you have to be to practice target shooting outdoors?
(Land office rules are plentiful, study chapter 4)

15–How much judgment is involved in deciding whether you can use deadly force in a situation?
(No easy answers to this, read everything you can find on the subject, study chapters 5 and 8, get training, and recognize that in using deadly force you accept very definite and substantial legal risks)

16–What are the main rules of firearm safety?
(More than 50 exist, study chapter 8)

17–What types of weapons are suitable for self defense, and what are the best choices for you?
(A very important topic, not covered in this book, you should discuss this at length with your instructor.)

18–How do the various types of firearms operate?
(This topic should be covered by your instructor)

19–What are the options for carrying a concealed handgun?
(This topic should be covered by your instructor)

20–Have any new laws passed that you should know about?
(This requires ongoing information and vigilance. Send Bloomfield Press a self-addressed stamped envelope for news of our next update)

21–Are you mentally prepared to use deadly force?
 (Mental conditioning for the use of deadly force is a critical component, and one that is not easily addressed. Until a moment arrives you may never truly know the answer to this question.)

As you can see, your preparation for carrying a concealed handgun can go well beyond the state-required minimums. Make the smart choice and exceed the minimum training by reading extensively, practicing regularly, keeping up on the important issues, and taking additional training programs.

JUDGMENTAL SHOOTING

All gun owners, and concealed-carry permit holders in particular, should study issues related to judgmental shooting. Anyone considering armed response needs an understanding of the issues involved.

The decision to use deadly force is rarely a clear-cut choice. Regardless of your familiarity with the laws, your degree of training, the quality of your judgmental skills and your physical location and condition at the time of a deadly threat, the demands placed on you at the critical moment are as intense as anything you will normally experience in your life, and your actual performance is an unknown.

Every situation is different. The answers to many questions relating to deadly force are subject to debate. To be prepared for armed response you must recognize that such situations are not black or white, and that your actions, no matter how well intentioned, will be evaluated by others, probably long after you act.

The chances that you will come away from a lethal encounter without any scars—legal, physical or psychological—are small, and the legal risks are substantial. That's why it's usually best to practice prevention and avoidance rather than confrontation, whenever possible.

Most people can think about it this way: You've gotten along this far in life without ever having pulled a weapon on someone, much less having fired it. The odds of that changing once you have a concealed-carry permit are about the same, practically zero.

A concealed handgun may make you feel more secure, but it doesn't change how safe your surroundings actually are, in the places you normally travel, one bit. And it certainly isn't safe to think of a firearm as a license (or a talisman) for walking through potentially dangerous areas you would otherwise avoid like the plague.

Remember that the person holding a gun after a shooting is frequently thought of as the bad guy—the perpetrator—even if it's you and you acted in self defense. The person who is shot often gets a different, more sympathetic name—the victim—and gets the benefit of a prosecutor even if, perhaps, you learn later it's a hardened criminal with a long record.

Maybe your defense will improve if it is indeed a serious repeat offender, but you won't know that until after the fact, and don't count on it. If you ever have to raise a gun to a criminal, you'll find out quickly how good they can be at portraying you as the bad guy and themselves as the helpless innocents, at the mercy of a crazed wacko—you.

Situational Analysis

Think about the deadly force encounters described below, and consider discussing them with your personal firearms-safety trainer:

1–If you are being seriously attacked by a man with a club, is it legal for you to aim for his leg so you can stop the attack without killing him?

2–If you enter your home and find a person looting your possessions are you justified in shooting?

3–If you enter your home and find a person looting your possessions, who runs out the back door as he hears you arrive, can you shoot him to stop him from escaping?

4–If you enter your home and find a person looting your possessions, who turns and whirls toward you when you enter, literally scaring you to death, may you shoot and expect to be justified?

5–If you enter your home and find a stranger in it who charges you with a knife, may you shoot?

6–A stranger in your home has just stabbed your spouse and is about to stab your spouse again. May you shoot the stranger from behind to stop the attack?

7–As you walk past a park at night, you notice a woman tied to a tree and a man tearing off her clothing. May you use deadly force to stop his actions?

8–A police officer is bleeding badly and chasing a man in prison coveralls who runs right past you. May you shoot the fleeing suspect while he is in close range to you?

9–You're in your home at night when a man with a ski mask on comes through an open window in the hallway. May you shoot?

10–You're in your home at night, sleeping, when a noise at the other end of the house awakens you. Taking your revolver you quietly walk over to investigate and notice a short person going through your silverware drawer, 45 feet from where you're standing. The person doesn't notice you. May you shoot ?

11–As you approach your parked car in a dark and remote section of a parking lot, three youthful toughs approach you from three separate directions. You probably can't unlock your vehicle and get in before they reach you and you're carrying a gun. What should you do?

12–From outside a convenience store you observe what clearly appears to be an armed robbery—four people are being held at gun point while the store clerk is putting money into a paper bag. You're armed. What should you do?

13–You're waiting to cross the street in downtown and a beggar asks you for money. He's insistent and begins to insult you when you refuse to ante up. Finally, he gets loud and belligerent and says he'll kill you if you don't give him ten dollars. May you shoot him?

14–You get in your car, roll down the windows, and before you can drive off a man sticks a knife in the window and orders you to get out. Can you shoot him?

15–You get in your car and before you start it a man points a gun at you and tells you to get out. You have a gun in the pocket on the door, another under the seat, and a gun in a holster in your pants. What should you do?

16–Before you get in your car, a man with a gun comes up from behind, demands your car keys, takes them, and while holding you at gun point, starts your car and drives away. Can you shoot at him while he's escaping?

17–You're walking to your car in the mall parking lot after a movie when two armed hoods jump out of a shadow and demand your money. You've got a gun in your back pocket. What should you do?

18–A masked person with a gun stops you on the street, demands and takes your valuables, then flees down the street on foot. You're carrying a concealed handgun. What should you do?

19–A youngster runs right by you down the street and an old lady shouts, "Stop him, he killed my husband!" May you shoot to stop his getaway?

20–You're at work when two ornery-looking dudes amble in. You can smell trouble, so you walk to a good vantage point behind a showcase. Sure enough, they pull guns and announce a stick-up. You and your four employees are armed and there are several customers in the store. What's your move?

21–Your friend and you have been drinking, and now you're arguing over a football bet. You say the spread was six points, he says four. There's $500 hanging in the balance of a five-point game, and it represents your mortgage payment. He pulls a knife and says, "Pay me or I'll slice you up." You've got a gun in your pocket. What should you do?

22–At a gas station, the lines are long, it's hot, and the guy next in line starts getting surly. You're not done pumping and he hits you in the face and tells you to finish up. He shuts off your pump and says he'll kick your butt if you don't move on. Should you pull your gun to put him in his place?

Observations about the situations presented:

1–The Hollywood-promoted idea of *shoot to wound* is incredibly poor in the real world for a host of reasons. If you wing an arm but hit an artery the person can die anyway—there is no such thing as "wounding-level force." Hitting the limb of a moving person may be one of the most difficult shots known, especially in the stressful emotional state where this would occur. If you miss you are jeopardizing your life which is severely threatened in the first place or you would have no justification to shoot at all. It wastes valuable ammunition which may be critical to stopping the lethal attack you face. It's an unlikely case where the justification to use deadly force would be justification to intentionally wound a person. Firing and missing is a different story, but a prosecutor can argue that if the threat wasn't sufficient to shoot to kill then there was no justification to shoot at all.

2–Not enough information is provided to make an informed choice.

3–No. The penalty for burglary is jail, not death, and you almost never have the right to kill to prevent a criminal from escaping. Once the danger to you is over—and it generally is once the criminal is fleeing—your right to use deadly force ends.

4–You need more information to make a responsible choice. Do you always enter your home prepared for mortal combat? Does your story have other holes a prosecutor will notice?

5–It's hard to imagine not being justified in this situation, but stranger things have happened.

6–It's hard to imagine not being justified in this situation, but stranger things have happened. Will the bullet exit the attacker and wound your spouse? In one bizarre case (Arizona 1996), the attacker was actually the husband, wearing a ski mask, and the shooter was the wife's father-in-law—the husband's dad. They didn't even suspect what really happened until they were at the hospital, where the wife learned she was a widow and the shooter realized he had killed his own son.

7–Probably not, since you don't know if the people are consenting adults who like this sort of thing. Even if a crime is being committed, shooting might be viewed as excessive force. A seasoned police officer might cautiously approach the couple, weapon drawn, and with words instead of force determine what's happening, and then make further choices depending on the outcome.

8–Not enough information is provided to make an informed choice. Keep in mind that you do not have the obligation to apprehend criminals that police have.

9–Probably, though a well-trained expert might instead confront the intruder from a secure position and succeed in holding the person for arrest, which is no easy task. The longer you must hold the suspect the greater the risk to you. Armed and from good cover, you might just convince the intruder to leave the way he came.

10–Probably not. The distance and lack of immediate threat will make for a difficult explanation when the police arrive, and if the perpetrator has an accomplice that you didn't notice, the danger to you is severe. If it turns out that the intruder is 11 years old your court defense will be extremely difficult. Remember, you're obligated to not shoot if you don't absolutely have to. A shot would be in conflict with a prime safety rule—clearly identify your target before firing. Has your training prepared you for this?

11–That's a good question, and you should never have parked there in the first place.

12–Call for assistance, go to a defensible position, continue to observe, and recognize that charging into such a volatile situation is incredibly risky for all parties.

13–You are never justified in using deadly force in response to verbal provocation alone, no matter how severe.

14–The prosecutor will make it clear that if you could have stepped on the gas and escaped, the threat to you would have ended, and the need to shoot did not exist. If you were boxed into a parking space, the need to defend yourself would be hard for a prosecutor to refute. These things often come down to the exact circumstances and the quality of the attorneys.

15–Get out quietly and don't provoke someone who has the drop on you. All your guns are no match for a drawn weapon. This is where a real understanding of tactics comes into play.

16–No. Once the threat to you is over, the justification for using lethal force ends.

17–Not enough information is provided to make an informed choice.

18–Anyone crazy enough to rob you at gun point must be considered capable of doing anything, and the smart move is to avoid further confrontation and stay alive. Chasing after him is extremely unwise and risky to you.

19–You don't have enough information. When in doubt, don't shoot.

20–This is where strategy and tactics are critical. If you allow your employees to carry and are prepared for armed defense of your premises you better get plenty of advanced training in gun fighting and self defense. You'll need it to survive, and you'll need it to meet the legal challenges later. If a customer gets shot by one of your own, even if you get the villains, you're in for big time trouble and grief. If no one gets hurt but the criminals, you'll be a hero, though the media might paint you as a wild-eyed vigilante. Either outcome remains burned in memory. Tough choice.

21–Too many killings occur between people who know each other. Your chance of a successful legal defense in a case like this are remote. Would he really have killed you? Probably not. Did you have any other options besides killing him? Probably so. Have you fought like this before? Maybe. What would the witnesses say? Nothing you could count on, and probably all the wrong things. The fact that you have a firearm and can use it doesn't mean you should, the likelihood of absolutely having to use it is small, and using it to settle a bet with a half-soused friend over a point spread may not be the worst thing you can do, but it's close.

22–Cap your tank and move on, you don't need the grief. When you are armed you must be even more reluctant to enter into a conflict than you otherwise might be. Your pride is not worth the price of an armed conflict.

RECOMMENDED READING

Knowledge is power, and the more you have the better off you are likely to be. Everyone concerned with personal safety, and gun owners in particular, should read books on crime avoidance, self defense and the use of deadly force. **If you have a firearm for self defense, decide to read about this critical subject.** A selection of some of the most highly regarded books on these topics appears at the back of *The Virginia Gun Owner's Guide* and are easily available directly from the publisher. If your instructor doesn't include these in your course, get them yourself. The single best book on the subject is probably *In The Gravest Extreme*, by Massad Ayoob.

You may also choose to obtain a complete copy of the Virginia criminal code, since the laws reproduced in *The Virginia Gun Owner's Guide* are a selected excerpt of gun laws only. Remember that no published edition of the law is complete without the legislation passed during the most recent session of the state congress, and that new federal laws may be passed at any time. An annotated edition of the law, available in major libraries, provides critical information in the form of court case summaries which clarify and expand on the meaning of the actual statutes.

THE NOBLE USES OF FIREARMS

In the great din of the national firearms debate it's easy to lose sight of the noble and respectable place firearms hold and have always held in American life. While some gun use in America is criminal and despicable, other applications appeal to the highest ideals our society cherishes, and are enshrined in and ensured by the statutes on the books:

- Protecting your family in emergencies
- Personal self defense
- Preventing and deterring crimes
- Detaining criminals for arrest
- Guarding our national borders
- Preserving our interests abroad
- Helping defend our allies
- Overcoming tyranny
- Emergency preparedness
- Obtaining food by hunting
- Historical preservation and study
- Olympic competition
- Sporting pursuits
- Target practice
- Recreational shooting

APPENDIX
GLOSSARY OF TERMS **A**

Words, when used in the law, often have special meanings you wouldn't expect from simply knowing the English language. For the complete legal description of these and other important terms, see each chapter of the criminal code and other legal texts dealing with language. The following plain-English descriptions are provided for your convenience only.

ALCOHOLIC = a person who through use of alcohol has become dangerous to the public or himself; or because of such alcohol use is medically determined to be in need of medical or psychiatric care, treatment, rehabilitation or counseling.

AMMUNITION = Cartridge, pellet, ball, missile or projectile adapted for use in a firearm.

ANTIQUE FIREARM = any firearm manufactured in or before 1898 and any replica of such a firearm not designed for using ammunition which is no longer manufactured in the United States and which is not readily available in the ordinary channels of commercial trade.

ARMOR-PIERCING AMMUNITION = Handgun ammunition designed primarily for penetrating metal or body armor. Referred to as *restricted* ammunition in statute.

ASSAULT FIREARM = Any semi-automatic center-fire rifle or pistol equipped with a magazine which will hold more than twenty rounds of ammunition or accept a silencer or has a folding stock.

BALLISTIC KNIFE = any knife with a detachable blade that is propelled by a spring-operated mechanism.

CIVIL DISORDER = any public disturbance within the United States or any territorial possessions thereof involving acts of violence by assemblages of three or more persons, which causes an immediate danger of or results in damage or injury to the property or person of any other individual.

CONCEALED HANDGUN = A handgun that can't be seen through ordinary observation or is disguised and unrecognizable as a handgun.

CONVICTED = Found guilty of an offense by a court, even if the sentence is probation, the offender is discharged from community supervision, or the offender is pardoned, unless the pardon is granted for proof of innocence.

CONSERVATOR OF THE PEACE = Anyone duly appointed with legal authority to make arrests. Includes all law enforcement officers, judges, clerks of court, and persons in charge of maintaining order in public areas such as private security guards, ship's captains, game wardens, prison guards, train conductors, airline pilots and bus drivers.

CRIME OF VIOLENCE = Committing or attempting to commit any of the following: murder, manslaughter, kidnapping, rape, mayhem, assault.

CRIMINAL INSTRUMENT = Anything which is normally legal but which is put to illegal use.

CULPABLE MENTAL STATE = An accountable state of mind. Specifically and in decreasing order of seriousness: intentionally, knowingly, recklessly or with criminal negligence, in the sense described by law.

CURTILAGE = The land and buildings immediately surrounding a house or dwelling.

DEALER = Anyone licensed as a firearms dealer by the federal government. The federal description of a dealer appears in Chapter 1.

DEADLY FORCE = Physical force which can cause death or serious bodily injury.

DEADLY WEAPON = Anything made or adapted for lethal use or for inflicting serious bodily injury, including a firearm.

EXPLOSIVE DEVICE = Dynamite and all other forms of high explosive. Any incendiary, fire bomb or similar device including "Molotov cocktails."

FIREARM = any handgun, shotgun, or rifle which expels a projectile by action of an explosion.

FIREARM SHOW = Any gathering, open to the public, not on the premises of a firearm dealer, for the purpose of trading or selling firearms.

FIREARM SILENCER = Any device that can muffle the sound of a firearm.

FELONY = A serious crime, typically carries a prison term of more than one year. A class 1 felony (capital murder) is the most serious, and has a possible sentence of death. A class 6 felony is the least serious, and carries a possible sentence of one year. Felony fines range from $2,500 to $100,000.

GOVERNMENT = The recognized political structure within the state.

HANDGUN = any pistol or revolver or other firearm originally designed, made and intended to fire a projectile by means of an explosion from one or more barrels when held in one hand.

HARM = Loss, disadvantage or injury to a person or someone for whom that person is responsible.

HOAX BOMB = A device that reasonably appears to be an explosive or incendiary device. A device that, by its design, causes alarm or reaction of any type by a public safety agency official or emergency volunteer agency is a hoax bomb.

INDIVIDUAL = A living human being.

INTOXICATED = Having an alcohol concentration of 0.08 or more, or having had enough alcoholic beverages to observably affect manner, disposition, speech, muscular movement, general appearance or behavior.

KNIFE = Any bladed hand instrument that can inflict serious bodily injury or death by cutting or stabbing.

KNUCKLES = A hard substance that can be worn on a fist and can inflict serious bodily injury or death by striking.

LAW = Formal rules by which society attempts to control itself. In Virginia, the law means the Virginia state statutes, the state Constitution, the U.S. Constitution and federal statutes, city ordinances, county commissioners court orders, county ordinances, published court precedents and more. "The law" is a thing too large for any one individual to know.

LAWFULLY ADMITTED FOR PERMANENT RESIDENCE = Lawfully given the privilege of residing permanently in the United States as an immigrant in accordance with the immigration laws.

LAW ENFORCEMENT OFFICER = Any full-time or part-time employee of a police department or sheriff's office who is responsible for the prevention and detection of crime and the enforcement of the penal, traffic or highway laws of this Commonwealth. Also included are agents of the Alcoholic Beverage Control, Virginia Marine Patrol, Department of Game and Inland Fisheries, State Lottery Department and Department of Motor Vehicles when fulfilling their duties.

MACHINE GUN = A firearm capable of shooting more than one shot, without manually reloading, by a single pull of the trigger.

MISDEMEANOR = A crime less serious than a felony. An offense against the law that carries a sentence of imprisonment of up to one year. Misdemeanor fines can run up to $2,500. Misdemeanors are classified as class 1 (most serious) to class 4 (least serious).

MUTATIS MUTANDIS = "When what must be changed has been changed." A legal term used to apply the provisions of one statute to a second statute, once the specifics such as section number have been changed.

PRIMA FACIE = A legal presumption meaning "on the face of it" or "at first sight." Prima facie evidence is presumed to be accurate unless convincing contradicting evidence is presented.

REASONABLE = The admittedly interpretable notion of what is "fair, proper, just, moderate, suitable to the end in view... being synonymous with rational, honest, equitable, fair, suitable, moderate, tolerable." (Black's Law Dictionary)

RESTRICTED AMMUNITION = See armor-piercing ammunition.

SAWED-OFF RIFLE = A rifle with a barrel length less than 16 inches or an overall length of less than 26 inches.

SAWED-OFF SHOTGUN = A smooth bore shotgun with a barrel length less than 18 inches. A rifled barrel shotgun with a length of less than 16 inches and a caliber greater than .225 (federal rules make no distinction as to caliber).

SERIOUS BODILY INJURY = Injury that causes permanent damage to or loss of a limb or organ, or creates a reasonable risk of death or death itself. Also, injury that causes serious and permanent disfigurement or impairment.

SPRING GUN = Any firearm or deadly weapon set to activate or discharge by means of a trip wire or any other remote device.

SPRING STICK = A spring-loaded metal stick activated by pushing a button which rapidly and forcefully telescopes the weapon to several times its original length.

STUN WEAPON = Any mechanism that is designed to emit an electronic, magnetic, or other type of charge used for the purpose of temporarily incapacitating a person.

SWITCHBLADE KNIFE = A knife with a blade that comes out of its handle automatically by centrifugal force, by gravity, or by pressing a button or other device on the handle.

TASER = Any mechanism that is designed to emit an electronic, magnetic, or other type of charge or shock through the use of a projectile for the purpose of temporarily incapacitating a person.

UNLAWFUL = Anything that's criminal or a tort.

UNSOUND MIND = The mental condition of someone who has been judged mentally incompetent or mentally ill, who has been found not guilty of a crime by reason of insanity, or who has been diagnosed by a licensed physician as being unable to manage themselves or their personal affairs.

APPENDIX B
Crime and Punishment Chart

EXPLANATIONS

Type of Crime: Illegal activities are divided into these ten categories, to match the punishment to the crime. The category may be affected by how the crime is committed.

Jail Term: These are the general ranges for a first offense involving a gun; many crimes have special sentences. A capital felony, in addition to life imprisonment, carries a possible death penalty for first degree murder, which is administered by lethal injection or electrocution. The method of execution is chosen by the prisoner, or if the prisoner refuses to choose, by injection (§53.1-234).

Fines: These are maximums, which may be lowered at court discretion. Fines can be payable immediately or a court may grant permission to pay by a certain date or in installments.

Statute of Limitations: A complex set of rules describes the length of time within which a person may be charged for a crime. The most serious crimes have no time limit for bringing a prosecution. (The limitations are found in Title 19.2.)

Offenses: The chart provides a partial list of offenses in each category, and exceptions often apply.

CRIME AND PUNISHMENT • Felonies

TYPE OF CRIME	PRISON SENTENCE FOR A FIRST OFFENSE	MAXIMUM FINE
Class 1 Felony	Death or Life in Jail	$100,000
	Capital murder.	

Class 2 Felony	20 Years to Life	$100,000

Attempted capital murder, first degree murder, aggravated malicious wounding, armed burglary, use of a machine gun or sawed-off shotgun/rifle in a crime of violence.

Class 3 Felony	5–20 Years	$100,000

Conspiracy to commit capital murder, second degree murder, malicious wounding, burglary, supplying prisoners with weapons, arson of an occupied building.

Class 4 Felony	2–10 Years	$100,000

Malicious discharge of a weapon in an occupied building, Discharge of a firearm within 1000 feet of school property, use of a machine gun for aggressive purposes, possession of a sawed-off shotgun/rifle, shooting at motor vehicles, false statements when attempting to procure a firearm.

Class 5 Felony	Up to 10 Years	$2,500

Manslaughter, possession of explosives, shooting from vehicles to endanger others, possession of plastic firearms, third offense of unlawful concealed weapon, "straw purchases" of a firearm, using restricted ammo in commission of a crime.

Class 6 Felony	Up to 5 Years	$2,500

Shooting in the commission of a felony, hoax explosives, possession of a stolen firearm, possession of a silencer, furnishing firearms to a minor, possession of a firearm on school property, fraudulent ID for a firearms purchase, possession of Striker 12 shotgun, furnishing firearms to felon.

CRIME AND PUNISHMENT • Misdemeanors

TYPE OF CRIME	JAIL SENTENCE FOR A FIRST OFFENSE	MAXIMUM FINE
Class 1 Misdemeanor	**Up to 1 Year**	**$2,500**

Reckless handling of a firearm, weapons in a courthouse, willful discharge of firearms in public, knowingly allowing access to firearms by children under twelve, brandishing a firearm, carrying a loaded "assault weapon" in a public place, first offense of unlawful concealed weapon.

Class 2 Misdemeanor	**Up to 6 Months**	**$1,000**

Deer hunting with a spotlight, hunting out of season, possessing false ID, obtaining criminal history information under false pretenses.

Class 3 Misdemeanor	**None**	**$500**

Trespassing by hunters, hunting under the influence of alcohol, hunting or fishing without a license, hunting with prohibited firearms, recklessly allowing access to firearms by children under fourteen.

Class 4 misdemeanor	**None**	**$250**

Carrying a dangerous weapon in a church, deer hunting from a boat, drinking while driving, spitting in public, selling; blackjacks, switchblades, ballistic knives.

THE PROPER AUTHORITIES C

Regulations on guns and their use come from a lot of places. Listed with each authority are the addresses and phones of the nearest offices. All cities are in Virginia unless indicated.

Federal Refuges
    Back Bay, Refuge Manager, 4005 Sandpiper Rd, Virginia Beach 23456
    Chincoteague, Refuge Manager, Box 62, Chincoteague 23336
    Dismal Swamp, Refuge Manager, Box 349, Suffolk 23434
    Eastern Shore, Refuge Manager, 5003 Hallett Circle
        Cape Charles 23310
    Presquile, Refuge Manager, Box 620, Hopewell 23860
Army Corps of Engineers 757-441-7500
Attorney General 804-786-2071
Bureau of Alcohol, Tobacco and Firearms 202-566-7591
    Dept. of the Treasury; Washington, DC 20226
Bureau of Indian Affairs 202-343-5116, 7163
    U.S. Dept. of Interior, Washington, DC 20240
Corporate Hunting Areas
    Appalachian Power Cooperative Management Areas
        Contact VDGIF, 804-525-7522, Route 6, Box 410, Forest 24551
    Bear Island Timberlands Co., L.P.
        Hunting Permits, PO Box 2119, Ashalnd 23005
    Chesapeake Forest Product Co.
        Eastern VA Region 804-843-5298
            Hunting Permits, 15th and Main Streets, West Point 23181
        Keysville Region 804-736-8505
            Hunting Permits, Box 450, Keysville 23947
        Pocomoke Region, 301-957-1521
            Hunting Permits, Box 300, Pocomoke City, MD 21851
    Glatfelter Pulp Wood Company, PO Box 868, Fredericksburg 22404
    Lester Properties, Forestland Department Manager,
        Post Office Drawer 4991, Martinsville 24115, 540-656-3250

City Governments
    Alexandria 703-838-4000
    Bedford 703-586-7102
    Buena Vista 703-466-2221
    Charlottesville 804-971-3101
    Clifton Forge 703-863-2501
    Colonial Heights 804-520-9265
    Covington 703-965-6300
    Danville 804-799-5100
    Emporia 804-634-3332
    Fairfax 703-385-7855
    Falls Church 703-241-5001
    Franklin 804-562-8504
    Fredericksburg 703-372-1010
    Galax 703-236-5773
    Hampton 804-727-6392
    Harrisonburg 703-434-6776
    Hopewell 804-541-2249
    Lexington 703-463-7133
    Lynchburg 804-847-1000
    Manassas 703-257-8200
    Manassas Park 703-335-8800
    Martinsville 703-368-3971
    Newport News 804-247-8411
    Norfolk 804-441-2831
    Norton 703-679-1160
    Petersburg 804-733-2301
    Poquoson 804-868-7151
    Portsmouth 804-398-8000
    Radford 703-731-3603
    Richmond 804-780-7970
    Roanoke 703-981-2000
    Salem 703-375-3000
    South Boston 804-575-4200
    Staunton 703-332-3200
    Suffolk 804-925-6339
    Virginia Beach 757-427-4242
    Waynesboro 703-942-6600
    Williamsburg 804-220-6100
    Winchester 703-667-1815
County Governments
    Accomack 804-787-5700
    Albemarle 804-296-5841
    Alleghany 703-962-4918
    Amelia 804-561-3039
    Amherst 804-946-9400
    Appomatox 804-352-2637

Arlington 703-358-3000
Augusta 703-245-5600
Bath 703-839-7221
Bedford 703-566-7601
Bland 703-368-4622
Botetourt 703-473-8220
Brunswick 804-848-3107
Buchanan 703-935-6501
Buckingham 804-969-4242
Campbell 804-332-5161
Caroline 804-633-5308
Carroll 703-728-3331
Charlotte 804-829-2401
Chesterfield 804-748-1000
Clarke 703-955-5100
Craig 703-864-5010
Culpeper 703-825-3035
Cumberland 804-492-3625
Dickenson 703-926-1676
Dinwiddie 804-469-4500
Essex 804-443-4331
Fairfax 703-324-2531
Fauquier 703-337-8680
Floyd 703-745-9300
Fluvanna 804-589-3138
Frederick 703-665-5600
Giles 540-921-2525
Gloucester 804-693-4042
Grayson 804-556-5300
Green 703-773-2471
Greensville 804-348-4205
Halifax 804-476-2141
Hanover 804-537-6005
Henrico 804-672-4000
Henry 703-368-5311
Highland 703-468-2447
Isle of Wight 804-357-3191
James City 804-253-6600
King and Queen 804-785-7955
King George 703-775-9181
King William 804-769-4927
Lancaster 804-462-6129
Lee 703-346-7714
Loudoun 703-770-0100
Louisa 703-967-0401
Lunenburg 804-696-2142
Madison 703-948-6700

Mathews 804-725-7172
Mecklenburg 804-738-6191
Middlesex 804-758-4330
Montgomery 703-382-6954
Nelson 804-263-4873
New Kent 804-966-9600
Northampton 804-678-0440
Northumberland 804-580-7666
Nottoway 804-645-8696
Orange 703-672-3313
Page 703-7434142
Patrick 703-694-6094
Pittsylvania 804-432-2041
Powhattan 804-598-5600
Prince Edward 804-392-8837
Prince George 804-732-2600
Prince William 703-792-6600
Pulaski 703-980-7705
Rappahannock 703-675-3342
Richmond County 804-333-3415
Roanoke 703-772-2006
Rockbridge 703-463-4361
Rockingham 703-564-3000
Russell 703-889-8000
Scott 703-386-6521
Shenandoah 703-459-2195
Smyth 703-783-3298
Southampton 804-653-2465
Spotsylvania 703-582-7010
Stafford 703-659-8600
Surry 804-294-5271
Tazwell 703-988-7541
Warren 703-636-4600
Washington 703-676-6202
Westmoreland 804-493-0130
Wise 703-328-2321
Wythe 703-223-6020
York 804-890-2320
Deptartment of Conservation and Recreation 804-786-1712
    203 Governor St. Suite 213, Richmond 23219
Dept. of Forestry Headquarters Office 804-977-6555
        PO Box 3758, Charlottesville 22903
    Cumberland State Forest 804-492-4121
        Route 1, Box 250, Cumberland 23040
    Appomattox-Buckingham State Forest 804-983-2175
        Route 3, Box 133, Dillwyn 23936

Dept. of Game and Inland Fisheries
  Main Office, Richmond 804-367-1000
    4010 West Broad St., PO Box 11104, Richmond 23230
  Region 1, Williamsburg 804-253-7072
    5806 Mooretown Rd., Williamsburg 23188
  Region 2, Forest, Rt. 6, Box 410, Forest 24551, 804-525-7522
  Region 3, Marion, Rt. 1, Box 107, Marion 24354, 540-783-4860
  Region 4, Verona, PO Box 996, Verona 24482, 540-248-9360
  Region 5, Fredericksburg 540-899-4169
    1320 Belman Rd., Fredericksburg 22401
  Ashland District 804-752-5503
    12108 Washington Hwy., Ashland 23005
  Blacksburg District 540-951-7923, 540-951-7923
    2206 S. Main St. Suite C, Blacksburg 24060
  Farmville District, HC 6 Box 46, Farmville 24060, 804-392-9645
  Suffok District, Godwin Blvd., Suffolk 23434, 804-255-0523, 5268
  Vinton District, 209 E. Cleaveland Ave., Vinton 24179, 540-857-7704
Military Areas Open for Hunting
  Fort A. P. HIll 804-633-8300
    USAG Fort A. P. Hill, Attn Wildlife Section, Bowling Green 22427
  Fort Pickett, HQ US Army Garrison 804-292-2618
    Attn: Game check station, Building 420, Fort Pickett 23824
  Marine Base, MCCDC Quantico 703-640-5523
  Radford Army Ammunition Plant, contact Game and Inland Fisheries at
    540-951-7923, VDGIF Blacksburg Field Office, 2206 S. Main St.
    Suite C, Blacksburg 24060
Hunt for the Hungry 800-352-4868
Law Libraries
  Fairfax County Law Library 703-246-2170
  Richmond City Law Library 804-780-6500
  Virginia Beach Wahab Law Library 757-427-4418
National Forests
  George Washington and Jefferson National Forrests 540-265-6054
National Rifle Association 800-336-7402
  11250 Waples Mill Rd., Fairfax 22030.
  Locally, contact the Virginia Shooting Sports Association
Norfolk Clerk of Court 804-664-4380
Secretary of the Commonwealth 804-786-2441
U.S. Forest Service PO Box 96090, Washington, DC 20090
  Forest Headquarters 540-265-6054
    5162 Vallypointe Parkway, Roanoke 24019
  Blacksburg Ranger District 540-552-4641
    110 Southpark Dr., Blacksburg 24060
  Clinch Ranger District, Route 3, Box 820, Wise 24293, 540-328-2931
  Deerfield Ranger District 540-885-8028
    Route 6, Box 419, Staunton 24401
  Dry River Ranger District 540-828-2591
    112 North River Rd., Bridgewater 22812

Glenwood Tanger District 540-291-2189
  PO Box 10, Natural Bridge Station 24579
James River Ranger District 540-962-2214
  810-A Madison Ave., Covington 24426
Lee Ranger District, 109 Molineu Rd., Edinburg 22824, 540-984-4101
Mount Rogers National Recreational Area, 540-783-5196
  Route 1, Box 303, Marion 24354
New Castle Ranger District 540-864-5195
  Box 246, New Castle 24127
Pedlar Ranger District 540-261-6105
  2424 Magnolia Ave., Buena Vista 24416
Warm Springs Ranger District 540-839-2521
  Hwy. 220 South, Route 2, Box 30 Hot Springs 24445
Wythe Ranger District, 155 Sherwood Forest Rd., Whtyevill 24382
Virginia Department of State Police
  Administrative HQ 804-674-2000
  Gun control 804-674-2026
Virginia Shooting Sports Association 800-526-1397, 540-672-5848
  PO Box 1258, Orange 22960
Virginia Wildlife Crimeline 800-237-5712
Virginia Wildlife Federation 804-648-3136

THE VIRGINIA GUN LAWS

Excerpts from the
Code of Virginia

APPENDIX
THE VIRGINIA GUN LAWS **D**

On the following pages are excerpts from official Virginia state law.

Virginia law covers a broad spectrum of subjects but **only gun laws for private citizens are included in this appendix.** A complete copy of the state law is available in major libraries, but keep in mind that those copies are incomplete (and in many instances inaccurate) without the new material from the last legislative session (which this book includes for 1996).

The laws reproduced here are *excerpts.* Only material related to bearing arms has been included. In some cases this means substantial portions of laws may have been edited. **For official legal proceedings do not rely on these excerpts**—obtain unedited texts and competent professional assistance.

How State Law Is Arranged

Each numbered part of the Code of Virginia is called a "section," represented by a "§" sign. This makes it easy to refer to any particular statute—just call it by its title and section numbers. For instance, Code of Virginia §18.2-308 is the part about concealed weapons. You say it like this, "Code of Virginia, section eighteen point two dash three oh eight."

Excerpt from the Constitution
of the Commonwealth of Virginia

Article 1, Section 13:
MILITIA; STANDING ARMIES;
MILITARY SUBORDINATE TO CIVIL POWER.

That a well regulated militia, composed of the body of the people, trained to arms, is the proper, natural, and safe defense of a free state, therefore, the right of the people to keep and bear arms shall not be infringed; that standing armies, in time of peace, should be avoided as dangerous to liberty; and that in all cases the military should be under strict subordination to, and governed by, the civil power.

VIRGINIA GUN LAWS

EXCERPTS FROM THE CODE OF VIRGINIA

<Cross-references and explanatory remarks appear in pointed brackets
and are not part of the statutes.>

Title 4.1   Alcoholic Beverage Control Code

Alcoholic Beverage Control Code §4.1-318.
Violations by armed persons; penalty.

No person shall unlawfully manufacture, transport or sell any alcoholic beverages,
and at the time of the unlawful manufacturing, transporting, or selling or aiding or
assisting in any manner in such act, shall carry on or about his person, or have
on or in any vehicle which he may be using to aid him in any such purpose, or
have in his possession, actual or constructive, at or within 100 yards of any place
where any such alcoholic beverages are being unlawfully manufactured,
transported or sold, any dangerous weapon as described in §18.2-308.
Any person convicted of a violation of this section shall be guilty of a Class 6 felony.

Alcoholic Beverage Control Code §4.1-336.
Contraband beverages and other articles subject to forfeiture.

All stills and distilling apparatus and materials for the manufacture of alcoholic
beverages, all alcoholic beverages and materials used in their manufacture, all
containers in which alcoholic beverages may be found, which are kept, stored,
possessed, or in any manner used in violation of the provisions of this title, and
any dangerous weapons as described in §18.2-308, which may be used, or
which may be found upon the person or in any vehicle which such person is
using, to aid such person in the unlawful manufacture, transportation or sale of
alcoholic beverages, or found in the possession of such person, or any horse,
mule or other beast of burden, any wagon, automobile, truck or vehicle of any
nature whatsoever which are found in the immediate vicinity of any place where
alcoholic beverages are being unlawfully manufactured and which such animal or
vehicle is being used to aid in the unlawful manufacture, shall be deemed
contraband and shall be forfeited to the Commonwealth.
Proceedings for the confiscation of the above property shall be in accordance with
§4.1-338 for all such property except motor vehicles which proceedings shall be
in accordance with §4.1-339 through 4.1-348.
Such dangerous weapons seized by any officer charged with the enforcement of this
title shall be forfeited to the Commonwealth upon the conviction of the person
owning or possessing such weapons and shall be sold by order of court and the
proceeds of such sale shall be paid into the Literary Fund.

Title 9   Commissions, Boards And Institutions Generally

Commissions, Boards And Institutions Generally §9-192.
Individual's right of access to and review and correction of information

A. Any individual who believes that criminal history record information is being maintained about him by the Central Criminal Records Exchange, or by the arresting law-enforcement agency in the case of offenses not required to be reported to such Exchange, shall have the right to inspect a copy of such criminal history record information at the Exchange or the arresting law-enforcement agency, respectively, for the purpose of ascertaining the completeness and accuracy of such information. The individual's right to access and review shall not extend to any information or data other than that defined in subdivision 4 of §9-169.

B. The Board shall issue regulations with respect to an individual's right to access and review criminal history record information about himself reported to the Central Criminal Records Exchange or, if not reported to the Exchange, maintained by the arresting law-enforcement agency. Such regulations shall provide for public notice of the right of access; access to criminal history record information by an individual or an attorney-at-law acting for an individual; identification required; places and times for review; review of Virginia records by individuals located in other states; assistance in understanding the record; obtaining a copy for purposes of initiating a challenge to the record; procedures for investigation of alleged incompleteness or inaccuracy; completion or correction of records if indicated; and notification of the individuals and agencies to whom an inaccurate or incomplete record has been disseminated.

C. If an individual believes information maintained about him to be inaccurate or incomplete, he may request the agency having custody or control of the records to purge, modify, or supplement them. Should the agency decline to so act, or should the individual believe the agency's decision to be otherwise unsatisfactory, the individual may request, in writing, review by the Board. The Board or its designee shall, in each case in which it finds prima facie basis for a complaint, conduct a hearing at which the individual may appear with counsel, present evidence, and examine and cross-examine witnesses. Written findings and conclusions shall be issued. Should the record in question be found to be inaccurate or incomplete, the criminal justice agency or agencies maintaining such information shall purge, modify, or supplement it in accordance with the findings and conclusions of the Board. Notification of purging, modification, or supplementation of criminal history record information shall be promptly made by the criminal justice agency maintaining such previously inaccurate information to any individuals or agencies to which the information in question was communicated, as well as to the individual whose records have been ordered so altered.

D. Criminal justice agencies shall maintain records of all agencies to whom criminal history record information was disseminated and the date upon which such information was disseminated and such other record matter for the number of years required by rules and regulations of the Board.

E. Any individual or agency aggrieved by any order or decision of the Board may appeal such order or decision in accordance with the provisions of the Administrative Process Act (§9-6.14:1 et seq.).

Title 15.1   Counties, Cities and Towns

Counties, Cities and Towns §15.1-29.15.
Control of firearms.

From and after January 1, 1987, no county, city or town shall adopt any ordinance
to govern the purchase, possession, transfer, ownership, carrying or transporting
of firearms, ammunition, or components or combination thereof other than those
expressly authorized by statute.

Nothing in this section shall affect the validity or invalidity of any ordinance adopted
prior to January 1, 1987. Nothing in this section shall have any effect on any
pending litigation.

Counties, Cities and Towns §15.1-29.20.
**Applicability of local noise ordinances to certain sport shooting
ranges**

No local ordinance regulating noise shall subject a sport shooting range to noise
control standards more stringent than those in effect at the time the construction
or operation of the range initially was approved. The operation or use of a sport
shooting range shall not be enjoined on the basis of noise, nor shall any person
be subject to action for nuisance or criminal prosecution in any matter relating to
noise resulting from the operation of the range, if the range is in compliance with
all ordinances relating to noise in effect at the time construction or operation of the
range was approved.

For purposes of this section, "sport shooting range" means an area or structure
designed for the use of rifles, shotguns, pistols, silhouettes, skeet, trap, black
powder, or any other similar sport shooting.

Counties, Cities and Towns §15.1-133.01:1.
**Disposal of unclaimed firearms or other weapons in possession of
sheriff or police.**

Any county, city, or town may destroy unclaimed firearms and other weapons
which have been in the possession of law-enforcement agencies for a period of
more than sixty days. For the purposes of this section, "unclaimed firearms and
other weapons" shall be defined the same as "unclaimed personal property" is
described in §15.1-133.01.

At the discretion of the chief of police, sheriff, or their duly authorized agents,
unclaimed firearms and other weapons may be destroyed by any means which
renders the firearms and other weapons permanently inoperable. Prior to the
destruction of such firearms and other weapons, the chief of police, sheriff, or
their duly authorized agents shall comply with the notice provision contained in
§15.1-133.01.

Counties, Cities and Towns §15.1-518.
**Prohibiting shooting of firearms or air-operated or gas-operated
weapons in certain areas**

Any county may prohibit the shooting of firearms or air-operated or gas-operated
weapons in any areas of the county which are in the opinion of the board of
supervisors so heavily populated as to make such conduct dangerous to the
inhabitants thereof.

Counties, Cities and Towns §15.1-518.1.
Prohibiting hunting in certain areas

The governing body of any county may by ordinance prohibit all hunting with firearms or other weapons in, or within one-half mile of, any subdivision or other area of such county which, in the opinion of the governing body, is so heavily populated as to make such hunting dangerous to the inhabitants thereof. Any such ordinance shall clearly describe each area in which hunting is prohibited, and shall further provide that appropriate signs shall be erected designating said boundaries thereof.

Counties, Cities and Towns §15.1-523.
Pistols and revolvers; license tax on dealers

The governing body of any county may impose a license tax of not more than twenty-five dollars on persons engaged in the business of selling pistols and revolvers to the public.

Counties, Cities and Towns §15.1-524.
Reports of sales

The governing body of any county may require sellers of pistols and revolvers to furnish the clerk of the circuit court of the county, within ten days after sale of any such weapon, with the name and address of the purchaser, the date of purchase, and the number, make and caliber of the weapon sold. The clerk shall keep a record of the reports.

Counties, Cities and Towns §15.1-525
Same; in certain counties

Chapter 297 of the Acts of 1944, approved March 29, 1944, requiring permits to sell or purchase pistols or revolvers in any county having a density of population of more than 1,000 a square mile, is continued in effect. <The specified statute follows.>

Chap. 297, An ACT to provide that in counties having a certain density of population, persons engaged in the business of selling pistols or revolvers at retail shall register with and obtain certain permits form the chief of police; to require any person desiring to purchase any such weapon to obtain a permit so to do; and to provide that no person obtaining a permit to sell shall sell, give or furnish any such weapon to any person unless he delivers to the dealer a permit obtained under the provisions of this act; and to prescribe penalties for violations. [H 366]

Be it enacted by the General Assembly of Virginia:

1. In any county having a density of population of more than one thousand a square mile, as shown by the last preceding United Sates census, any person, firm or corporation engaged in the business of selling pistols or revolvers at retail shall, before making any such sale, register as such a dealer with the chief of police of the county and obtain from him a permit to sell such weapons to persons entitled to buy them, which permit he shall issue upon his being satisfied with the fitness of the dealer to engage in such business. Such permits shall be issued for a period of one year.

Any person desiring to buy at retail or otherwise acquire a pistol or revolver shall first apply to the chief of police, hereinafter called the Chief, for a permit so to do, and shall at the same time give the Chief such information as he requires concerning his fitness to own and possess such weapon. The Chief may grant such permit, or refuse same or defer the application until he has made an independent investigation of the applicant; provided no permit shall be granted to any person under the age of eighteen years, nor until the Chief is satisfied that the applicant is a proper person to own and have the weapon in his possession. No dealer holding a permit issued hereunder shall sell, give, barter, exchange or furnish a pistol or revolver to any person unless he delivers to the dealer the permit of the Chief as required in this act. Upon the delivery of any such weapon to any person by the dealer, he shall endorse on the permit the date of delivery, the make and calibre of the pistol or revolver, and shall return the permit to the Chief no later than the day following that on which the weapon was sold or furnished.

The Chief shall make and preserve in his office a record of all permits issued by him hereunder, showing thereon the dates when and the persons to whom issued.

Any person violating any provision of this act shall be guilty of a misdemeanor.

Counties, Cities and Towns §15.1-865.
Dangerous, etc., business or employment; transportation of offensive substances; explosive or inflammable substances; fireworks; compound bows, crossbows; firearms

A municipal corporation may regulate or prohibit the conduct of any dangerous, offensive or unhealthful business, trade or employment; the transportation of any offensive substance; the manufacture, storage, transportation, possession and use of any explosive or inflammable substance; and the use and exhibition of fireworks and the discharge of firearms. A municipal corporation may also require the maintenance of safety devices on storage equipment for such substances or items.

A municipal corporation may prohibit a person from shooting a compound bow or crossbow at or upon the property of another without permission.

Title 16.1   Courts Not of Record

Courts Not of Record §16.1-246.
When and how child may be taken into immediate custody
No child may be taken into immediate custody except:
C. 1. When a child has committed a misdemeanor offense involving
(i) shoplifting in violation of §18.2-103
(ii) assault and battery or
(iii) carrying a weapon on school property in violation of §18.2-308.1 and, although the offense was not committed in the presence of the officer who makes the arrest, the arrest is based on probable cause on reasonable complaint of a person who observed the alleged offense;

Courts Not of Record §16.1-269.1.
Conditions for transfer to circuit court
A. If a juvenile fourteen years of age or older is charged with an offense which would be a felony if committed by an adult, the court shall, on motion of the attorney for the Commonwealth and prior to a hearing on the merits, hold a transfer hearing and may retain jurisdiction or transfer such juvenile for proper criminal proceedings to the appropriate circuit court having criminal jurisdiction of such offenses if committed by an adult. Any transfer to the appropriate circuit court shall be subject to the following conditions:
4. b. The seriousness and number of alleged offenses, including
(iv) whether the alleged offense involved the use of a firearm or other dangerous weapon by brandishing, threatening, displaying or otherwise employing such weapon.

Courts Not of Record §16.1-278.9.
Delinquent children; loss of driving privileges for alcohol, firearm and drug offenses
A. If a court has found facts which would justify a finding that a child at least thirteen years of age at the time of the offense is delinquent and such finding involves;
(vii) the unlawful use or possession of a handgun or possession of a "streetsweeper" as defined below, the court shall order that the child be denied a driver's license. In addition to any other penalty authorized by this section, if the offense involves a violation designated under clause (vii), the denial of driving privileges shall be for a period of not less than thirty days, except when the offense involves possession of a concealed handgun or, a striker 12, commonly called a "streetsweeper," or any semi-automatic folding stock shotgun of like kind with a spring tension drum magazine capable of holding twelve shotgun shells, in which case the denial of driving privileges shall be for a period of two years unless the offense is committed by a child under the age of sixteen, in which event the child's ability to apply for a driver's license shall be delayed for a period of two years following his sixteenth birthday.

Courts Not of Record §16.1-285.1.
Commitment of serious offenders

A. In the case of a juvenile fourteen years of age or older who has been found guilty of an offense which would be a felony if committed by an adult, and either

(i) the juvenile is on parole for an offense which would be a felony if committed by an adult,

(ii) the juvenile was committed to the state for an offense which would be a felony if committed by an adult within the immediately preceding twelve months or

(iii) the felony offense is punishable by a term of confinement of greater than twenty years if the felony was committed by an adult, and the court finds that commitment under this section is necessary to meet the rehabilitative needs of the juvenile and would serve the best interests of the community, then the court may order the juvenile committed to the Department of Youth and Family Services for placement in a learning center for the period of time prescribed pursuant to this section.

B. Prior to committing any juvenile pursuant to this section, the court shall consider:

2. The seriousness and number of the present offenses, including:

(iii) whether the offense involved the use of a firearm or other dangerous weapon by brandishing, displaying, threatening with or otherwise employing such weapon;

Courts Not of Record §16.1-305.1.
Disclosure of disposition in certain delinquency cases

Upon disposition of a proceeding in a court of competent jurisdiction in which a juvenile is adjudicated delinquent or convicted of a crime based upon a violation of the law involving

(i) the unlawful purchase, possession or use of a weapon, the clerk of the court in which the disposition is entered shall, within fifteen days if there has been no notice of an appeal, provide written notice of the disposition ordered by the court, including the nature of the offense upon which the adjudication or conviction was based, to the superintendent of the school division in which the child is enrolled at the time of the disposition or, if he is not then enrolled in school, the division in which he was enrolled at the time of the offense.

Title 17   Courts of Record

Courts of Record §17-47.4.
Disposition of papers in ended cases
B. The following records for cases ending on or after January 1, 1913, may be
   destroyed in their entirety at the discretion of the clerk of each circuit court after
   having been retained for ten years:
2. Concealed weapons permit applications;

Courts of record §17-116.05:1.
Petitions for appeal; cases over which Court of Appeals does not have jurisdiction
A. Any aggrieved party may present a petition for appeal to the Court of Appeals
   from;
(ii) any final decision of a circuit court on an application for a concealed weapons
   permit pursuant to subsection D of §18.2-308.

Title 18.2   Crimes and Offenses Generally

Crimes and Offenses Generally §18.2-10.
Punishment for conviction of felony
The authorized punishments for conviction of a felony are:
(a) For Class 1 felonies, death, or imprisonment for life and, subject to subdivision
(g), a fine of not more than $100,000.
(b) For Class 2 felonies, imprisonment for life or for any term not less than twenty
years and, subject to subdivision (g), a fine of not more than $100,000.
(c) For Class 3 felonies, a term of imprisonment of not less than five years nor more
than twenty years and, subject to subdivision (g), a fine of not more than
$100,000.
(d) For Class 4 felonies, a term of imprisonment of not less than two years nor more
than ten years and, subject to subdivision (g), a fine of not more than $100,000.
(e) For Class 5 felonies, a term of imprisonment of not less than one year nor more
than ten years, or in the discretion of the jury or the court trying the case without
a jury, confinement in jail for not more than twelve months and a fine of not more
than $2,500, either or both.
(f) For Class 6 felonies, a term of imprisonment of not less than one year nor more
than five years, or in the discretion of the jury or the court trying the case without
a jury, confinement in jail for not more than twelve months and a fine of not more
than $2,500, either or both.
(g) Except as specifically authorized in subdivision (e) or (f), or in Class 1 felonies for
which a sentence of death is imposed, the court shall impose either a sentence of
imprisonment together with a fine, or imprisonment only. However, if the
defendant is not a natural person, the court shall impose only a fine.
For any felony offense committed on or after January 1, 1995, the court may impose
an additional term of not less than six months nor more than three years, which
shall be suspended conditioned upon successful completion of a period of post-
release supervision pursuant to §19.2-295.2 and compliance with such other
terms as the sentencing court may require. However, such additional term may
only be imposed when the sentence includes an active term of incarceration in a
correctional facility.

Crimes and Offenses Generally §18.2-11. Punishment for conviction of misdemeanor
The authorized punishments for conviction of a misdemeanor are:
(a) For Class 1 misdemeanors, confinement in jail for not more than twelve months
and a fine of not more than $2,500, either or both.
(b) For Class 2 misdemeanors, confinement in jail for not more than six months and
a fine of not more than $1,000, either or both.
(c) For Class 3 misdemeanors, a fine of not more than $500.
(d) For Class 4 misdemeanors, a fine of not more than $250.

Crimes and Offenses Generally §18.2-31.
Capital murder defined; punishment
The following offenses shall constitute capital murder, punishable as a Class 1
felony:
1. The willful, deliberate, and premeditated killing of any person in the commission of
abduction, as defined in §18.2-48, when such abduction was committed with the
intent to extort money or a pecuniary benefit;
2. The willful, deliberate, and premeditated killing of any person by another for hire;

3. The willful, deliberate, and premeditated killing of any person by a prisoner confined in a state or local correctional facility as defined in §53.1-1, or while in the custody of an employee thereof;
4. The willful, deliberate, and premeditated killing of any person in the commission of robbery or attempted robbery while armed with a deadly weapon;
5. The willful, deliberate, and premeditated killing of any person in the commission of, or subsequent to, rape or attempted rape, forcible sodomy or attempted forcible sodomy or object sexual penetration;
6. The willful, deliberate, and premeditated killing of a law-enforcement officer as defined in §9-169(9) when such killing is for the purpose of interfering with the performance of his official duties;
7. The willful, deliberate, and premeditated killing of more than one person as a part of the same act or transaction;
8. The willful, deliberate, and premeditated killing of a child under the age of twelve years in the commission of abduction as defined in §18.2-48 when such abduction was committed with the intent to extort money or a pecuniary benefit, or with the intent to defile the victim of such abduction; and
9. The willful, deliberate, and premeditated killing of any person in the commission of or attempted commission of a violation of §18.2-248, involving a Schedule I or II controlled substance, when such killing is for the purpose of furthering the commission or attempted commission of such violation. If any one or more subsections, sentences, or parts of this section shall be judged unconstitutional or invalid, such adjudication shall not affect, impair, or invalidate the remaining provisions thereof but shall be confined in its operation to the specific provisions so held unconstitutional or invalid.

Crimes and Offenses Generally §18.2-51
Shooting, stabbing, etc., with intent to maim, kill, etc.

If any person maliciously shoot, stab, cut, or wound any person or by any means cause him bodily injury, with the intent to maim, disfigure, disable, or kill, he shall, except where it is otherwise provided, be guilty of a Class 3 felony. If such act be done unlawfully but not maliciously, with the intent aforesaid, the offender shall be guilty of a Class 6 felony.

Crimes and Offenses Generally §18.2-51.2
Aggravated malicious wounding;   penalty

If any person maliciously shoots, stabs, cuts or wounds any other person, or by any means causes bodily injury, with the intent to maim, disfigure, disable or kill, he shall be guilty of a Class 2 felony if the victim is thereby severely injured and is caused to suffer permanent and significant physical impairment.

Crimes and Offenses Generally §18.2-53.1
Use or display of firearm in committing felony

It shall be unlawful for any person to use or attempt to use any pistol, shotgun, rifle, or other firearm or display such weapon in a threatening manner while committing or attempting to commit murder, rape, forcible sodomy, inanimate or animate object sexual penetration as defined in §18.2-67.2, robbery, carjacking, burglary, malicious wounding as defined in §18.2-51, malicious bodily injury to a law-enforcement officer as defined in §18.2-51.1, aggravated malicious wounding as defined in §18.2-51.2, malicious wounding by mob as defined in §18.2-41 or abduction. Violation of this section shall constitute a separate and distinct felony and any person found guilty thereof shall be sentenced to a term of imprisonment of three years for a first conviction, and for a term of five years for a second or subsequent conviction under the provisions of this section. Notwithstanding any other provision of law, the sentence prescribed for a violation of the provisions of this section shall not be suspended in whole or in part, nor shall anyone convicted hereunder be placed on probation. Such punishment shall be separate and apart from, and shall be made to run consecutively with, any punishment received for the commission of the primary felony.

Crimes and Offenses Generally §18.2-56.1
Reckless handling of firearms; reckless handling while hunting

A. It shall be unlawful for any person to handle recklessly any firearm so as to endanger the life, limb or property of any person. Any person violating this section shall be guilty of a Class 1 misdemeanor.

B. If this section is violated while the person is engaged in hunting, trapping or pursuing game, the trial judge may, in addition to the penalty imposed by the jury or the court trying the case without a jury, revoke such person's hunting or trapping license or privilege to hunt or trap while possessing a firearm for a period of one year to life.

C. Upon a revocation pursuant to subsection B hereof, the clerk of the court in which the case is tried pursuant to this section shall forthwith send to the Department of Game and Inland Fisheries

(i) such person's revoked hunting or trapping license or notice that such person's privilege to hunt or trap while in possession of a firearm has been revoked and

(ii) a notice of the length of revocation imposed. The Department shall keep a list which shall be furnished upon request to any law-enforcement officer, Commonwealth's attorney or court in this Commonwealth, and such list shall contain the names and addresses of all persons whose license or privilege to hunt or trap while in possession of a firearm has been revoked and the court which took such action.

D. If any person whose license to hunt and trap, or whose privilege to hunt and trap while in possession of a firearm, has been revoked pursuant to this section, thereafter hunts or traps while in possession of a firearm, he shall be guilty of a Class 1 misdemeanor, and, in addition to any penalty imposed by the jury or the court trying the case without a jury, the trial judge may revoke such person's hunting or trapping license, or privilege to hunt or trap while in possession of a firearm, for an additional period not to exceed five years. The clerk of the court shall notify the Department of Game and Inland Fisheries as is provided in subsection C herein.

Crimes and Offenses Generally §18.2-56.2.
Allowing access to firearms by children; penalty

A. It shall be unlawful for any person to recklessly leave a loaded, unsecured firearm in such a manner as to endanger the life or limb of any child under the age of fourteen. Any person violating the provisions of this subsection shall be guilty of a Class 3 misdemeanor.

B. It shall be unlawful for any person knowingly to authorize a child under the age of twelve to use a firearm except when the child is under the supervision of an adult. Any person violating this subsection shall be guilty of a Class 1 misdemeanor. For purposes of this subsection, "adult" shall mean a parent, guardian, person standing in loco parentis to the child or a person twenty-one years or over who has the permission of the parent, guardian, or person standing in loco parentis to supervise the child in the use of a firearm.

Crimes and Offenses Generally §18.2-57.1.
Assault and battery against law-enforcement officers; penalty; lesser included offenses

If any person commits an assault or an assault and battery against another by the shooting of any pistol, shotgun, rifle or other firearm, knowing or having reason

to know that such other person is a law-enforcement officer, as defined
hereinafter, engaged in the performance of his public duties as a law-enforcement
officer, such person shall be guilty of a Class 1 misdemeanor and, upon
conviction, the sentence of such person shall include a mandatory, minimum term
of confinement in jail for six months.

Nothing in this section shall be construed to affect the right of any person charged
with a violation of this section from asserting and presenting evidence in support
of any defenses to the charge that may be available under common law.

As used in this section the term "mandatory minimum" means that the sentence it
describes shall be served with no suspension of sentence in whole or in part, and
no probation being given by the court.

Crimes and Offenses Generally §18.2-58.
How punished

If any person commit robbery by partial strangulation, or suffocation, or by striking
or beating, or by other violence to the person, or by assault or otherwise putting
a person in fear of serious bodily harm, or by the threat or presenting of firearms,
or other deadly weapon or instrumentality whatsoever, he shall be guilty of a
felony and shall be punished by confinement in a state correctional facility for life
or any term not less than five years.

Crimes and Offenses Generally §18.2-58.1
Carjacking; penalty

A. Any person who commits carjacking, as herein defined, shall be guilty of a felony
punishable by imprisonment for life or a term not less than fifteen years.

B. As used in this section, "carjacking" means the intentional seizure or seizure of
control of a motor vehicle of another with intent to permanently or temporarily
deprive another in possession or control of the vehicle of that possession or
control by means of partial strangulation, or suffocation, or by striking or beating,
or by other violence to the person, or by assault or otherwise putting a person in
fear of serious bodily harm, or by the threat or presenting of firearms, or other
deadly weapon or instrumentality whatsoever. "Motor vehicle" shall have the
same meaning as set forth in §46.2-100.

Crimes and Offenses Generally §18.2-67.3
Aggravated sexual battery

A. An accused shall be guilty of aggravated sexual battery if he or she sexually
abuses the complaining witness, and

c. The accused uses or threatens to use a dangerous weapon.

Crimes and Offenses Generally §18.2-85.
Manufacture, possession, use, etc., of fire bombs or explosive materials or devices; penalties

Any person who
(i) possesses materials with which fire bombs or explosive materials or devices can
be made with the intent to manufacture fire bombs or explosive materials or
devices or,

(ii) manufactures, transports, distributes, possesses or uses a fire bomb or explosive
materials or devices shall be guilty of a Class 5 felony. Any person who
constructs, uses, places, sends, or causes to be sent any hoax explosive device
so as to intentionally cause another person to believe that such device is a bomb
or explosive shall be guilty of a Class 6 felony.

Nothing in this section shall prohibit the authorized manufacture, transportation,
distribution, use or possession of any material, substance, or device by a member
of the armed forces of the United States, fire fighters or law-enforcement officers,

nor shall it prohibit the manufacture, transportation, distribution, use or possession of any material, substance or device to be used solely for scientific research, educational purposes or for any lawful purpose.

Crimes and Offenses Generally §18.2-89
Burglary; how punished

If any person break and enter the dwelling house of another in the nighttime with intent to commit a felony or any larceny therein, he shall be guilty of burglary, punishable as a Class 3 felony; provided, however, that if such person was armed with a deadly weapon at the time of such entry, he shall be guilty of a Class 2 felony.

Crimes and Offenses Generally §18.2-90
Entering dwelling house, etc., with intent to commit murder, rape or robbery

If any person in the nighttime enters without breaking or in the daytime breaks and enters or enters and conceals himself in a dwelling house or an adjoining, occupied outhouse or in the nighttime enters without breaking or at any time breaks and enters or enters and conceals himself in any office, shop, manufactured home, storehouse, warehouse, banking house, or other house, or any ship, vessel or river craft or any railroad car, or any automobile, truck or trailer, if such automobile, truck or trailer is used as a dwelling or place of human habitation, with intent to commit murder, rape or robbery, he shall be deemed guilty of statutory burglary, which offense shall be a Class 3 felony. However, if such person was armed with a deadly weapon at the time of such entry, he shall be guilty of a Class 2 felony.

Crimes and Offenses Generally §18.2-91
Entering dwelling house, etc., with intent to commit larceny, assault and battery or other felony

If any person commits any of the acts mentioned in §18.2-90 with intent to commit larceny, assault and battery or any felony other than murder, rape or robbery, he shall be guilty of statutory burglary, punishable by confinement in a state correctional facility for not less than one or more than twenty years or, in the discretion of the jury or the court trying the case without a jury, be confined in jail for a period not exceeding twelve months or fined not more than $2,500, either or both. However, if the person was armed with a deadly weapon at the time of such entry, he shall be guilty of a Class 2 felony.

Crimes and Offenses Generally §18.2-92
Breaking and entering dwelling house with intent to commit other misdemeanor

If any person break and enter a dwelling house while said dwelling is occupied, either in the day or nighttime, with the intent to commit any misdemeanor except assault and battery or trespass, he shall be guilty of a Class 6 felony. However, if the person was armed with a deadly weapon at the time of such entry, he shall be guilty of a Class 2 felony.

Crimes and Offenses Generally §18.2-93
Entering bank, armed, with intent to commit larceny

If any person, armed with a deadly weapon, shall enter any banking house, in the daytime or in the nighttime, with intent to commit larceny of money, bonds, notes, or other evidence of debt therein, he shall be guilty of a Class 2 felony.

Crimes and Offenses Generally §18.2-95
Grand larceny defined; how punished

Any person who
(i) commits larceny from the person of another of money or other thing of value of
$5 or more,
(ii) commits simple larceny not from the person of another of goods and chattels of
the value of $200 or more, or
(iii) commits simple larceny not from the person of another of any handgun, rifle or
shotgun, regardless of the handgun's, rifle's or shotgun's value, shall be guilty of
grand larceny, punishable by imprisonment in a state correctional facility for not
less than one nor more than twenty years or, in the discretion of the jury or court
trying the case without a jury, be confined in jail for a period not exceeding twelve
months or fined not more than $2,500, either or both.

Crimes and Offenses Generally §18.2-108.1.
Theft or receipt of stolen firearm

1. Any person who commits simple larceny of a firearm not from the person shall be
guilty of a Class 6 felony.
2. Any person who buys or receives a firearm from another person or aids in
concealing a firearm, knowing that the firearm was stolen, shall be guilty of a Class
6 felony and may be proceeded against although the principal offender is not
convicted.

Crimes and Offenses Generally §18.2-134.
Trespass on posted property

Any person who goes on the lands, waters, ponds, boats or blinds of another,
which have been posted in accordance with the provisions of §18.2-134.1, to
hunt, fish or trap except with the written consent of or in the presence of the
owner or his agent shall be guilty of a Class 1 misdemeanor.

Crimes and Offenses Generally §18.2-136
**Right of certain hunters to go on lands of another; carrying firearms
or bows and arrows prohibited**

Fox hunters and coon hunters, when the chase begins on other lands, may follow
their dogs on prohibited lands, and hunters of all other game, when the chase
begins on other lands, may go upon prohibited lands to retrieve their dogs, but
may not carry firearms or bows and arrows on their persons or hunt any game
while thereon. The use of vehicles to retrieve dogs on prohibited lands shall be
allowed only with the permission of the landowner or his agent.

Crimes and Offenses Generally §18.2-154.
**Shooting at or throwing missiles, etc., at train, car, vessel, etc.;
penalty**

Any person who maliciously shoots at, or maliciously throws any missile at or
against, any train or cars on any railroad or other transportation company or any
vessel or other watercraft, or any motor vehicle or other vehicles when occupied
by one or more persons, whereby the life of any person on such train, car,
vessel, or other watercraft, or in such motor vehicle or other vehicle, may be put
in peril, shall be guilty of a Class 4 felony. In the event of the death of any such
person, resulting from such malicious shooting or throwing, the person so
offending shall be deemed guilty of murder, the degree to be determined by the
jury or the court trying the case without a jury.

If any such act is committed unlawfully, but not maliciously, the person so offending shall be guilty of a Class 6 felony and, in the event of the death of any such person, resulting from such unlawful act, the person so offending shall be deemed guilty of involuntary manslaughter.

If any person commits a violation of this section by maliciously or unlawfully shooting, with a firearm, at a conspicuously marked law-enforcement, fire or rescue squad vehicle, ambulance or any other emergency medical vehicle, the sentence imposed shall include a mandatory, minimum term of imprisonment of one year which shall not be suspended in whole or in part.

Crimes and Offenses Generally §18.2-204.1
Fraudulent use of birth certificates, drivers' licenses, etc.

A. It shall be unlawful for any person to obtain or possess the birth certificate of another for the purpose of establishing a false identity for himself or for another person.

B. It shall be unlawful for any person to possess, sell or transfer any document for the purpose of establishing a false status, occupation, membership, license or identity for himself or any other person.

C. Any person who shall violate the provisions of this section is guilty of a Class 1 misdemeanor, except when the birth certificate or document is obtained, possessed, sold, or transferred with the intent to use such certificate or document to purchase a firearm, in which case a violation of this section shall be punishable as a Class 6 felony.

D. The provisions of this section shall not apply to members of state, federal, county, city or town law-enforcement agencies in the performance of their duties.

Crimes and Offenses Generally §18.2-279.
Discharging firearms or missiles within or at building or dwelling house

If any person maliciously discharges a firearm within any building when occupied by one or more persons in such a manner as to endanger the life or lives of such person or persons, or maliciously shoots at, or maliciously throws any missile at or against any dwelling house or other building when occupied by one or more persons, whereby the life or lives of any such person or persons may be put in peril, the person so offending shall be guilty of a Class 4 felony. In the event of the death of any person, resulting from such malicious shooting or throwing, the person so offending shall be guilty of murder, the degree to be determined by the jury or the court trying the case without a jury.

If any such act be done unlawfully, but not maliciously, the person so offending shall be guilty of a Class 6 felony; and, in the event of the death of any person resulting from such unlawful shooting or throwing, the person so offending shall be guilty of involuntary manslaughter. If any person willfully discharges a firearm within or shoots at any school building whether occupied or not, he shall be guilty of a Class 4 felony.

Crimes and Offenses Generally §18.2-280.
Willfully discharging firearms in public places

A. If any person willfully discharges or causes to be discharged any firearm in any street in a city or town, or in any place of public business or place of public gathering, he shall be guilty of a Class 1 misdemeanor.

B. If any person willfully discharges or causes to be discharged any firearm upon any public, private or parochial elementary, middle or high school, including the buildings and grounds or upon public property within 1,000 feet of such school property, he shall be guilty of a Class 4 felony.

C. This section shall not apply to any law-enforcement officer in the performance of his official duties nor to any other person whose said willful act is otherwise justifiable or excusable at law in the protection of his life or property, or is otherwise specifically authorized by law. In addition, subsection B shall not apply to any otherwise lawful discharge while actually engaged in lawful hunting, a program or curriculum sponsored by or conducted with permission of the school or while in or on an established shooting range.

Crimes and Offenses Generally §18.2-281.
Setting spring gun or other deadly weapon

It shall be unlawful for any person to set or fix in any manner any firearm or other deadly weapon so that it may be discharged or activated by a person coming in contact therewith or with any string, wire, spring, or any other contrivance attached thereto or designed to activate such weapon remotely. Any person violating this section shall be guilty of a Class 6 felony.

Crimes and Offenses Generally §18.2-282.
Pointing, holding, or brandishing firearm or object similar in appearance; penalty

A. It shall be unlawful for any person to point, hold or brandish any firearm, as hereinafter described, or any object similar in appearance to a firearm, whether capable of being fired or not, in such manner as to reasonably induce fear in the mind of another or hold a firearm in a public place in such a manner as to reasonably induce fear in the mind of another of being shot or injured. However, this section shall not apply to any person engaged in excusable or justifiable self-defense. Persons violating the provisions of this section shall be guilty of a Class 1 misdemeanor or, if the violation occurs upon any public, private or parochial elementary, middle or high school, including buildings and grounds or upon public property within 1,000 feet of such school property, he shall be guilty of a Class 6 felony.
B. Any police officer in the performance of his duty, in making an arrest under the provisions of this section, shall not be civilly liable in damages for injuries or death resulting to the person being arrested if he had reason to believe that the person being arrested was pointing, holding, or brandishing such firearm, or object which was similar in appearance to a firearm, with intent to induce fear in the mind of another.
C. For purposes of this section, the word "firearm" shall mean any weapon in which ammunition may be used or discharged by explosion or pneumatic pressure. The word "ammunition," as used herein, shall mean a cartridge, pellet, ball, missile or projectile adapted for use in a firearm.

Crimes and Offenses Generally §18.2-283.
Carrying dangerous weapon to place of religious worship

If any person carry any gun, pistol, bowie knife, dagger or other dangerous weapon, without good and sufficient reason, to a place of worship while a meeting for religious purposes is being held at such place he shall be guilty of a Class 4 misdemeanor.

Crimes and Offenses Generally §18.2-283.1.
Carrying weapon into courthouse

It shall be unlawful for any person to possess in or transport into any courthouse in this Commonwealth any
(i) gun or other weapon designed or intended to propel a missile or projectile of any kind,

(ii) frame, receiver, muffler, silencer, missile, projectile or ammunition designed for use with a dangerous weapon and

(iii) any other dangerous weapon, including explosives, tasers, stun weapons and those weapons specified in subsection A of §18.2-308. Any such weapon shall be subject to seizure by a law-enforcement officer. A violation of this section is punishable as a Class 1 misdemeanor, and upon the person's conviction, the weapon seized shall be forfeited to the Commonwealth and disposed of as provided in subsection A of §18.2-308.

The provisions of this section shall not apply to any police officer, sheriff, law-enforcement agent or official, game warden, conservator of the peace, magistrate, court officer, or judge while in the conduct of such person's official duties.

Crimes and Offenses Generally §18.2-284.
Selling or giving toy firearms

No person shall sell, barter, exchange, furnish, or dispose of by purchase, gift or in any other manner any toy gun, pistol, rifle or other toy firearm, if the same shall, by means of powder or other explosive, discharge blank or ball charges. Any person violating the provisions of this section shall be guilty of a Class 4 misdemeanor. Each sale of any of the articles hereinbefore specified to any person shall constitute a separate offense.

Nothing in this section shall be construed as preventing the sale of what are commonly known as cap pistols.

Crimes and Offenses Generally §18.2-285.
Hunting with firearms while under influence of intoxicant or narcotic drug

It shall be unlawful for any person to hunt with firearms in the Commonwealth of Virginia while under the influence of alcohol, or while under the influence of any narcotic drug or any other self-administered intoxicant or drug of whatsoever nature. Any person violating the provisions of this section shall be guilty of a Class 3 misdemeanor. Game wardens, sheriffs and all other law-enforcement officers shall enforce the provisions of this section.

Crimes and Offenses Generally §18.2-286.
Shooting in or across road or in street

If any person discharges a firearm, crossbow or bow and arrow in or across any road, or within the right-of-way thereof, or in a street of any city or town, he shall, for each offense, be guilty of a Class 4 misdemeanor.

The provisions of this section shall not apply to firing ranges or shooting matches maintained, and supervised or approved, by law-enforcement officers and military personnel in performance of their lawful duties.

Crimes and Offenses Generally §18.2-286.1.
Shooting from vehicles so as to endanger persons; penalty

Any person who, while in or on a motor vehicle, intentionally discharges a firearm so as to create the risk of injury or death to another person or thereby cause another person to have a reasonable apprehension of injury or death shall be guilty of a Class 5 felony. Nothing in this section shall apply to a law-enforcement officer in the performance of his duties.

Crimes and Offenses Generally §18.2-287.
Counties may regulate carrying of loaded firearms on public highways

The governing body of any county is hereby empowered to adopt ordinances making it unlawful for any person to carry or have in his possession while on any part of a public highway within such county a loaded firearm when such person is not authorized to hunt on the private property on both sides of the highway along which he is standing or walking; and to provide a penalty for violation of such ordinance not to exceed a fine of $100. The provisions of this section shall not apply to persons carrying loaded firearms in moving vehicles, nor to persons acting at the time in defense of persons or property.

Crimes and Offenses Generally §18.2-287.1.
Transporting a loaded rifle or shotgun

The governing body of any county or city is hereby empowered to adopt ordinances making it unlawful for any person to transport, possess or carry a loaded shotgun or loaded rifle in any vehicle on any public street, road, or highway within such locality. Any violation of such ordinance shall be punishable by a fine of not more than $100. Game wardens, sheriffs and all other law-enforcement officers shall enforce the provisions of this section. No ordinance adopted pursuant to this section shall be enforceable unless the governing body adopting such ordinance so notifies the Director of the Department of Game and Inland Fisheries by registered mail prior to May 1 of the year in which such ordinance is to take effect.

The provisions of this section shall not apply to duly authorized law-enforcement officers or military personnel in the performance of their lawful duties, nor to any person who reasonably believes that a loaded rifle or shotgun is necessary for his personal safety in the course of his employment or business.

Crimes and Offenses Generally §18.2-287.2.
Wearing of body armor while committing a violent crime; penalty

Any person who, while committing a crime of violence as described in §18.2-288 (2), has in his possession a firearm or knife and is wearing body armor designed to diminish the effect of the impact of a bullet or projectile shall be guilty of a Class 4 felony.

Crimes and Offenses Generally §18.2-287.4.
Carrying loaded firearms in public areas prohibited; penalty

It shall be unlawful for any person to carry a loaded firearm on or about his person on any public street, road, alley, sidewalk, public right-of-way, or in any public park or any other place of whatever nature that is open to the public
(i) in any city with a population of 160,000 or more or
(ii) in any county having an urban county executive form of government or any county or city surrounded thereby or adjacent thereto or in any county having a county manager form of government. The provisions of this section shall not apply to law-enforcement officers, licensed security guards, military personnel in the performance of their lawful duties, or any person having a valid permit to carry such firearm or to any person actually engaged in lawful hunting or lawful recreational shooting activities at an established shooting range or shooting contest. Any person violating the provisions of this section shall be guilty of a Class 1 misdemeanor.
For purposes of this section, "firearm" means any;
(i) semi-automatic center-fire rifle or pistol which expels a projectile by action of an explosion and is equipped at the time of the offense with a magazine which will

hold more than twenty rounds of ammunition or designed by the manufacturer to accommodate a silencer or equipped with a folding stock or;

(ii) shotgun with a magazine which will hold more than seven rounds of the longest ammunition for which it is chambered.

Any firearm carried in violation of this section may be forfeited to the Commonwealth pursuant to the provisions of §18.2-310.

The exemptions set out in §18.2-308 shall apply, mutatis mutandis, to the provisions of this section.

<The following laws, through §18.2-298, are known as the Uniform Machine Gun Act.>

Crimes and Offenses Generally §18.2-288
Definitions

When used in this article:

1. "Machine gun" applies to any weapon which shoots or is designed to shoot automatically more than one shot, without manual reloading, by a single function of the trigger.
2. "Crime of violence" applies to and includes any of the following crimes or an attempt to commit any of the same, namely, murder, manslaughter, kidnapping, rape, mayhem, assault with intent to maim, disable, disfigure or kill, robbery, burglary, housebreaking, breaking and entering and larceny.
3. "Person" applies to and includes firm, partnership, association or corporation.

Crimes and Offenses Generally §18.2-289
Use of machine gun for crime of violence

Possession or use of a machine gun in the perpetration or attempted perpetration of a crime of violence is hereby declared to be a Class 2 felony.

Crimes and Offenses Generally §18.2-290.
Use of machine gun for aggressive purpose

Unlawful possession or use of a machine gun for an offensive or aggressive purpose is hereby declared to be a Class 4 felony.

Crimes and Offenses Generally §18.2-291.
What constitutes aggressive purpose

Possession or use of a machine gun shall be presumed to be for an offensive or aggressive purpose:

1. When the machine gun is on premises not owned or rented for bona fide permanent residence or business occupancy by the person in whose possession the machine gun may be found;
2. When the machine gun is in the possession of, or used by, a person who has been convicted of a crime of violence in any court of record, state or federal, of the United States of America, its territories or insular possessions;
3. When the machine gun has not been registered as required in §18.2-295; or
4. When empty or loaded shells which have been or are susceptible of use in the machine gun are found in the immediate vicinity thereof.

Crimes and Offenses Generally §18.2-292.
Presence prima facie evidence of use

The presence of a machine gun in any room, boat or vehicle shall be prima facie evidence of the possession or use of the machine gun by each person occupying the room, boat, or vehicle where the weapon is found.

Crimes and Offenses Generally §18.2-293
What article does not apply to

The provisions of this article <Uniform Machine Gun Act> shall not be applicable to:
1. The manufacture for, and sale of, machine guns to the armed forces or law-enforcement officers of the United States or of any state or of any political subdivision thereof, or the transportation required for that purpose; and
2. Machine guns and automatic arms issued to the national guard of Virginia by the United States or such arms used by the United States army or navy or in the hands of troops of the national guards of other states or territories of the United States passing through Virginia, or such arms as may be provided for the officers of the State Police or officers of penal institutions.

Crimes and Offenses Generally §18.2-293.1.
What article does not prohibit

Nothing contained in this article <Uniform Machine Gun Act> shall prohibit or interfere with:
1. The possession of a machine gun for scientific purposes, or the possession of a machine gun not usable as a weapon and possessed as a curiosity, ornament, or keepsake; and
2. The possession of a machine gun for a purpose manifestly not aggressive or offensive.
Provided, however, that possession of such machine guns shall be subject to the provisions of §18.2-295.

Crimes and Offenses Generally §18.2-294.
Manufacturer's and dealer's register; inspection of stock

Every manufacturer or dealer shall keep a register of all machine guns manufactured or handled by him. This register shall show the model and serial number, date of manufacture, sale, loan, gift, delivery or receipt of every machine gun, the name, address, and occupation of the person to whom the machine gun was sold, loaned, given or delivered, or from whom it was received. Upon demand every manufacturer or dealer shall permit any marshal, sheriff or police officer to inspect his entire stock of machine guns, parts, and supplies therefor, and shall produce the register, herein required, for inspection. A violation of any provisions of this section shall be punishable as a Class 3 misdemeanor.

Crimes and Offenses Generally §18.2-295.
Registration of machine guns

Every machine gun in this Commonwealth shall be registered with the Department of State Police within twenty-four hours after its acquisition or, in the case of semi-automatic weapons which are converted, modified or otherwise altered to become machine guns, within twenty-four hours of the conversion, modification or alteration. Blanks for registration shall be prepared by the Superintendent of State Police, and furnished upon application. To comply with this section the application as filed shall be notarized and shall show the model and serial number of the gun, the name, address and occupation of the person in possession, and from whom and the purpose for which, the gun was acquired or altered. The Superintendent of State Police shall upon registration required in this section forthwith furnish the registrant with a certificate of registration, which shall be valid as long as the registrant remains the same. Certificates of registration shall be retained by the registrant and produced by him upon demand by any peace officer. Failure to keep or produce such certificate for inspection shall be a Class 3 misdemeanor, and any peace officer, may without warrant, seize the machine gun and apply for its confiscation as provided in §18.2-296. Upon transferring a registered machine gun, the transferor shall forthwith notify the Superintendent in writing, setting forth the date of transfer and name and address of the transferee. Failure to give the required notification shall constitute a Class 3 misdemeanor. Registration data shall not be subject to inspection by the public.

Crimes and Offenses Generally §18.2-296.
Search warrants for machine guns

Warrant to search any house or place and seize any machine gun possessed in violation of this article may issue in the same manner and under the same restrictions as provided by law for stolen property, and any court of record, upon application of the attorney for the Commonwealth, a police officer or conservator of the peace, may order any machine gun, thus or otherwise legally seized, to be confiscated and either destroyed or delivered to a peace officer of the Commonwealth or a political subdivision thereof.

Crimes and Offenses Generally §18.2-299.
Definitions

When used in this article:

"Sawed-off' shotgun" applies to any weapon, loaded or unloaded, originally designed as a shoulder weapon, utilizing a self-contained cartridge from which a number of ball shot pellets or projectiles may be fired simultaneously from a smooth or rifled bore by a single function of the firing device and which has a barrel length of less than eighteen inches for smooth bore weapons and sixteen inches for rifled weapons. Weapons of less than .225 caliber shall not be included.

"Sawed-off' rifle" means a rifle of any caliber, loaded or unloaded, which expels a projectile by action of an explosion and is designed as a shoulder weapon with a barrel or barrels length of less than sixteen inches or which has been modified to an overall length of less than twenty-six inches.

Crimes and Offenses Generally §18.2-300.
Possession or use of "sawed-off" shotgun or rifle

A. Possession or use of a "sawed-off" shotgun or "sawed-off" rifle in the perpetration or attempted perpetration of a crime of violence is a Class 2 felony.

B. Possession or use of a "sawed-off" shotgun or "sawed-off" rifle for any other purpose, except as permitted by this article and official use by those persons permitted possession by §18.2-303, is a Class 4 felony.

Crimes and Offenses Generally §18.2-303.
What article does not apply to

The provisions of this article shall not be applicable to:

1. The manufacture for, and sale of, "sawed-off" shotguns or "sawed-off" rifles to the armed forces or law-enforcement officers of the United States or of any state or of any political subdivision thereof, or the transportation required for that purpose; and

2. "Sawed-off" shotguns, "sawed-off" rifles and automatic arms issued to the National Guard of Virginia by the United States or such arms used by the United States Army or Navy or in the hands of troops of the national guards of other states or territories of the United States passing through Virginia, or such arms as may be provided for the officers of the State Police or officers of penal institutions.

Crimes and Offenses Generally §18.2-303.1.
What article does not prohibit

Nothing contained in this article shall prohibit or interfere with the possession of a "sawed-off" shotgun or "sawed-off" rifle for scientific purposes, the possession of a "sawed-off" shotgun or "sawed-off" rifle possessed in compliance with federal law or the possession of a "sawed-off" shotgun or "sawed-off" rifle not usable as a firing weapon and possessed as a curiosity, ornament, or keepsake.

Crimes and Offenses Generally §18.2-304.
Manufacturer's and dealer's register; inspection of stock

Every manufacturer or dealer shall keep a register of all "sawed-off" shotguns and "sawed-off" rifles manufactured or handled by him. This register shall show the model and serial number, date of manufacture, sale, loan, gift, delivery or receipt of every "sawed-off" shotgun and "sawed-off" rifle, the name, address, and occupation of the person to whom the "sawed-off" shotgun or "sawed-off" rifle was sold, loaned, given or delivered, or from whom it was received. Upon demand every manufacturer or dealer shall permit any marshal, sheriff or police officer to inspect his entire stock of "sawed-off" shotguns and "sawed-off" rifles, and "sawed-off" shotgun or "sawed-off" rifle barrels, and shall produce the register, herein required, for inspection. A violation of any provision of this section shall be punishable as a Class 3 misdemeanor.

Crimes and Offenses Generally §18.2-306.
Search warrants for "sawed-off" shotguns and rifles; confiscation and destruction

Warrant to search any house or place and seize any "sawed-off" shotgun or "sawed-off" rifle possessed in violation of this article may issue in the same manner and under the same restrictions as provided by law for stolen property, and any court of record, upon application of the attorney for the Commonwealth, a police officer or conservator of the peace, may order any "sawed-off" shotgun or "sawed-off" rifle thus or otherwise legally seized, to be confiscated and either destroyed or delivered to a peace officer of the Commonwealth or a political subdivision thereof.

Crimes and Offenses Generally §18.2-308.
Personal protection; carrying concealed weapons; when lawful to carry

A. If any person carries about his person, hidden from common observation,

(i) any pistol, revolver, or other weapon designed or intended to propel a missile of any kind, or

(ii) any dirk, bowie knife, switchblade knife, ballistic knife, razor, slingshot, spring stick, metal knuckles, blackjack, or

(iii) any flailing instrument consisting of two or more rigid parts connected in such a manner as to allow them to swing freely, which may be known as a nun chahka, nun chuck, nunchaku, shuriken, or fighting chain, or

(iv) any disc, of whatever configuration, having at least two points or pointed blades which is designed to be thrown or propelled and which may be known as a throwing star or oriental dart, or

(v) any weapon of like kind as those enumerated in this subsection, he shall be guilty of a Class 1 misdemeanor. A second violation of this section or a conviction under this section subsequent to any conviction under any substantially similar ordinance of any county, city, or town shall be punishable as a Class 6 felony, and a third or subsequent such violation shall be punishable as a Class 5 felony. Any weapon used in the commission of a violation of this section shall be forfeited to the Commonwealth and may be seized by an officer as forfeited, and such as may be needed for police officers, conservators of the peace, and the Division of Forensic Science shall be devoted to that purpose, subject to any registration requirements of federal law, and the remainder shall be disposed of as provided in §18.2-310. For the purpose of this section, a weapon shall be deemed to be hidden from common observation when it is observable but is of such deceptive appearance as to disguise the weapon's true nature.

B. This section shall not apply to:

1. Any person while in his own place of abode or the curtilage thereof;

2. Any police officers, including Capitol Police officers, sergeants, sheriffs, deputy sheriffs or regular game wardens appointed pursuant to Chapter 2 (§29.1-200 et seq.) of Title 29.1;

3. Any regularly enrolled member of a target shooting organization who is at, or going to or from, an established shooting range, provided that the weapons are unloaded and securely wrapped while being transported;

4. Any regularly enrolled member of a weapons collecting organization who is at, or going to or from, a bona fide weapons exhibition, provided that the weapons are unloaded and securely wrapped while being transported;

5. Any person carrying such weapons between his place of abode and a place of purchase or repair, provided the weapons are unloaded and securely wrapped while being transported;

6. Campus police officers appointed pursuant to Chapter 17 (§23-232 et seq.) of Title 23;

7. Any person actually engaged in lawful hunting, as authorized by the Board of Game and Inland Fisheries, under inclement weather conditions necessitating temporary protection of his firearm from those conditions; and

8. Any State Police officer retired from the Department of State Police following at least fifteen years of service, other than a person terminated for cause, provided such officer carries with him written proof of consultation with and favorable review of the need to carry a concealed weapon issued by the Superintendent of State Police.

C. This section shall also not apply to any of the following individuals while in the discharge of their official duties, or while in transit to or from such duties:

1. Carriers of the United States mail;
2. Officers or guards of any state correctional institution;
4. Conservators of the peace, except that the following conservators of the peace shall not be permitted to carry a concealed weapon without obtaining a permit as provided in subsection D hereof: (a) notaries public; (b) registrars; (c) drivers, operators or other persons in charge of any motor vehicle carrier of passengers for hire; (d) commissioners in chancery;
5. Noncustodial employees of the Department of Corrections designated to carry weapons by the Director of the Department of Corrections pursuant to §53.1-29;
6. Law-enforcement agents of the Armed Forces of the United States and federal agents who are otherwise authorized to carry weapons by federal law while engaged in the performance of their duties;
7. Law-enforcement agents of the United States Naval Criminal Investigative Service; and
8. Harbormaster of the City of Hopewell.
D. Any person twenty-one years of age or older may apply in writing to the clerk of the circuit court of the county or city in which he resides for a two-year permit to carry a concealed handgun. The application shall be made under oath before a notary or other person qualified to take oaths and shall be made on a form prescribed by the Supreme Court, requiring only that information necessary to determine eligibility for the permit. The court, after consulting the law-enforcement authorities of the county or city and receiving a report from the Central Criminal Records Exchange, shall issue the permit within forty-five days of receipt of the completed application unless it appears that the applicant is disqualified, except that any permit issued prior to July 1, 1996, shall be issued within ninety days of receipt of the completed application.
E. The following persons shall be deemed disqualified from obtaining a permit:
1. An individual who is ineligible to possess a firearm pursuant to §18.2-308.1:1, §18.2-308.1:2 or §18.2-308.1:3 or the substantially similar law of any other state or of the United States.
2. An individual who was ineligible to possess a firearm pursuant to §18.2-308.1:1 and who was discharged from the custody of the Commissioner pursuant to §19.2-182.7 less than five years before the date of his application for a concealed handgun permit.
3. An individual who was ineligible to possess a firearm pursuant to §18.2-308.1:2 and whose competency or capacity was restored pursuant to §37.1-134.1 less than five years before the date of his application for a concealed handgun permit.
4. An individual who was ineligible to possess a firearm under §18.2-308.1:3 and who was released from commitment less than five years before the date of this application for a concealed handgun permit.
5. An individual who is subject to a restraining order, or to a protective order and prohibited by §18.2-308.1:4 from purchasing or transporting a firearm.
6. An individual who is prohibited by §18.2-308.2 from possessing or transporting a firearm, except that a permit may be obtained in accordance with subsection C of that section.
7. An individual who has been convicted of two or more misdemeanors within the three-year period immediately preceding the application, if one of the misdemeanors was a Class 1 misdemeanor, but the judge shall have the discretion to deny a permit for two or more misdemeanors that are not Class 1. Traffic infractions or reckless driving shall not be considered for purposes of this disqualification.

8. An individual who is addicted to, or is an unlawful user or distributor of, marijuana or any controlled substance.

9. An individual who has been convicted of a violation of §18.2-266 <drunk driving> or a substantially similar local ordinance or of public drunkenness within the three-year period immediately preceding the application, or who is a habitual drunkard as determined pursuant to §4.1-333.

10. An alien other than an alien lawfully admitted for permanent residence in the United States.

11. An individual who has been discharged from the Armed Forces of the United States under dishonorable conditions.

12. An individual who is a fugitive from justice.

13. An individual who it is alleged, in a sworn written statement submitted to the court by the sheriff, chief of police or the attorney for the Commonwealth, that in the opinion of such sheriff, chief of police or attorney for the Commonwealth, is likely to use a weapon unlawfully or negligently to endanger others. The statement of the sheriff, chief of police or Commonwealth's attorney shall be based upon personal knowledge or upon the sworn written statement of a competent person having personal knowledge.

14. An individual who has been convicted of any assault, assault and battery, sexual battery, discharging of a firearm in violation of §18.2-280 or §18.2-286.1 or brandishing of a firearm in violation of §18.2-282 within the three-year period immediately preceding the application.

15. An individual who has been convicted of stalking.

16. An individual whose previous convictions or adjudications of delinquency were based on an offense which would have been at the time of conviction a felony if committed by an adult under the laws of any state, the District of Columbia, the United States or its territories. For purposes of this disqualifier, only convictions occurring within sixteen years following the later of the date of

(i) the conviction or adjudication or

(ii) release from any incarceration imposed upon such conviction or adjudication shall be deemed to be "previous convictions."

17. An individual who has a felony charge pending or a charge pending for an offense listed in subdivision 14 or 15.

18. An individual who has received mental health treatment or substance abuse treatment in a residential setting within five years prior to the date of his application for a concealed handgun permit.

F. The making of a materially false statement in an application under this section shall constitute perjury, punishable as provided in §18.2-434.

G. The court may further require proof that the applicant has demonstrated competence with a handgun and the applicant may demonstrate such competence by one of the following:

1. Completing any hunter education or hunter safety course approved by the Department of Game and Inland Fisheries or a similar agency of another state;

2. Completing any National Rifle Association firearms safety or training course;

3. Completing any firearms safety or training course or class available to the general public offered by a law-enforcement agency, junior college, college, or private or public institution or organization or firearms training school utilizing instructors certified by the National Rifle Association or the Department of Criminal Justice Services;

4. Completing any law-enforcement firearms safety or training course or class offered for security guards, investigators, special deputies, or any division or

subdivision of law enforcement or security enforcement;

5. Presenting evidence of equivalent experience with a firearm through participation in organized shooting competition or military service;

6. Obtaining or previously having held a license to carry a firearm in this Commonwealth or a locality thereof, unless such license has been revoked for cause;

7. Completing any firearms training or safety course or class conducted by a state-certified or National Rifle Association-certified firearms instructor; or

8. Completing any other firearms training which the court deems adequate. A photocopy of a certificate of completion of any of the courses or classes; an affidavit from the instructor, school, club, organization, or group that conducted or taught such course or class attesting to the completion of the course or class by the applicant; or a copy of any document which shows completion of the course or class or evidences participation in firearms competition shall constitute evidence of qualification under this subsection.

H. The permit to carry a concealed handgun shall specify the name, address, date of birth, gender, social security number, height, weight, color of hair, color of eyes, and signature of the permittee; the signature of the judge issuing the permit, or of the clerk of court who has been authorized to sign such permits by the issuing judge; the date of issuance; and the expiration date. The person issued the permit shall have such permit on his person at all times during which he is carrying a concealed handgun and must display the permit and a photo-identification issued by a government agency of the Commonwealth or by the United States Department of Defense or United States State Department (passport) upon demand by a law-enforcement officer.

I. Persons who previously have held a concealed weapons permit shall be issued, upon application, a new two-year permit unless there is good cause shown for refusing to reissue a permit. If the circuit court denies the permit, the specific reasons for the denial shall be stated in the order of the court denying the permit. Upon denial of the application and request of the applicant made within ten days, the court shall place the matter on the docket for an ore tenus hearing. The applicant may be represented by counsel, but counsel shall not be appointed. The final order of the court shall include the court's findings of fact and conclusions of law.

J. Any person convicted of an offense that would disqualify that person from obtaining a permit under subsection E or who violates subsection F shall forfeit his permit for a concealed handgun to the court. Any person permitted to carry a concealed weapon under this section, who is under the influence of alcohol or illegal drugs while carrying such weapon in a public place, shall be guilty of a Class 1 misdemeanor.

J1. An individual who has a felony charge pending or a charge pending for an offense listed in subdivision 14 or 15, holding a permit for a concealed handgun, may have such permit suspended by such court before which such charge is pending.

J2. No person shall carry a concealed handgun into any place of business or special event for which a license to sell or serve alcoholic beverages on premises has been granted by the Virginia Alcoholic Beverage Control Board under Title 4.1 of the Code of Virginia; provided nothing herein shall prohibit any owner or event sponsor or his employees from carrying a concealed handgun while on duty at such place of business or at such special event if such person has a concealed handgun permit.

K. No fee shall be charged for the issuance of such permit to a person who has retired from service as a magistrate in the Commonwealth or as a law-enforcement officer with the Department of State Police, or with a sheriff or police department, bureau or force of any political subdivision of the Commonwealth of Virginia, after completing twenty years' service or after reaching age fifty-five nor to any person who has retired after completing twenty years' service or after reaching age fifty-five from service as a law-enforcement officer with the United States Federal Bureau of Investigation, Bureau of Alcohol, Tobacco and Firearms, Secret Service Agency, Drug Enforcement Administration or Naval Criminal Investigative Service. The clerk shall charge a fee of ten dollars for the processing of an application or issuing of a permit, including his costs associated with the consultation with law-enforcement agencies. The local law-enforcement agencies may charge a fee not to exceed thirty-five dollars to cover the cost of conducting an investigation pursuant to this section. The State Police may charge a fee not to exceed five dollars to cover their costs associated with processing the application. The order issuing such permit shall be provided to the State Police and the law-enforcement agencies of the county or city. The State Police shall enter the permittee's name and description in the Virginia Criminal Information Network so that the permit's existence will be made known to law-enforcement personnel accessing the Network for investigative purposes.

L. Any person denied a permit to carry a concealed weapon under the provisions of this section may, within thirty days of the final decision, present a petition for review to the Court of Appeals or any judge thereof. The petition shall be accompanied by a copy of the original papers filed in the circuit court, including a copy of the order of the circuit court denying the permit. Subject to the provisions of §17-116.07 <allows constitutional issues to go to Supreme Court> B, the decision of the Court of Appeals or judge shall be final. Notwithstanding any other provision of law, if the decision to deny the permit is reversed upon appeal, taxable costs incurred by the person shall be paid by the Commonwealth.

O. The granting of a concealed handgun permit shall not thereby authorize the possession of any handgun or other weapon on property or in places where such possession is otherwise prohibited by law or is prohibited by the owner of private property.

P. The provisions of this statute or the application thereof to any person or circumstances which are held invalid shall not affect the validity of other provisions or applications of this statute which can be given effect without the invalid provisions or applications. This section is to reiterate §1-17.1 <severability clause> and is not meant to add or delete from that provision.

Crimes and Offenses Generally §18.2-308.1.
Possession of firearm, stun weapon, or other weapon on school property prohibited

If any person has in his possession any
(i) stun weapon or taser as defined in this section or
(ii) weapon, other than a firearm, designated in subsection A of §18.2-308 upon
(i) the property of any public, private or parochial elementary, middle or high school, including buildings and grounds,
(ii) that portion of any property open to the public used for school-sponsored functions or extracurricular activities while such functions or activities are taking place, or
(iii) any school bus owned or operated by any such school, he shall be guilty of a Class 1 misdemeanor. If any person has in his possession any firearm designed or intended to propel a missile of any kind while such person is upon
(i) any public, private or parochial elementary, middle or high school, including buildings and grounds,
(ii) that portion of any property open to the public used for school-sponsored functions or extracurricular activities while such functions or activities are taking place, or
(iii) any school bus owned or operated by any such school, he shall be guilty of a Class 6 felony.

The exemptions set out in §18.2-308 shall apply, mutatis mutandis, to the provisions of this section. The provisions of this section shall not apply to persons who possess such weapon or weapons as a part of the curriculum or other programs sponsored by the school or any organization permitted by the school to use its premises or to any law-enforcement officer while engaged in his duties as such. In addition, this section shall not apply to possession of an unloaded firearm which is in a closed container in or upon a motor vehicle or an unloaded shotgun or rifle in a firearms rack in or upon a motor vehicle.

Crimes and Offenses Generally §18.2-308.1:1.
Possession or transportation of firearms by persons acquitted by reason of insanity; penalty; permit

A. It shall be unlawful for any person acquitted by reason of insanity and committed to the custody of the Commissioner of Mental Health, Mental Retardation and Substance Abuse Services, pursuant to §19.2-181, on a charge of treason, any felony or any offense punishable as a misdemeanor under Title 54.1 or a Class 1 or Class 2 misdemeanor under this title, except those misdemeanor violations of
(i) Article 2 (§18.2-266 et seq.) of Chapter 7 of this title <Boundaries, Jurisdiction and Emblems of the Commonwealth, now 7.1>,
(ii) Article 2 (§18.2-415 et seq.) of Chapter 9 of this title <Commissions, Boards and Institutions Generally>, or
(iii) §18.2-119, or
(iv) an ordinance of any county, city, or town similar to the offenses specified in (i), (ii), or (iii), to knowingly and intentionally possess or transport any firearm. A violation of this section shall be punishable as a Class 1 misdemeanor.
B. Any person so acquitted may, upon discharge from the custody of the Commissioner, petition the circuit court in which he resides for a permit to possess or carry a firearm. The court may, in its discretion and for good cause shown, grant the petition and issue a permit, in which event the provisions of subsection A do not apply.

Crimes and Offenses Generally §18.2-308.1:2.
Purchase, possession or transportation of firearm by persons adjudicated legally incompetent or mentally incapacitated; penalty

A. It shall be unlawful for any person who has been adjudicated legally incompetent pursuant to §37.1-128.02 or §37.1-134 or mentally incapacitated pursuant to §37.1-128.1 or §37.1-132 and whose competency or capacity has not been restored pursuant to §37.1-134.1, to purchase, possess, or transport any firearm. A violation of this subsection shall be punishable as a Class 1 misdemeanor.

B. Any firearm possessed or transported in violation of this section shall be forfeited to the Commonwealth and disposed of as provided in §18.2-310.

Crimes and Offenses Generally §18.2-308.1:3.
Purchase, possession or transportation of firearm by persons involuntarily committed; penalty

A. It shall be unlawful for any person involuntarily committed pursuant to §37.1-67.3 to purchase, possess or transport a firearm during the period of such person's commitment. A violation of this subsection shall be punishable as a Class 1 misdemeanor.

B. Any firearm possessed or transported in violation of this section shall be forfeited to the Commonwealth and disposed of as provided in §18.2-310.

C. Any person prohibited from purchasing, possessing or transporting firearms under this subsection may, at any time following his release from commitment, petition the circuit court in the city or county in which he resides to restore his right to purchase, possess or transport a firearm. The court may, in its discretion and for good cause shown, grant the petition. The clerk shall certify and forward forthwith to the Central Criminal Records Exchange, on a form provided by the Exchange, a copy of any such order.

Crimes and Offenses Generally §18.2-308.1:4.
Purchase or transportation of firearm by persons subject to protective orders; penalty

A. It shall be unlawful for any person who is subject to a protective order entered pursuant to §16.1-253.1, 16.1-253.4, or §16.1-279.1 or to an order entered pursuant to subsection E of §18.2-60.3 to purchase or transport any firearm while the order is in effect. A violation of this subsection shall be punishable as a Class 1 misdemeanor.

B. Any firearm purchased or transported in violation of this section shall be forfeited to the Commonwealth and disposed of as provided in §18.2-310.

Crimes and Offenses Generally §18.2-308.1:5
Purchase or transportation of firearm by persons convicted of certain drug offenses prohibited

Any person who, within a thirty-six consecutive month period, has been convicted of two misdemeanor offenses under §18.2-250 or §18.2-250.1 shall be ineligible to purchase or transport a handgun. However, upon expiration of a period of five years from the date of the second conviction and provided the person has not been convicted of any such offense within that period, the ineligibility shall be removed.

Crimes and Offenses Generally §18.2-308.2.

Possession or transportation of firearms or concealed weapons by convicted felons; penalties; petition for permit; when issued

A. It shall be unlawful for

(i) any person who has been convicted of a felony or

(ii) any person under the age of twenty-nine who was found guilty as a juvenile fourteen years of age or older at the time of the offense of a delinquent act which would be a felony if committed by an adult, whether such conviction or adjudication occurred under the laws of this Commonwealth, or any other state, the District of Columbia, the United States or any territory thereof, to knowingly and intentionally possess or transport any firearm or to knowingly and intentionally carry about his person, hidden from common observation, any weapon described in §18.2-308A. A violation of this section shall be punishable as a Class 6 felony. Any firearm or any concealed weapon possessed, transported or carried in violation of this section shall be forfeited to the Commonwealth and disposed of as provided in §18.2-310.

B. The prohibitions of subsection A shall not apply to

(i) any person who possesses a firearm or other weapon while carrying out his duties as a member of the armed forces of the United States or of the National Guard of Virginia or of any other state,

(ii) any law-enforcement officer in the performance of his duties, or

(iii) any person who has been pardoned or whose political disabilities have been removed pursuant to Article V, Section 12 of the Constitution of Virginia <Governor's pardon> provided the Governor, in the document granting the pardon or removing the person's political disabilities, may expressly place conditions upon the reinstatement of the person's right to ship, transport, possess or receive firearms.

C. Any person prohibited from possessing, transporting or carrying a firearm under subsection A, may petition the circuit court of the jurisdiction in which he resides for a permit to possess or carry a firearm. The court may, in its discretion and for good cause shown, grant such petition and issue a permit. The provisions of this section shall not apply to any person who has been granted a permit pursuant to this subsection.

Crimes and Offenses Generally §18.2-308.2:01.

Possession or transportation of certain firearms by aliens

It shall be unlawful for any person who is not a citizen of the United States or who is not a person lawfully admitted for permanent residence to knowingly and intentionally possess or transport any assault firearm or to knowingly and intentionally carry about his person, hidden from common observation, an assault firearm. A violation of this section shall be punishable as a Class 6 felony. Any firearm possessed, transported or carried in violation of this section shall be forfeited to the Commonwealth and disposed of as provided in §18.2-310.

Crimes and Offenses Generally §18.2-308.2:1.

Prohibiting the selling, etc., of firearms to certain felons

Any person who sells, barters, gives or furnishes, or has in his possession or under his control with the intent of selling, bartering, giving or furnishing, any firearm to any person he knows is prohibited from possessing or transporting a firearm pursuant to §18.2-308.1:1, §18.2-308.2 or §18.2-308.7 shall be guilty of a Class 6 felony. However, this prohibition shall not be applicable when the person convicted of the felony, adjudicated delinquent or acquitted by reason of insanity has

(i) been issued a permit pursuant to §18.2-308.2 C or §18.2-308.1:1 B,

(ii) been pardoned or had his political disabilities removed in accordance with §18.2-308.2 B or

(iii) obtained a permit to ship, transport, possess or receive firearms pursuant to the laws of the United States. Any firearm sold, bartered, given or furnished or possessed or controlled with intent to do so in violation of this section shall be forfeited to the Commonwealth and disposed of as provided in §18.2-310.

Crimes and Offenses Generally §18.2-308.2:2.

Criminal history record information check required for the transfer of certain firearms; firearm safety information to be provided

A. Any person purchasing from a dealer a firearm as herein defined shall consent in writing, on a form to be provided by the Department of State Police, to have the dealer obtain criminal history record information. Such form shall include only, in addition to the information required by subdivision B 1, the identical information required to be included on the firearms transaction record required by regulations administered by the Bureau of Alcohol, Tobacco and Firearms of the U.S. Department of the Treasury, except that the copies of such forms mailed or delivered to the Department of State Police shall not include any information related to the firearm purchased or transferred.

B. 1. No dealer shall sell, rent, trade or transfer from his inventory any such firearm to any other person who is a resident of Virginia until he has
<Note that the portion of law which follows was enacted with an indexing error; three parts are labeled "(i)" and "(ii)", and two parts labeled "(iii)".>

(i) obtained written consent as specified in subsection A, and provided the Department of State Police with the name, birth date, gender, race, and social security and/or any other identification number and the number of firearms by category intended to be sold, rented, traded or transferred and

(ii) requested and received criminal history record information by a telephone call to the State Police.

To establish personal identification and residence in Virginia for purposes of this section, a dealer must require any prospective purchaser to present one photo-identification form issued by a governmental agency of the Commonwealth or by the United States Department of Defense, and other documentation of residence.

Except where the photo-identification was issued by the United States Department of Defense, the other documentation of residence shall show an address identical to that shown on the photo-identification form, such as evidence of currently paid personal property tax or real estate tax, or a current

(i) lease,

(ii) utility or telephone bill,

(iii) voter registration card,

(iv) bank check,

(v) passport,

(vi) automobile registration, or

(vii) hunting or fishing license; other current identification allowed as evidence of residency by Part 178.124 of Title 27 of the Code of Federal Regulations <describes ID requirements for federal 4473 firearm transaction record form> and ATF Ruling 79-7 <allows multiple pieces of ID that, when taken as a group, provide all required information>; or other documentation of residence determined to be acceptable by the Department of Criminal Justice Services, that corroborates that the prospective purchaser currently resides in Virginia. Where the photo-identification was issued by the Department of Defense, permanent orders may be used as documentation of residence. Additionally, when the photo-identification presented to a dealer by the prospective purchaser is a driver's license or other photo-identification issued by the Department of Motor Vehicles, and such identification form contains a date of issue, the dealer shall not, except for a renewed driver's license or other photo-identification issued by the Department of Motor Vehicles, sell or otherwise transfer a firearm to the prospective purchaser until thirty days after the date of issue of an original or duplicate driver's license unless the prospective purchaser also presents a copy of his Virginia Department of Motor Vehicles driver's record showing that the original date of issue of the driver's license was more than thirty days prior to the attempted purchase.

In addition, no dealer shall sell, rent, trade or transfer from his inventory any assault firearm to any person who is not a citizen of the United States or who is not a person lawfully admitted for permanent residence. To establish citizenship or lawful admission for a permanent residence for purposes of purchasing an assault firearm, a dealer shall require a prospective purchaser to present a certified birth certificate or a certificate of birth abroad issued by the United States State Department, a certificate of citizenship or a certificate of naturalization issued by the Immigration and Naturalization Service, an unexpired U.S. passport, a United States citizen identification card, a current voter registration card, a current selective service registration card, or an immigrant visa or other documentation of status as a person lawfully admitted for permanent residence issued by the Immigration and Naturalization Service.

Upon receipt of the request for a criminal history record information check, the State Police shall

(i) review its criminal history record information to determine if the buyer or transferee is prohibited from possessing or transporting a firearm by state or federal law,

(ii) inform the dealer if its record indicates that the buyer or transferee is so prohibited, and

(iii) provide the dealer with a unique reference number for that inquiry.

2. The State Police shall provide its response to the requesting dealer during the dealer's call, or by return call without delay. If the criminal history record information check indicates the prospective purchaser or transferee has a criminal record or has been acquitted by reason of insanity and committed to the custody of the Commissioner of Mental Health, Mental Retardation and Substance Abuse Services, the State Police shall have until the end of the dealer's next business day to advise the dealer if its records indicate the buyer or transferee is prohibited from possessing or transporting a firearm by state or federal law. If not so advised by the end of the dealer's next business day, a dealer who has fulfilled the requirements of subdivision B 1 of this subsection may immediately complete the sale or transfer and shall not be deemed in violation of this section with respect to such sale or transfer. In case of electronic failure or other circumstances beyond the control of the State Police, the dealer shall be advised immediately of the reason for such delay and be given an estimate of the length of such delay. After such notification, the State Police shall, as soon as possible but in no event later than the end of the dealer's next business day, inform the requesting dealer if its records indicate the buyer or transferee is prohibited from possessing or transporting a firearm by state or federal law. A dealer who fulfills the requirements of subdivision B 1 of this subsection and is told by the State Police that a response will not be available by the end of the dealer's next business day may immediately complete the sale or transfer and shall not be deemed in violation of this section with respect to such sale or transfer.

3. Except as required by subsection D of §9-192 <relates to checking your own criminal history file>, the State Police shall not maintain records longer than thirty days, except for multiple handgun transactions for which records shall be

maintained for twelve months, from any dealer's request for a criminal history record information check pertaining to a buyer or transferee who is not found to be prohibited from possessing and transporting a firearm under state or federal law. However, the log on requests made may be maintained for a period of twelve months, and such log shall consist of the name of the purchaser, the dealer identification number, the unique approval number and the transaction date.

4. On the last day of the week following the sale or transfer of any firearm, the dealer shall mail or deliver the written consent form required by subsection A to the Department of State Police. The State Police shall immediately initiate a search of all available criminal history record information to determine if the purchaser is prohibited from possessing or transporting a firearm under state or federal law. If the search discloses information indicating that the buyer or transferee is so prohibited from possessing or transporting a firearm, the State Police shall inform the chief law-enforcement officer in the jurisdiction where the sale or transfer occurred and the dealer without delay.

5. Notwithstanding any other provisions of this section, rifles and shotguns may be purchased by persons who are citizens of the United States or persons lawfully admitted for permanent residence but residents of other states under the terms of subsections A and B upon furnishing the dealer with proof of citizenship or status as a person lawfully admitted for permanent residence and one photo-identification form issued by a governmental agency of the person's state of residence and one other form of identification determined to be acceptable by the Department of Criminal Justice Services.

C. No dealer shall sell, rent, trade or transfer from his inventory any firearm, other than a rifle or a shotgun, to any person who is not a resident of Virginia unless he has first obtained from the Department of State Police a report indicating that a search of all available criminal history record information has not disclosed that the person is prohibited from possessing or transporting a firearm under state or federal law. The dealer shall obtain the required report by mailing or delivering the written consent form required under subsection A to the State Police within twenty-four hours of its execution. If the dealer has complied with the provisions of this subsection and has not received the required report from the State Police within ten days from the date the written consent form was mailed to the Department of State Police, he shall not be deemed in violation of this section for thereafter completing the sale or transfer.

D. Nothing herein shall prevent a resident of this Commonwealth, at his option, from buying, renting or receiving a firearm from a dealer by obtaining a criminal history record information check through the dealer as provided in subsection C.

E. If any buyer or transferee is denied the right to purchase a firearm under this section, he may exercise his right of access to and review and correction of criminal history record information under §9-192 or institute a civil action as provided in §9-194, provided any such action is initiated within thirty days of such denial.

F. Any dealer who willfully and intentionally requests, obtains, or seeks to obtain criminal history record information under false pretenses, or who willfully and intentionally disseminates or seeks to disseminate criminal history record information except as authorized in this section shall be guilty of a Class 2 misdemeanor.

H. The Department of Criminal Justice Services shall promulgate regulations to ensure the identity, confidentiality and security of all records and data provided by the Department of State Police pursuant to this section.

I. The provisions of this section shall not apply to

(i) transactions between persons who are licensed as firearms importers or collectors, manufacturers or dealers pursuant to 18 U.S.C. §921 et seq.,

(ii) purchases by or sales to any law-enforcement officer or agent of the United States, the Commonwealth or any local government,

(iii) antique firearms or

(iv) transactions in any county, city or town that has a local ordinance adopted prior to January 1, 1987, governing the purchase, possession, transfer, ownership, conveyance or transportation of firearms which is more stringent than this section.

J. All licensed firearms dealers shall collect a fee of two dollars for every transaction for which a criminal history record information check is required pursuant to this section, except that a fee of five dollars shall be collected for every transaction involving an out-of-state resident. Such fee shall be transmitted to the Department of State Police by the last day of the month following the sale for deposit in a special fund for use by the State Police to offset the cost of conducting criminal history record information checks under the provisions of this section.

K. Any person willfully and intentionally making a materially false statement on the consent form required in subsection B or C shall be guilty of a Class 5 felony.

L. Except as provided in §18.2-308.2:1, any dealer who willfully and intentionally sells, rents, trades or transfers a firearm in violation of this section shall be guilty of a Class 6 felony.

M. Any person who purchases a firearm with the intent to

(i) resell or otherwise provide such firearm to any person who he knows or has reason to believe is ineligible to purchase or otherwise receive from a dealer a firearm for whatever reason or

(ii) transport such firearm out of the Commonwealth to be resold or otherwise provided to another person who the transferor knows is ineligible to purchase or otherwise receive a firearm, shall be guilty of a Class 5 felony. However, if the violation of this subsection involves such a transfer of more than one firearm, the person shall be sentenced to a mandatory minimum term of imprisonment of five years, which shall not be suspended in whole or in part nor shall the person be eligible for parole during that period.

N. Any person who is ineligible to purchase or otherwise receive or possess a firearm in the Commonwealth who solicits, employs or assists any person in violating subsection M shall be guilty of a Class 5 felony and shall be sentenced to a mandatory minimum term of imprisonment of five years, which shall not be suspended in whole or in part nor shall the person be eligible for parole during that period.

O. All driver's licenses issued on or after July 1, 1994, shall carry a letter designation indicating whether the driver's license is an original, duplicate or renewed driver's license.

P. The Department of Education, in conjunction with the Department of Game and Inland Fisheries, shall develop a standard informational form and posted notice to be furnished to each licensed firearms dealer in the Commonwealth at no cost to the dealer. The form and notice shall provide basic information of the laws governing the purchase, possession and use of firearms by juveniles and adults. Copies of the form shall be made available by the dealer whenever a firearm is purchased. Every firearms dealer shall conspicuously post the written notice which shall be at least eight and one-half inches by eleven inches in size and printed in boldface type of a minimum size of ten points. A licensed firearms dealer shall not be liable for damages for injuries resulting from the discharge of a firearm purchased from the dealer if, at the time of the purchase, the dealer failed to provide the form or failed to post the written notice.

Q. Except as provided in subdivisions 1, 2 and 3 of this subsection, it shall be unlawful for any person who is not a licensed firearms dealer to purchase more than one handgun within any thirty-day period. A violation of this subsection shall be punishable as a Class 1 misdemeanor.

1. Purchases in excess of one handgun within a thirty-day period may be made upon completion of an enhanced background check, as described herein, by special application to the Department of State Police listing the number and type of handguns to be purchased and transferred for lawful business or personal use, in a collector series, for collections, as a bulk purchase from estate sales and for similar purposes. Such applications shall be signed under oath by the applicant on forms provided by the Department of State Police, shall state the purpose for the purchase above the limit, and shall require satisfactory proof of residency and identity. Such application shall be in addition to the firearms sales report required by the Bureau of Alcohol, Tobacco and Firearms (ATF). The Superintendent of State Police shall promulgate regulations, pursuant to the Administrative Process Act (§9-6.14:1 et seq.), for the implementation of an application process for purchases of handguns above the limit.

Upon being satisfied that these requirements have been met, the Department of State Police shall forthwith issue to the applicant a nontransferable certificate which shall be valid for seven days from the date of issue. The certificate shall be surrendered to the dealer by the prospective purchaser prior to the consummation of such sale and shall be kept on file at the dealer's place of business for inspection as provided in §54.1-4201 for a period of not less than two years. Upon request of any local law-enforcement agency, and pursuant to its regulations, the Department of State Police may certify such local law-enforcement agency to serve as its agent to receive applications and, upon authorization by the Department of State Police, issue certificates forthwith pursuant to this subsection. Applications and certificates issued under this subsection shall be maintained as records as provided in subdivision 3 of subsection B. The Department of State Police shall make available to local law-enforcement agencies all records concerning certificates issued pursuant to this subsection and all records provided for in subdivision 3 of subsection B.

2. The provisions of this subsection shall not apply to:

a. A law-enforcement agency;

b. An agency duly authorized to perform law-enforcement duties;

c. State and local correctional facilities;

d. A private security company licensed to do business within the Commonwealth;

e. The purchase of antique firearms as herein defined; or

f. A person whose handgun is stolen or irretrievably lost who deems it essential that such handgun be replaced immediately. Such person may purchase another handgun, even if the person has previously purchased a handgun within a thirty-day period, provided

(i) the person provides the firearms dealer with a copy of the official police report or a summary thereof, on forms provided by the Department of State Police, from the law-enforcement agency that took the report of the lost or stolen handgun;

(ii) the official police report or summary thereof contains the name and address of the handgun owner, the description of the handgun, the location of the loss or theft, the date of the loss or theft, and the date the loss or theft was reported to the law-enforcement agency; and

(iii) the date of the loss or theft as reflected on the official police report or summary thereof occurred within thirty days of the person's attempt to replace the handgun. The firearms dealer shall attach a copy of the official police report or summary thereof to the original copy of the Virginia firearms transaction report completed for the transaction and retain it for the period prescribed by the Department of State Police.

3. For the purposes of this subsection, "purchase" shall not include the exchange or replacement of a handgun by a seller for a handgun purchased from such seller by the same person seeking the exchange or replacement within the thirty-day period immediately preceding the date of exchange or replacement.

Crimes and Offenses Generally §18.2-308.3.
Use or attempted use of restricted ammunition in commission or attempted commission of crimes prohibited; penalty

A. When used in this section:
"Restricted firearm ammunition" applies to bullets, projectiles or other types of ammunition that are:

(i) coated with or contain, in whole or in part, polytetrafluorethylene or a similar product,

(ii) commonly known as "KTW" bullets or "French Arcanes," or

(iii) any cartridges containing bullets coated with a plastic substance with other than lead or lead alloy cores, jacketed bullets with other than lead or lead alloy cores, or cartridges of which the bullet itself is wholly comprised of a metal or metal alloy other than lead. This definition shall not be construed to include shotgun shells or solid plastic bullets.

B. It shall be unlawful for any person to knowingly use or attempt to use restricted firearm ammunition while committing or attempting to commit a crime. Violation of this section shall constitute a separate and distinct felony and any person found guilty thereof shall be guilty of a Class 5 felony.

Crimes and Offenses Generally §18.2-308.4.
Possession of firearms while in possession of certain controlled substances

A. Any person unlawfully in possession of a controlled substance classified in Schedule I or II of the Drug Control Act (§54.1-3400 et seq.) of Title 54.1 who simultaneously with knowledge and intent possesses any firearm, shall be guilty of a Class 6 felony.

B. It shall be unlawful for any person to possess, use, or attempt to use any pistol, shotgun, rifle, or other firearm or display such weapon in a threatening manner while committing or attempting to commit the illegal manufacture, sale, distribution, or the possession with the intent to manufacture, sell, or distribute a controlled substance classified in Schedule I or Schedule II of the Drug Control Act (§54.1-3400 et seq.) of Title 54.1 or more than one pound of marijuana. Violation of this subsection shall constitute a separate and distinct felony and any person convicted thereof shall be sentenced to a term of imprisonment of three years for a first conviction and for a term of five years for a second or subsequent conviction under this subsection. Notwithstanding any other provision of law, the sentence prescribed for a violation of this subsection shall not be suspended in whole or in part, nor shall anyone convicted hereunder be placed on probation or parole for this offense. Such punishment shall be separate and apart from, and shall be made to run consecutively with, any punishment received for the commission of the primary felony.

C. Any firearm possessed in violation of this section shall be forfeited to the Commonwealth pursuant to the provisions of §18.2-310.

Crimes and Offenses Generally §18.2-308.5.
Manufacture, import, sale, transfer or possession of plastic firearm prohibited

It shall be unlawful for any person to manufacture, import, sell, transfer or possess any plastic firearm. As used in this section "plastic firearm" means any firearm, including machine guns and sawed-off shotguns as defined in this chapter, containing less than 3.7 ounces of electromagnetically detectable metal in the barrel, slide, cylinder, frame or receiver of which, when subjected to inspection by X-ray machines commonly used at airports, does not generate an image that accurately depicts its shape. A violation of this section shall be punishable as a Class 5 felony.

Any firearm manufactured, imported, sold, transferred or possessed in violation of this section shall be forfeited to the Commonwealth and disposed of in accordance with §18.2-310.

Crimes and Offenses Generally §18.2-308.6.
Possession of unregistered firearm mufflers or silencers prohibited; penalty

It shall be unlawful for any person to possess any firearm muffler or firearm silencer which is not registered to him in the National Firearms Registration and Transfer Record. A violation of this section shall be punishable as a Class 6 felony.

Crimes and Offenses Generally §18.2-308.7.
Possession or transportation of certain firearms by persons under the age of eighteen; penalty

It shall be unlawful for any person under eighteen years of age to knowingly and intentionally possess or transport a handgun or assault firearm anywhere in the Commonwealth. A violation of this section shall be a Class 1 misdemeanor. Any handgun possessed or transported in violation of this section shall be forfeited to the Commonwealth and disposed of as provided in §18.2-310.

This section shall not apply to:
1. Any person
(i) while in his home or on his property,
(ii) while in the home or on the property of his parent, grandparent, or legal guardian; or
(iii) while on the property of another who has provided prior permission, and with the prior permission of his parent or legal guardian if the person has the landowner's written permission on his person while on such property;
2. Any person who, while accompanied by an adult, is at, or going to and from, a lawful shooting range or firearms educational class, provided that the weapons are unloaded while being transported;
3. Any person actually engaged in lawful hunting or going to and from a hunting area or preserve, provided that the weapons are unloaded while being transported; and
4. Any person while carrying out his duties in the armed forces of the United States or the National Guard of this Commonwealth or any other state.

Crimes and Offenses Generally §18.2-308.8.
Importation, sale, possession or transfer of Striker 12's prohibited; penalty

It shall be unlawful for any person to import, sell, possess or transfer the following firearms: the Striker 12, commonly called a "streetsweeper," or any semi-automatic folding stock shotgun of like kind with a spring tension drum magazine capable of holding twelve shotgun shells. A violation of this section shall be punishable as a Class 6 felony.

Crimes and Offenses Generally §18.2-309.
Furnishing certain weapons to minors; penalty

A. If any person sells, barters, gives or furnishes, or causes to be sold, bartered, given or furnished, to any minor a dirk, switchblade knife or bowie knife, having good cause to believe him to be a minor, such person shall be guilty of a Class 1 misdemeanor.
B. If any person sells, barters, gives or furnishes, or causes to be sold, bartered, given or furnished, to any minor a handgun, having good cause to believe him to be a minor, such person shall be guilty of a Class 6 felony. This subsection shall not apply to any transfer made between family members or for the purpose of engaging in a sporting event or activity.

Crimes and Offenses Generally §18.2-310.
Forfeiture of certain weapons used in commission of criminal offense

All pistols, shotguns, rifles, dirks, bowie knives, switchblade knives, ballistic knives, razors, slingshots, brass or metal knuckles, blackjacks, stun weapons and tasers, and other weapons used by any person in the commission of a criminal offense, shall, upon conviction of such person, be forfeited to the Commonwealth by order of the court trying the case. The court shall dispose of such weapons as it deems proper by entry of an order of record. Such disposition may include the destruction of the weapons or, subject to any registration requirements of federal law, sale of the firearms to a licensed dealer in such firearms in accordance with the provisions of Chapter 22 (§19.2-369 et seq.) of Title 19.2 regarding sale of property forfeited to the Commonwealth.

The proceeds of any sale of such weapon shall be paid in accordance with the provisions of Article VIII, Section 8 of the Constitution of Virginia. In addition, the court may authorize the seizing law-enforcement agency to use the weapon for a period of time as specified in the order. When the seizing agency ceases to so use the weapon, it shall be disposed of as otherwise provided in this section.

However, upon petition to the court and notice to the attorney for the Commonwealth, the court, upon good cause shown, shall return any such weapon to its lawful owner after conclusion of all relevant proceedings if such owner
(i) did not know and had no reason to know of the conduct giving rise to the forfeiture and
(ii) is not otherwise prohibited by law from possessing the weapon. The owner shall acknowledge in a sworn affidavit to be filed with the record in the case or cases that he has retaken possession of the weapon involved.

Crimes and Offenses Generally §18.2-311.
Prohibiting the selling or having in possession blackjacks, etc.

If any person sells or barters, or exhibits for sale or for barter, or gives or furnishes, or causes to be sold, bartered, given or furnished, or has in his possession, or under his control, with the intent of selling, bartering, giving or furnishing, any blackjack, brass or metal knuckles, any disc of whatever configuration having at least two points or pointed blades which is designed to be thrown or propelled and which may be known as a throwing star or oriental dart, switchblade knife, ballistic knife, or like weapons, such person shall be guilty of a Class 4 misdemeanor. The having in one's possession of any such weapon shall be prima facie evidence, except in the case of a conservator of the peace, of his intent to sell, barter, give or furnish the same.

Crimes and Offenses Generally §18.2-311.1.
Removing, altering, etc., serial number or other identification on firearm

Any person, firm, association or corporation who or which intentionally removes, defaces, alters, changes, destroys or obliterates in any manner or way or who or which causes to be removed, defaced, altered, changed, destroyed or obliterated in any manner or way the name of the maker, model, manufacturer's or serial number, or any other mark or identification on any pistol, shotgun, rifle, machine gun or any other firearm shall be guilty of a Class 1 misdemeanor.

Crimes and Offenses Generally §18.2-311.2.
Third conviction of firearm offenses; penalty

On a third or subsequent conviction of any offense contained in Article 4, 5, 6, or 7 of Chapter 7 (§18.2-247 et seq.) of Title 18.2, which would ordinarily be punished as a Class 1 misdemeanor, where it is alleged in the information or indictment on which the person is convicted, that
(i) such person has been twice previously convicted of a violation of any Class 1 misdemeanor or felony offense contained in either Article 4, 5, 6, or 7 of Chapter 7 of Title 18.2 or §18.2-53.1, or of a substantially similar offense under the law of any other jurisdiction of the United States, and
(ii) each such violation occurred on a different date, such person shall be guilty of a Class 6 felony.

Crimes and Offenses Generally §18.2-312.
Illegal use of tear gas, phosgene and other gases

If any person maliciously release or cause or procure to be released in any private home, place of business or place of public gathering any tear gas, mustard gas, phosgene gas or other noxious or nauseating gases or mixtures of chemicals designed to, and capable of, producing vile or injurious or nauseating odors or gases, and bodily injury results to any person from such gas or odor, the offending person shall be guilty of a Class 3 felony.
If such act be done unlawfully, but not maliciously, the offending person shall be guilty of a Class 6 felony.
Nothing herein contained shall prevent the use of tear gas or other gases by police officers or other peace officers in the proper performance of their duties, or by any person or persons in the protection of person, life or property.

Crimes and Offenses Generally §18.2-405
What constitutes a riot; punishment

Any unlawful use, by three or more persons acting together, of force or violence which seriously jeopardizes the public safety, peace or order is riot.
If such person carried, at the time of such riot, any firearm or other deadly or dangerous weapon, he shall be guilty of a Class 5 felony.

Crimes and Offenses Generally §18.2-406
What constitutes an unlawful assembly; punishment

Whenever three or more persons assembled share the common intent to advance some lawful or unlawful purpose by the commission of an act or acts of unlawful force or violence likely to jeopardize seriously public safety, peace or order, and the assembly actually tends to inspire persons of ordinary courage with well-grounded fear of serious and immediate breaches of public safety, peace or order, then such assembly is an unlawful assembly. Every person who participates in any unlawful assembly shall be guilty of a Class 1 misdemeanor. If any such person carried, at the time of his participation in an unlawful assembly, any firearm or other deadly or dangerous weapon, he shall be guilty of a Class 5 felony.

Crime and Offenses Generally §18.2-433.1
Definitions (Unlawful Paramilitary Activity)

As used in this article:

"Civil disorder" means any public disturbance within the United States or any territorial possessions thereof involving acts of violence by assemblages of three or more persons, which causes an immediate danger of or results in damage or injury to the property or person of any other individual.

"Explosive or incendiary device" means

(i) dynamite and all other forms of high explosives,

(ii) any explosive bomb, grenade, missile, or similar device, or

(iii) any incendiary bomb or grenade, fire bomb, or similar device, including any device which consists of or includes a breakable container including a flammable liquid or compound, and a wick composed of any material which, when ignited, is capable of igniting such flammable liquid or compound, and can be carried or thrown by one individual acting alone.

"Firearm" means any weapon which is designed to or may readily be converted to expel any projectile by the action of an explosive; or the frame or receiver of any such weapon.

"Law-enforcement officer" means any officer as defined in subdivision 9 of §9-169 or any such officer or member of the armed forces of the United States, any state, any political subdivision of a state, or the District of Columbia, and such term shall specifically include, but shall not be limited to, members of the National Guard, as defined in §101 (9) of Title 10, United States Code, members of the organized militia of any state or territory of the United States, the Commonwealth of Puerto Rico, or the District of Columbia, not included within the definition of National Guard as defined by such S§101 (9), and members of the armed forces of the United States.

Crimes and Offenses Generally §18.2-433.2.
Paramilitary activity prohibited

A. person shall be guilty of unlawful paramilitary activity, punishable as a Class 5 felony if he:

1. Teaches or demonstrates to any other person the use, application, or making of any firearm, explosive or incendiary device, or technique capable of causing injury or death to persons, knowing or having reason to know or intending that such training will be employed for use in, or in furtherance of, a civil disorder; or

2. Assembles with one or more persons for the purpose of training with, practicing with, or being instructed in the use of any firearm, explosive or incendiary device, or technique capable of causing injury or death to persons, intending to employ such training for use in, or in furtherance of, a civil disorder.

Crimes and Offenses Generally §18.2-433.3
Exceptions (Unlawful Paramilitary activities)

Nothing contained in this article shall be construed to apply to:

1. Any act of a law-enforcement officer performed in the otherwise lawful performance of the officer's official duties;

2. Any activity, undertaken without knowledge of or intent to cause or further a civil disorder, which is intended to teach or practice self-defense or self-defense techniques such as karate clubs or self-defense clinics, and similar lawful activity;
3. Any facility, program or lawful activity related to firearms instruction and training intended to teach the safe handling and use of firearms; or
4. Any other lawful sports or activities related to the individual recreational use or possession of firearms, including but not limited to hunting activities, target shooting, self-defense and firearms collection.

Notwithstanding any language contained herein, no activity of any individual, group, organization or other entity engaged in the lawful display or use of firearms or other weapons or facsimiles thereof shall be deemed to be in violation of this statute.

Crimes and Offenses Generally §18.2-434
What deemed perjury;   punishment and penalty

If any person to whom an oath is lawfully administered on any occasion willfully swear falsely on such occasion touching any material matter or thing, or if a person falsely make oath that any other person is eighteen years of age in order to obtain a marriage license for such other person, he shall be guilty of perjury, punishable as a Class 5 felony. Upon the conviction of any person for perjury, such person thereby shall be adjudged forever incapable of holding any office of honor, profit or trust under the Constitution of Virginia, or of serving as a juror.

Crimes and Offenses Generally §18.2-474.1.
Delivery of drugs, firearms, explosives, etc., to prisoners

Notwithstanding the provisions of §18.2-474, any person who shall willfully in any manner deliver, attempt to deliver, or conspire with another to deliver to any prisoner confined under authority of the Commonwealth of Virginia, or of any political subdivision thereof, any drug which is a controlled substance regulated by the Drug Control Act in Chapter 34 of Title 54.1 or marijuana, shall be guilty of a Class 5 felony. Any person who shall willfully in any manner so deliver or attempt to deliver or conspire to deliver to any such prisoner, firearms, ammunitions, or explosives of any nature shall be guilty of a Class 3 felony.
Nothing herein contained shall be construed to repeal or amend §18.2-473.

Title 19.2   Criminal Procedure

Criminal Procedure §19.2-53.
What may be searched and seized

Search warrants may be issued for the search of or for specified places, things or
persons, and seizure therefrom of the following things as specified in the warrant:
1. Weapons or other objects used in the commission of crime;

Criminal Procedure §19.2-59.1
Strip searches prohibited; exceptions; how strip searches conducted

A. No person in custodial arrest for a traffic infraction, Class 3 or Class 4
misdemeanor, or a violation of a city, county, or town ordinance, which is
punishable by no more than thirty days in jail shall be strip searched unless there
is reasonable cause to believe on the part of a law-enforcement officer authorizing
the search that the individual is concealing a weapon. All strip searches
conducted under this section shall be performed by persons of the same sex as
the person arrested and on premises where the search cannot be observed by
persons not physically conducting the search.

Criminal Procedure §19.2-386.11.
Judgment of condemnation; destruction

A. If the forfeiture is established, the judgment shall be that the property be
condemned as forfeited to the Commonwealth subject to any remission granted
under subsection A of §19.2-386.10 and further that the same be sold, unless
(i) a sale thereof has been already made under §19.2-386.7,
(ii) the court determines that the property forfeited is of such minimal value that the
sale would not be in the best interest of the Commonwealth or
(iii) the court finds that the property may be subject to return to a participating
agency. If the court finds that the property may be subject to return to an agency
participating in the seizure in accordance with subsection C of §19.2-386.14, the
order shall provide for storage of the property until the determination to return it
is made or, if return is not made, for sale of the property as provided in this
section and §19.2-386.12. If sale has been made, the judgment shall be against
the proceeds of sale, subject to the rights of any lien holder whose interest is not
forfeited. If the property condemned has been delivered to the claimant under
§19.2-386.6, further judgment shall be against the obligors in the bond for the
penalty thereof, to be discharged by the payment of the appraised value of the
property, upon which judgment, process of execution shall be awarded and the
clerk shall endorse thereon, "No security is to be taken."
C. Contraband, the sale or possession of which is unlawful, weapons and property
not sold because of the minimal value thereof, may be ordered destroyed by the
court.

Criminal Procedure §19.2-389.1.
Dissemination of juvenile record information

Record information maintained in the Central Criminal Records Exchange pursuant to
the provisions of §16.1-299 shall be disseminated only
(i) to make the determination as provided in §18.2-308.2 and §18.2-308.2:2 of
eligibility to possess or purchase a firearm.

Title 22.1 Education

Education §22.1-3.2
Notice of student's school status required as condition of admission

Prior to admission to any public school of the Commonwealth, a school board shall
  require the parent, guardian, or other person having control or charge of a child
  of school age to provide, upon registration, a sworn statement or affirmation
  indicating whether the student has been expelled from school attendance at a
  private school or in a public school division of the Commonwealth or in another
  state for an offense in violation of school board policies relating to weapons,
  alcohol or drugs, or for the willful infliction of injury to another person. Any
  person making a materially false statement or affirmation shall be guilty upon
  conviction of a Class 3 misdemeanor. The registration document shall be
  maintained as a part of the student's scholastic record.

Education §22.1-277.01.
**Expulsion of students under certain circumstances; Board of
  Education designated agency; local school board application for
  assistance; reporting; exceptions**

A. In compliance with the federal Improving America's Schools Act of 1994 (Part F--
  "Gun-Free Schools Act of 1994"), a school board shall expel from school
  attendance for a period of not less than one year any student whom such school
  board has determined, in accordance with the procedures set forth in §22.1-277,
  to have brought a firearm onto school property or to a school-sponsored activity
  as prohibited by §18.2-308.1, or to have brought a firearm as defined in
  subsection D of this section on school property or to a school-sponsored
  activity. A school board may, however, determine, based on the facts of the
  particular case, that special circumstances exist and another disciplinary action or
  term of expulsion is appropriate.
D. As used in this section;
"Firearm" means any weapon prohibited on school property or at a school-
  sponsored activity pursuant to §18.2-308.1, or
(i) any weapon, including a starter gun, which will, or is designed or may readily be
  converted to, expel a projectile by the action of an explosive;
(ii) the frame or receiver of any such weapon;
(iii) any firearm muffler or firearm silencer; or
(iv) any destructive device.
E. The exemptions set out in §18.2-308 shall apply, mutatis mutandis, to the
  provisions of this section. The provisions of this section shall not apply to
  persons who possess such firearm or firearms as a part of the curriculum or
  other programs sponsored by the schools in the school division or any
  organization permitted by the school to use its premises or to any law-
  enforcement officer while engaged in his duties as such. In addition, this section
  shall not apply to possession of an unloaded firearm which is in a closed
  container in or upon a motor vehicle or an unloaded shotgun or rifle in a firearms
  rack in or upon a motor vehicle.

Education §22.1-278
**Guidelines for school board policies;   school board regulations
governing student conduct;   Board standards for compliance with
federal law requiring expulsion under certain circumstances by
school board**

B. The Board of Education shall establish standards to ensure compliance with the
federal Improving America's Schools Act of 1994 (Part F--"Gun-Free Schools Act
of 1994"), in accordance with Sec. 22.1-277.01, to be effective on July 1, 1995.
This subsection shall not be construed to diminish the authority of the Board of
Education or the Governor concerning decisions on whether, or the extent to
which, Virginia shall participate in the federal Improving America's Schools Act of
1994, or to diminish the Governor's authority to coordinate and provide policy
direction on official communications between the Commonwealth and the United
States government.

Education §22.1-280.1.
Reports of certain acts to school authorities

A. Reports shall be made to the principal or his designee on all incidents involving
(iv) the illegal carrying of a firearm onto school property. The principal or his
designee shall submit a report of all such incidents to the superintendent of the
school division. The division superintendent shall annually report all such
incidents to the Department of Education for the purpose of recording the
frequency of such incidents on forms which shall be provided by the Department.
A division superintendent who knowingly fails to comply or secure compliance
with the reporting requirements of this subsection shall be subject to the sanctions
authorized in §22.1-65.

Title 29.1 Game, Inland Fisheries and Boating

Game, Inland Fisheries and Boating §29.1-208
Searches and seizures

All game wardens are vested with the authority to search any person arrested as provided in §29.1-205 together with any box, can, package, barrel or other container, hunting bag, coat, suit, trunk, grip, satchel or fish basket carried by, in the possession of, or belonging to such person. Game wardens shall also have the authority, immediately subsequent to such arrest, to enter and search any refrigerator, building, vehicle, or other place in which the officer making the search has reasonable ground to believe that the person arrested has concealed or placed any wild bird, wild animal or fish, which will furnish evidence of a violation of the hunting, trapping and inland fish laws. Such a search may be made without a warrant, except that a dwelling may not be searched without a warrant. Should any container as described in this section reveal any wild bird, wild animal or fish, or any part thereof, which has been illegally taken, possessed, sold, purchased or transported, the game warden shall seize and hold as evidence the container, together with such wild bird, wild animal or fish, and any unlawful gun, net, or other device of any kind for taking wild birds, wild animals or fish which he may find.

Game, Inland Fisheries and Boating §29.1-300.1.
Certification of competence in hunter education

A. Except as provided in subsection B of this section, no hunting license shall be issued to
(i) a person who has never obtained a license to hunt in any state or country, or
(ii) a person who is under the age of sixteen, unless such a person presents to the Board of Game and Inland Fisheries or one of its authorized license vendors, a certificate of completion in hunter education issued or authorized by the Board under the hunter education program, or proof that he holds the equivalent certificate obtained from an authorized agency or association of another state or country.
B. Except as provided in subsection A of §29.1-301, any person under the age of twelve may purchase a Virginia hunting license, except a special lifetime hunting and fishing license issued pursuant to §29.1-302.1, without completing a hunter education program as required in subsection A of this section, provided that no person under the age of twelve shall hunt unless accompanied and directly supervised by an adult who has, on his person, a valid Virginia hunting license. The adult shall be responsible for such supervision. For the purposes of this section, "adult" means the parent or legal guardian of the person under age twelve, or such person over the age of eighteen designated by the parent or legal guardian.
"Accompanied and directly supervised" means that the adult is within sight of the person under the age of twelve.
C. This section shall not apply to persons while on horseback hunting foxes with hounds but without firearms.

Game, Inland Fisheries and Boating §29.1-301
Exemptions from license requirements

A. No license shall be required of landowners, their spouses, or their children and minor grandchildren, resident or nonresident, to hunt, trap and fish within the boundaries of their own lands and inland waters or while within such boundaries or upon any private permanent extension therefrom, to fish in any abutting public waters.

B. No license shall be required of any stockholder owning fifty percent or more of the stock of any domestic corporation owning land in this Commonwealth, his or her spouse and children and minor grandchildren, resident or nonresident, to hunt, trap and fish within the boundaries of lands and inland waters owned by the domestic corporation.

C. No license shall be required of bona fide tenants, renters or lessees to hunt, trap or fish within the boundaries of the lands or waters on which they reside or while within such boundaries or upon any private permanent extension therefrom, to fish in any abutting public waters if such individuals have the written consent of the landlord upon their person. A guest of the owner of a private fish pond shall not be required to have a fishing license to fish in such pond.

D. No license shall be required of resident persons under sixteen years old to fish.

E. No license shall be required of a resident person sixty-five years of age or over to hunt or trap on private property in the county or city in which he resides. An annual license at a fee of one dollar shall be required of a resident person sixty-five years of age or older to fish in any inland waters of the Commonwealth which shall be in addition to a license to fish for trout as specified in subsection B of §29.1-310. A resident sixty-five years of age or older may, upon proof of age satisfactory to the Department and the payment of a one-dollar fee, apply for and receive from any authorized agent of the Department a nontransferable annual license permitting such person to hunt or an annual license permitting such person to trap in all cities and counties of the Commonwealth. Any lifetime license issued pursuant to this article prior to July 1, 1988, shall remain valid for the lifetime of the person to whom it was issued. Any license issued pursuant to this section includes any damage stamp required pursuant to Article 3 (§29.1-352 et seq.) of this chapter.

G. No license shall be required to trap rabbits with box traps.

H. No license shall be required of resident persons under sixteen years of age to trap when accompanied by any person eighteen years of age or older who possesses a valid state license to trap in this Commonwealth.

I. No license to hunt, trap or fish shall be required of any Indian who habitually resides on an Indian reservation; however, such Indian must have on his person an identification card or paper signed by the chief of his reservation, setting forth that the person named is an actual resident upon such reservation. Such card or paper shall create a presumption of residence, which may be rebutted by proof of actual residence elsewhere.

Game, Inland Fisheries and Boating §29.1-307
Special muzzleloading license

There shall be a license for hunting with a muzzleloader during the special muzzleloading seasons, which shall be in addition to the license required to hunt small game. The fee for the special license shall be twelve dollars for a resident and twenty-five dollars for a nonresident. The special muzzleloader license may be obtained from the clerk or agent whose duty it is to sell licenses in any county or city.

Game, Inland Fisheries and Boating §29.1-519.
Guns, pistols, revolvers, etc., which may be used; penalty

A. All wild birds and wild animals may be hunted with the following weapons unless shooting is expressly prohibited:

1. A shotgun not larger than ten gauge;

2. An automatic-loading or hand-operated repeating shotgun capable of holding not more than three shells the magazine of which has been cut off or plugged with a one-piece filler incapable of removal through the loading end, so as to reduce the capacity of the gun to not more than three shells at one time in the magazine and chamber combined;
3. A rifle; or
4. A bow and arrow.
B. A pistol, muzzle-loading pistol or revolver may be used to hunt nuisance species of birds and animals between sunrise and sunset except over inland waters, and raccoons during the legal hunting hours for said species.
C. In the counties west of the Blue Ridge Mountains, and counties east of the Blue Ridge where rifles of a caliber larger than .22 caliber may be used for hunting wild birds and animals, game birds and animals may be hunted with pistols or revolvers firing cartridges rated in manufacturers' tables at 350 foot pounds of energy or greater and under the same restrictions and conditions as apply to rifles, provided that no cartridge shall be used with a bullet of less than .23 caliber. In no event shall pistols or revolvers firing cartridges rated in manufacturers' tables at 350 foot pounds of energy or greater be used if rifles of a caliber larger than .22 caliber are not authorized for hunting purposes.
D. The use of muzzle-loading pistols and .22 caliber rimfire handguns is permitted for hunting small game where .22 caliber rifles are permitted.
E. The hunting of wild birds and wild animals with fully automatic firearms, defined as a machine gun in §18.2-288, is prohibited.
F. The hunting of wild birds or wild animals with
(i) weapons other than those authorized by this section or
(ii) weapons that have been prohibited by this section shall be punishable as a Class 3 misdemeanor.

Game, Inland Fisheries and Boating §29.1-521.
Unlawful to hunt, trap, possess, sell or transport wild birds and wild animals except as permitted; penalty

A. The following shall be unlawful:
1. To hunt or kill any wild bird or wild animal, including any nuisance species, with a gun, firearm or other weapon on Sunday, which is hereby declared a rest day for all species of wild bird and wild animal life, except raccoons, which may be hunted until 2:00 a.m. on Sunday mornings.
3. To hunt or attempt to kill or trap any species of wild bird or wild animal after having obtained the daily bag or season limit during such day or season.
4. To occupy any baited blind or other baited place for the purpose of taking or attempting to take any wild bird or wild animal or to put out bait or salt for any wild bird or wild animal for the purpose of taking or killing them. However, this shall not apply to baiting nuisance species of animals and birds, or to baiting traps for the purpose of taking fur-bearing animals that may be lawfully trapped.
5. To kill or capture any wild bird or wild animal adjacent to any area while a field or forest fire is in progress.
6. To shoot or attempt to take any wild bird or wild animal from an automobile or other vehicle, except as provided in §29.1-521.3.
10. To hunt, trap, take, capture, kill, attempt to take, capture or kill, possess, deliver for transportation, transport, cause to be transported, by any means whatever, receive for transportation or export, or import, at any time or in any manner, any wild bird or wild animal or the carcass or any part thereof, except as specifically permitted by law and only by the manner or means and within the numbers stated. However, the provisions of this section shall not be construed to prohibit the use or transportation of legally taken turkey carcasses, or portions thereof, for the purposes of making or selling turkey callers.

B. A violation of subdivisions 1 through 10 of subsection A of this section shall be punishable as a Class 3 misdemeanor.

Game, Inland Fisheries and Boating §29.1-521.2
Violation of §18.2-286 while hunting; forfeiture of certain weapons; revocation of license

A. Any firearm, crossbow or bow and arrow used by any person to hunt any game bird or game animal in a manner which violates §18.2-286 may, upon conviction of such person violating §18.2-286, be forfeited to the Commonwealth by order of the court trying the case. The forfeiture shall be enforced as provided in Chapter 22 (§19.2-369 et seq.) of Title 19.2. The officer or other person seizing the property shall immediately give notice to the attorney for the Commonwealth.
B. The court may revoke the current hunting license, if any, of a person hunting any game bird or game animal in a manner that constitutes a violation of §18.2-286. The court may prohibit the issuance of any hunting license to that person for a period of up to five years. If found hunting during this prohibited period, the person shall be guilty of a Class 2 misdemeanor. Notification of such revocation or prohibition shall be forwarded to the Department pursuant to subsection C of §18.2-56.1.

Game, Inland Fisheries and Boating §29.1-521.3
Shooting wild birds and wild animals from stationary vehicles by disabled persons

Any person, upon application to a game warden and the presentation of a medical doctor's written statement based on a physical examination that such person is permanently unable to walk due to impaired mobility, may, in the discretion of the game warden, be issued a permit to shoot wild birds and wild animals from a stationary automobile or other vehicle during established open hunting seasons and in accordance with other laws and regulations. Permits issued pursuant to this section shall
(i) be issued on a form provided by the Department,
(ii) not authorize shooting from a stationary vehicle less than 50 feet from nor in or across any public road or highway subject to the provisions of §29.1-526,
(iii) be issued for the lifetime of the permittee and be issued only to those persons who are properly licensed to hunt, and
(iv) be nontransferable. Any permit found in the possession of any person not entitled to such permit shall be subject to confiscation by a game warden.

Game, Inland Fisheries and Boating §29.1-523
Killing deer by use of certain lights; acts raising presumption of attempt to kill

Any person who kills or attempts to kill any deer between a half hour after sunset and a half hour before sunrise by use of a light attached to any vehicle or a spotlight or flashlight shall be guilty of a Class 2 misdemeanor. The flashing of a light attached to any vehicle or a spotlight or flashlight from any vehicle between a half hour after sunset and half hour before sunrise by any person or persons, then in possession of a rifle, shotgun, pistol, crossbow, or bow and arrow or speargun, without good cause, shall raise a presumption of an attempt to kill deer in violation of this section. Every person in or on any such vehicle shall be deemed a principal in the second degree and subject to the same punishment as a principal in the first degree. Every person who, in any manner, aids, abets or acts in concert with any person or persons violating this section shall be deemed a principal in the second degree and subject to the same punishment as a principal in the first degree.

In addition to the penalty prescribed herein, the court shall revoke the current hunting license, if any, of the person convicted of violating this section and prohibit the issuance of any hunting license to that person for the next license year. If found hunting during this prohibited period, the person shall be guilty of a Class 2 misdemeanor. Notification of such revocation or prohibition shall be forwarded to the Department pursuant to subsections C and D of §18.2-56.1. This section shall not apply to persons duly authorized to kill deer according to the provisions of §29.1-529.

Game, Inland Fisheries and Boating §29.1-524.
Forfeiture of vehicles and weapons used for killing or attempt to kill

Every vehicle, rifle, shotgun, pistol, crossbow, bow and arrow, or speargun used with the knowledge or consent of the owner or lienholder thereof, in killing or attempting to kill deer between a half hour after sunset and a half hour before sunrise in violation of §29.1-523, and every vehicle used in the transportation of the carcass, or any part thereof, of a deer so killed shall be forfeited to the Commonwealth. Upon being condemned as forfeited in proceedings under Chapter 22 (§19.2-369 et seq.) of Title 19.2, the proceeds of sale shall be disposed of according to law.

Game, Inland Fisheries and Boating §29.1-525.
Employment of lights under certain circumstances upon places used by deer

A. Any person in any vehicle and then in possession of any rifle, shotgun, pistol, crossbow, bow and arrow or speargun who employs a light attached to the vehicle or a spotlight or flashlight to cast a light beyond the water or surface of the roadway upon any place used by deer shall be guilty of a Class 2 misdemeanor. Every person in or on any such vehicle shall be deemed prima facie a principal in the second degree and subject to the same punishment as a principal in the first degree. This subsection shall not apply to a landowner in possession of a weapon when he is on his own land and is making a bona fide effort to protect his property from damage by deer and not for the purpose of killing deer unless the landowner is in possession of a permit to do so pursuant to the provisions of §29.1-529.

B. Any person in any motor vehicle who deliberately employs a light attached to such vehicle or a spotlight or flashlight to cast a light beyond the surface of the roadway upon any place used by deer, except upon his own land or upon land on which he has an easement or permission for such purpose, shall be guilty of a Class 4 misdemeanor. Every person in or on any such vehicle shall be deemed prima facie a principal in the second degree and subject to the same punishment as a principal in the first degree.

C. In addition to the penalties prescribed in subsection A of this section, the court shall revoke the current hunting license, if any, of the person convicted of a violation of subsection A of this section and prohibit the issuance of any hunting license to that person for the next license year. In addition to the penalties prescribed in subsection B of this section, the court may revoke the current hunting license, if any, of the person convicted of a violation of subsection B of this section and prohibit the issuance of any hunting license to that person for the next license year. If a person convicted of a violation of subsection A or subsection B of this section is found hunting during the prohibited period, the person shall be guilty of a Class 2 misdemeanor. Notification of such revocation or prohibition shall be forwarded to the Department pursuant to subsections C and D of §18.2-56.1.

Game, Inland Fisheries and Boating §29.1-526.
Counties and cities may prohibit hunting or trapping near primary and secondary highways

The governing body of any county or city may prohibit by ordinance the hunting, with a firearm, of any game bird or game animal while the hunting is on or within 100 yards of any primary or secondary highway in such county or city and may provide that any violation of the ordinance shall be a Class 3 misdemeanor. In addition, the governing body of any county or city may prohibit by ordinance the trapping of any game animal or furbearer within fifty feet of the shoulder of any primary or secondary highway in the county or city and may provide that any violation of the ordinance shall be a Class 3 misdemeanor. No such ordinance shall prohibit such trapping where the written permission of the landowner is obtained. It shall be the duty of the governing body enacting an ordinance under the provisions of this section to notify the Director by registered mail no later than May 1 of the year in which the ordinance is to take effect. If the governing body fails to make such notice, the ordinance shall be unenforceable.

For the purpose of this section, the terms "hunt" and "trap" shall not include the necessary crossing of highways for the bona fide purpose of going into or leaving a lawful hunting or trapping area.

Game, Inland Fisheries and Boating §29.1-527.
Counties, cities or towns may prohibit hunting near public schools and county, city, town or regional parks

The governing body of any county, city or town may prohibit by ordinance, shooting or hunting with a firearm, or prohibit hunters from traversing an area while in possession of a loaded firearm, within 100 yards of any property line of a public school or a county, city, town or regional park. The governing body may, in such ordinance, provide that any violation thereof shall be a Class 4 misdemeanor. Nothing in this section shall give any county, city or town the authority to enforce such an ordinance on lands within a national or state park or forest, or wildlife management area.

Game, Inland Fisheries and Boating §29.1-528.
Counties or cities may prohibit hunting with certain firearms

A. The governing body of any county or city may, by ordinance, prohibit hunting in such county or city with a shotgun loaded with slugs, or with a rifle of a caliber larger than .22 rimfire. However, such ordinance may permit the hunting of groundhogs with a rifle of a caliber larger than .22 rimfire between March 1 and August 31. Such ordinance may also permit the use of muzzle-loading rifles during the prescribed open seasons for the hunting of game species. Any such ordinance may also specify permissible type of ammunition to be used for such hunting.

B. No such ordinance shall be enforceable unless the governing body notifies the Director by registered mail prior to May 1 of the year in which the ordinance is to take effect.

C. In adopting an ordinance pursuant to the provisions of this section the governing body of any county or city may provide that any person who violates the provisions of the ordinance shall be guilty of a Class 3 misdemeanor.

Game, Inland Fisheries and Boating §29.1-530.
Open and closed season for trapping, bag limits, etc.

B. In addition, the following general rules shall be applicable to any person trapping in the Commonwealth:

3. Licensed trappers may shoot wild animals caught in traps during the open hunting season if the trapper has a license to hunt.

Game, Inland Fisheries and Boating §29.1-530.1
Blaze orange clothing required at certain times

During any firearms deer season, except during the special season for hunting deer with a muzzle-loading rifle only, in counties and cities designated by the Board, every hunter, or any person accompanying a hunter, shall wear a blaze orange hat or blaze orange upper body clothing that is visible from 360 degrees or display at least 100 square inches of solid blaze orange material at shoulder level within body reach visible from 360 degrees.

Any person violating the provisions of this section shall, upon conviction, pay a fine of twenty-five dollars.

Violations of this section shall not be admissible in any civil action for personal injury or death as evidence of negligence, contributory negligence or assumption of the risk.

This section shall not apply when

(i) hunting waterfowl from stationary or floating blinds,

(ii) hunting waterfowl over decoys,

(iii) hunting waterfowl in wetlands as defined in §62.1-13.2,

(iv) hunting waterfowl from a boat or other floating conveyance,

(v) participating in hunting dog field trials permitted by the Board of Game and Inland Fisheries, or

(vi) on horseback while hunting foxes with hounds but without firearms.

Game, Inland Fisheries and Boating §29.1-549.
Hunting deer from watercraft; confiscation of watercraft and weapons used

A. Any person who kills or attempts to kill any deer while the person is in a boat or other type watercraft shall be guilty of a Class 4 misdemeanor.

B. Every boat or other watercraft and their motors, and any rifle, shotgun, crossbow, bow and arrow, or speargun used with the knowledge or consent of the owner or lienholder thereof, in killing or attempting to kill deer in violation of this section, shall be forfeited to the Commonwealth, and upon being condemned as forfeited in proceedings under Chapter 22 (§19.2-369 et seq.) of Title 19.2 the proceeds of sale shall be disposed of according to law.

Game, Inland Fisheries and Boating §29.1-556.
Unlawful devices to be destroyed

Any firearm, trap, net, or other device of any kind or nature for taking wild birds, wild animals, or fish, except as specifically permitted by law, shall be considered unlawful. Any person who violates the provisions of this section shall be guilty of a Class 3 misdemeanor, and the device shall be forfeited to the Commonwealth. Nets, traps or other such devices, excluding firearms, shall be destroyed by the game warden if the owner or user of the device cannot be located within thirty days. Unlawful fixed devices may be destroyed by the game warden at the place where the devices are found.

Title 37.1   Institutions for the Mentally Ill

Institutions for the Mentally Ill; Mental Health Generally §37.1-67.3
Involuntary admission and treatment

The clerk shall certify and forward forthwith to the Central Criminal Records
Exchange, on a form provided by the Exchange, a copy of any order for
involuntary commitment to a hospital. The copy of the form and the order shall
be kept confidential in a separate file and used only for the purpose of conducting
a firearms transaction record check authorized by §18.2-308.2:2.

Institutions for the Mentally Ill; Mental Health Generally §37.1-129.
**Clerk to index findings of legal incompetency or restoration of
competency; notice to Commissioner, Secretary of Board of
Elections and CCRE**

A. A copy of the findings of the court, if the person is found to be legally
   incompetent, or restored to competency, shall be filed by the judge with the clerk
   of the court of the county or city in which deeds are admitted to record. The
   clerk shall properly index the same in the index to deed books by reference to the
   order book and page whereon such order is spread and shall immediately notify
   the Commissioner in accordance with §37.1-147, and the Secretary of the State
   Board of Elections with such information as required by §24.2-410.
B. The clerk shall certify and forward forthwith to the Central Criminal Records
   Exchange, on a form provided by the Exchange, a copy of any order adjudicating
   a person legally incompetent pursuant to §37.1-128.02 or §37.1-134 or mentally
   incapacitated under §37.1-128.1 or §37.1-134.5 and any order of restoration of
   competency or capacity under §37.1-134.1. The copy of the form and the order
   shall be kept confidential in a separate file and used only for the purpose of
   conducting a firearms transaction record check authorized by §18.2-308.2:2.

Title 44   Military and Emergency Laws

Military and Emergency Laws §44-54.12.
Arms, equipment and facilities

The Virginia State Defense Force, to the extent authorized by the Governor and
   funded by the General Assembly, shall be equipped as needed for training and for
   state active duty. The Adjutant General, by regulation or otherwise, may
   authorize the use of privately owned real and personal property if deemed in the
   best interest of the Commonwealth.
To the extent permitted by federal law and contracts with the federal government or
   localities and to the extent that space is available, the Adjutant General in his
   discretion may authorize the use of armories and other facilities of the National
   Guard, other state facilities under his control, and all or portions of privately
   owned facilities under contract for the storage and maintenance of arms,
   equipment and supplies of the Virginia State Defense Force and for the assembly,
   drill, training and instruction of its members.
Members of the Virginia State Defense Force shall not be armed with firearms during
   the performance of training duty or state active duty, except under circumstances
   and in instances authorized by the Governor.

Title 46.2   Motor Vehicles

Motor Vehicles §46.2-345.
Issuance of special identification cards; fee; confidentiality; penalties

A. On the application of any person who is a resident of the Commonwealth and who does not possess a license to drive a motor vehicle, the Department shall issue a special identification card to the person provided:

G. Any person who uses a false or fictitious name or gives a false or fictitious address in any application for an identification card, or any renewal, or knowingly makes a false statement or conceals a material fact or otherwise commits a fraud in any such application shall be guilty of a Class 2 misdemeanor. However, where the name or address is given, or false statement is made, or fact is concealed, or fraud committed, with the intent to purchase a firearm or where the identification card is obtained for the purpose of committing any offense punishable as a felony, a violation of this section shall constitute a Class 4 felony.

Motor Vehicles §46.2-348.
Fraud or false statements in applications for license; penalties

Any person who uses a false or fictitious name or gives a false or fictitious address in any application for a driver's license, or any renewal or duplicate thereof, or knowingly makes a false statement or conceals a material fact or otherwise commits a fraud in his application shall be guilty of a Class 2 misdemeanor. However, where the license is used, or the fact concealed, or fraud is done, with the intent to purchase a firearm, a violation of this section shall be punishable as a Class 4 felony.

Motor Vehicles §46.2-749.6
Special license plates for supporters of the National Rifle Association

On receipt of an application therefor, the Commissioner shall issue special license plates to supporters of the National Rifle Association.

Title 52   Police (State)

Police (State) §52-4.4.
Duties relating to criminal history record information checks required by licensed firearms dealers

The Superintendent of the Department of State Police shall establish a toll-free telephone number which shall be operational seven days a week between the hours of 8:00 a.m. and 10:00 p.m. for purposes of responding to inquiries from licensed firearms dealers, as such term is defined in 18 U.S.C. §921 et seq., pursuant to the provisions of §18.2-308.2:2. The Department shall hire and train such personnel as are necessary to administer the provisions of this section.

Police (State) §52-8.4:1.
Regulations for firearms shows

The Superintendent of State Police shall provide a form for use by promoters of firearms shows for the purpose of notifying the State Police and the chief of police, or the sheriff in localities without police departments, of their intent to conduct a firearms show pursuant to §54.1-4201.1.

Police (State) §52-25.1.
Reporting of confiscated firearms

The Superintendent shall establish and maintain within the Department of State Police a Criminal Firearms Clearinghouse as a central repository of information regarding all firearms seized, forfeited, found or otherwise coming into the possession of any state or local law-enforcement agency of the Commonwealth which are believed to have been used in the commission of a crime. The Superintendent shall adopt and promulgate regulations prescribing the form for reporting this information and the time and manner of submission of the form.

In addition to any other information which the Superintendent may require, the form shall require

(i) the serial number or other identifying information on the firearm, if available,

(ii) a brief description of the circumstances under which the firearm came into the possession of the law-enforcement agency, including the crime which was or may have been committed with the firearm,

(iii) the name of or other identifying information on the person from whom the firearm was taken,

(iv) the original place of sale and, if known, the chain of possession of the firearm, and

(v) the disposition of the firearm.

Title 53.1   Prisons and Other Methods of Correction

Prisons and Other Methods of Correction §53.1-151.
Eligibility for parole

A. Except as herein otherwise provided, every person convicted of a felony and sentenced and committed by a court under the laws of this Commonwealth to the Department of Corrections, whether or not such person is physically received at a Department of Corrections facility, or as provided for in §19.2-308.1:

4. B. 1. Any person convicted of three separate felony offenses of

(i) murder,

(ii) rape or

(iii) robbery by the presenting of firearms or other deadly weapon, or any combination of the offenses specified in subdivisions (i), (ii) or (iii) when such offenses were not part of a common act, transaction or scheme shall not be eligible for parole.

Prisons and Other Methods of Correction §53.1-203.
Felonies by prisoners; penalties

It shall be unlawful for a prisoner in a state, local or community correctional facility or in the custody of an employee thereof to:

7. Introduce into a correctional facility or have in his possession firearms or ammunition for firearms;

Prisoners and Other Methods of Correction §53.1-233.
Death chamber; who to execute death sentence

The Director is hereby authorized and directed to provide and maintain a permanent death chamber and necessary appurtenant facilities within the confines of a state correctional facility. The death chamber shall have all the necessary appliances for the proper execution of prisoners by electrocution or by continuous intravenous injection of a substance or combination of substances sufficient to cause death. Any such substance shall be applied until the prisoner is pronounced dead by a physician licensed in the Commonwealth. All prisoners upon whom the death penalty has been imposed shall be executed in the death chamber. Each execution shall be conducted by the Director or one or more assistants designated by him.

Prisoners and Other Methods of Correction §53.1-234.
Transfer of prisoner; how death sentence executed; who to be present

The clerk of the circuit court in which is pronounced the sentence of death against any person shall, after such judgment becomes final in the circuit court, deliver a certified copy thereof to the Director. Such person so sentenced to death shall be confined prior to the execution of the sentencing a state correctional facility designated by the Director. Not less than fifteen days before the time fixed in the judgment of the court for the execution of the sentence, the Director shall cause the condemned prisoner to be conveyed to the state correctional facility housing the death chamber.

The Director, or the assistants appointed by him, shall at the time named in the sentence, unless a suspension of execution is ordered, cause the prisoner under sentence of death to be electrocuted or injected with a lethal substance, until he is dead. The method of execution shall be chosen by the prisoner. In the event the prisoner refuses to make a choice at least fifteen days prior to the scheduled execution, the method of execution shall be by lethal injection.

Execution by lethal injection shall be permitted in accordance with procedures developed by the Department. At the execution there shall be present the Director or an assistant, a physician employed by the Department or his assistant, such other employees of the Department as may be required by the Director and, in addition thereto, at least six citizens who shall not be employees of the Department. In addition, the counsel for the prisoner and a clergyman may be present.

Title 54.1   Professions and Occupations

Professions and Occupations §54.1-2967.
Physicians and others rendering medical aid to report certain wounds

Any physician or other person who renders any medical aid or treatment to any person for any wound which such physician or other person knows or has reason to believe is a wound inflicted by a weapon specified in §18.2-308 and which wound such physician or other person believes or has reason to believe was not self-inflicted shall as soon as practicable report such fact, including the wounded person's name and address, if known, to the sheriff or chief of police of the county or city in which treatment is rendered. If such medical aid or treatment is rendered in a hospital or similar institution, such physician or other person rendering such medical aid or treatment shall immediately notify the person in charge of such hospital or similar institution, who shall make such report forthwith.

Any physician or other person failing to comply with this section shall be guilty of a Class 3 misdemeanor. Any person participating in the making of a report pursuant to this section or participating in a judicial proceeding resulting therefrom shall be immune from any civil liability in connection therewith, unless it is proved that such person acted in bad faith or with malicious intent.

Professions and Occupations §54.1-4200
Definitions

For the purpose of this chapter, unless the context requires a different meaning:

"Dealer in firearms" means
(i) any person, firm, partnership, or corporation engaged in the business of selling, trading or transferring firearms at wholesale or retail;
(ii) any person, firm, partnership, or corporation engaged in the business of making or fitting special barrels, stocks, or trigger mechanisms to firearms; or
(iii) any person, firm, partnership, or corporation that is a pawnbroker.

"Engaged in business" means as applied to a dealer in firearms a person, firm, partnership, or corporation that devotes time, attention, and labor to dealing in firearms as a regular course of trade or business with the principal objective of livelihood and profit through repetitive purchase or resale of firearms, but such term shall not involve a person who makes occasional sales, exchanges, or purchases of firearms for the enhancement of a personal collection or for a hobby, or who sells all or part of his personal collection of firearms.

"Firearms show" means any gathering or exhibition, open to the public, not occurring on the permanent premises of a dealer in firearms, conducted principally for the purposes of exchanging, selling or trading firearms as defined in Sec. 18.2-308.2:2.

Professions and Occupations §54.1-4201.
Inspection of records

A. Every dealer in firearms shall keep at his place of business, for not less than a period of two years, the original consent form required to be completed by §18.2-308.2:2 for each firearm sale.
B. Every dealer in firearms shall admit to his place of business during regular business hours the chief law-enforcement officer, or his designee, of the jurisdiction in which the dealer is located, or any law-enforcement official of the Commonwealth, and shall permit such law-enforcement officer, in the course of a bona fide criminal investigation, to examine and copy those records related to the acquisition or disposition of a particular firearm required by this section. This section shall not be construed to authorize the seizure of any records.

Professions and Occupations §54.1-4201.1.
Notification by sponsor of firearms show to State Police and local law-enforcement authorities required; records; penalty

A. No promoter of a firearms show shall hold such show without giving notice at least thirty days prior to the show to the State Police and the sheriff or chief of police of the locality in which the firearms show will be held. The notice shall be given on a form provided by the State Police. A separate notice shall be required for each firearms show.

The promoter shall, not later than seventy-two hours prior to the opening of the show, by mail, by hand or by fax, transmit to the authorities to which prior notice is required, a list of vendors or exhibitors who have registered to sell or exhibit in the show.

The promoter shall maintain for the duration of the show a list of all vendors or exhibitors in the show and a copy of the prior notice for immediate inspection by any law-enforcement authorities, and within seventy-two hours after the conclusion of the show, by mail, by hand or by fax, transmit a copy of the complete vendor or exhibitor list to the law-enforcement authorities to which prior notice was required. The vendor or exhibitor list shall contain the full name and residence address and the business name and address, if any, of the vendors or exhibitors.

B. A willful violation of this section shall be a Class 3 misdemeanor.
C. The provisions of this section shall not apply to firearms shows held in any town with a population of not less than 1,995 and not more than 2,010, according to the 1990 United States census.

Professions and Occupations §54.1-4202.
Penalties for violation of the provisions of this chapter

Any person convicted of a first offense for willfully violating the provisions of this chapter shall be guilty of a Class 2 misdemeanor. Any person convicted of a second or subsequent offense under the provisions of this chapter shall be guilty of a Class 1 misdemeanor.

Title 55   Property and Conveyances

Property and Conveyances §55-248.9.
Prohibited provisions in rental agreements

A. A rental agreement shall not contain provisions that the tenant:
6. Agrees as a condition of tenancy in public housing to a prohibition or restriction of any lawful possession of a firearm within individual rental units unless required by federal law or regulation.
B. A provision prohibited by subsection A of this section included in a rental agreement is unenforceable. If a landlord brings an action to enforce any of said prohibited provisions, the tenant may recover actual damages sustained by him and reasonable attorney's fees.

Title 58.1   Taxation

Taxation §58.1-3504
Classification of certain household goods and personal effects for taxation; governing body may exempt

A. Notwithstanding any provision of §58.1-3503, household goods and personal effects are hereby defined as separate items of taxation and classified as follows:
2. Household and kitchen furniture, including gold and silver plates, plated ware, watches and clocks, sewing machines, refrigerators, automatic refrigerating machinery of any type, vacuum cleaners and all other household machinery, books, firearms and weapons of all kinds.

Title 59.1   Trade and Commerce

Trade and Commerce §59.1-148.1.
Purchase of firearms in contiguous state

Any resident of the Commonwealth of Virginia, including a corporation or other business entity maintaining a place of business in this Commonwealth, who may lawfully purchase and receive delivery of a rifle or shotgun in this Commonwealth, may purchase a rifle or shotgun in a contiguous state and transport or receive the same into the Commonwealth of Virginia provided the sale meets the lawful requirements of each such state, meets all lawful requirements of any federal statute, and is made by a licensed importer, licensed manufacturer, licensed dealer, or licensed collector.

Trade and Commerce §59.1-148.2.
Sale of firearms to resident of contiguous state

Any importer, manufacturer, dealer or collector licensed to sell rifles or shotguns in this Commonwealth may sell such firearms to a resident of a contiguous state provided the sale meets the lawful requirements of each state as well as the requirements of any federal statute pertaining thereto.

Trade and Commerce §59.1-148.3.
Purchase of handguns of certain officers

A. The Department of State Police, the Department of Game and Inland Fisheries, the Department of Alcoholic Beverage Control, the Marine Resources Commission, the Capitol Police, any sheriff, and any local police department may allow any full-time sworn law-enforcement officer or deputy, the State Corporation Commission may allow any agent, inspector, or investigator appointed pursuant to §56-334, and any institution of higher learning named in §23-14 may allow any campus police officer appointed pursuant to Chapter 17 (§23-232 et seq.) of Title 23, retiring on or after July 1, 1991, who retires after at least twenty years of service or as a result of a service-incurred disability to purchase the service handgun issued to him by the agency or institution at a price of one dollar for the weapon.

B. The agencies listed above may allow any full-time sworn law-enforcement officer who retires with ten or more years of service, but less than twenty, to purchase the service handgun issued to him by the agency at a price equivalent to the weapon's fair market value on the date of the officer's retirement. Any full-time sworn law-enforcement officer employed by any of the agencies listed above who is retired for disability as a result of a nonservice-incurred disability may purchase the service handgun issued to him by the agency at a price equivalent to the weapon's fair market value on the date of the officer's retirement. Determinations of fair market value may be made by reference to a recognized pricing guide.

C. The agencies listed above may allow the immediate survivor of any full-time sworn law-enforcement officer

(i) who is killed in the line of duty or

(ii) who dies in service and has at least twenty years of service to purchase the service handgun issued to the officer by the agency at a price of one dollar for the weapon.

D. The governing board of any institution of higher learning named in §23-14 may allow any campus police officer appointed pursuant to Chapter 17 (§23-232 et seq.) of Title 23 who retires on or after July 1, 1991, to purchase the service handgun issued to him at a price equivalent to the weapon's fair market value on the date of the officer's retirement. Determinations of fair market value may be made by reference to a recognized pricing guide.

E. The Department of State Police may allow any full-time sworn state police law-enforcement officer who retires as a result of a service-incurred disability and who was on disability leave at the time the Department issued 10-mm semiautomatic handguns to its officers to purchase one of the 10-mm semiautomatic handguns used by the Department of State Police at a price of one dollar.

F. The Department of State Police may allow any officer who at the time of his retirement was a full-time sworn law-enforcement officer and who retires after twenty years of state service, even if a portion of his service was with another state agency, to purchase the service handgun issued to him by the Department at a price of one dollar for the weapon.

Trade and Commerce §59.1-148.4.
Sale of firearms by law-enforcement agencies prohibited; exception

A law-enforcement agency of this Commonwealth shall not sell or trade any firearm owned and used or otherwise lawfully in its possession except

(i) to another law-enforcement agency of the Commonwealth,

(ii) to a licensed firearms dealer,

(iii) to the persons as provided in §59.1-148.3 or

(iv) as authorized by a court in accordance with §18.2-310.

NOTES

NOTES

About The Pensus Group

This book has been produced in cooperation with The Pensus Group. Pensus is an eclectic firm, comprised of individuals and companies active in diversified businesses. These range from commercial real estate development and public-private partnerships to marinas and an all-purpose outdoor western theme town, Cowtown. One division of the firm helps equip law enforcement agencies in 14 states, and Pensus owns Shooter's World, in Phoenix, Ariz., one of the largest retail gun ranges in America.

With the exception of a number of professional and scholarly papers (the principals all hold advanced degrees) *The Gun Owner's Guide Series* represents their initial venture in the book publishing field.

About Alan Korwin

Alan Korwin is a professional writer and management consultant with two decades of experience in business, technical, news and promotional communication. He is a founder and two-term past president of the Arizona Book Publishing Association, on the national publicity committee of the Society for Technical Communication, and a former board member of the Society of Professional Journalists, Valley of the Sun Chapter.

Mr. Korwin helped forge the largest enclave of technologists in the state, as steering committee chair for the Arizona Coalition for Computer Technologies; he did the publicity for Pulitzer Prize cartoonist Steve Benson's 4th book; he wrote a business plan which raised $5 million in venture capital and launched SkyMall; in an executive-level strategic plan he helped American Express define its worldwide telecommunications strategy for the 1990s; and he had a hand in developing ASPED, Arizona's economic strategic plan. Korwin's writing appears regularly in local and national publications, and he serves an extensive business client base.

In 1990 Mr. Korwin introduced a unique seminar entitled, *Instant Expertise—How To Find Out Practically Anything, Fast.* The 4-hour course reveals the trade secrets he uses to gather any information short of espionage—and this is not about databases. He also teaches writing (How To Get Yourself Published At Last), publishing (The Secret of Self-Publishing), phone power (How to Supercharge Your Telephones) and publicity (The Secret of Free Publicity), at colleges, for businesses and privately. His talk on Constitutional issues (The Pen and The Sword, Constitutional Rights Under Attack) is a real eye opener.

Alan Korwin is originally from New York City, where his clients included IBM, AT&T, NYNEX and others, many with real names. In 1986, finally married, he moved to the Valley of the Sun. It was a joyful and successful move.

About Steve Maniscalco

Steve Maniscalco served in the U.S. Navy from 1980 to 1986, achieving the rank of Petty Officer First Class. As a Submarine Sonar Technician he traveled extensively throughout the Atlantic, Arctic and Mediterranean Oceans and the Caribbean Islands. Steve observed that, remarkably, it all looks like the inside of a nuclear submarine.

Since 1986, Steve has worked for the U.S. government as a technical writer and an electronic technician. The majority of his government service was in the Norfolk, Va., area as a sailor and then as a civilian employee.

Steve moved to Phoenix, Ariz., in 1994, and made the switch from submarines to F-16 jet aircraft, writing technical manuals for aircraft trainers at Luke Air Force base. He is an active competitive shooter, having participated in literally hundreds of matches.

In 1995, Steve approached Bloomfield Press, proposing to co-author a book about Virginia gun laws. Steve brings to *The Virginia Gun Owner's Guide* his ambition as a writer, his passion for competitive shooting and an abiding interest in Constitutional issues.

Mr. Maniscalco recently quit his secure government position to devote himself as a full-time dad to his new son, Steven Blaise, a full-time husband to his wife, Leslie and a full-time writer to just about anyone who will pay him fairly for quality work. You are holding a sample of his abilities in your hands. To see his work as a web-page designer visit www.bloomfieldpress.com.

Order these books about firearms and personal safety from
BLOOMFIELD PRESS

"It doesn't make sense to own a gun and not know the rules." This is an ongoing theme at Bloomfield Press. No matter where you stand in the raging debates over a citizen's rights to bear arms, you must admit that if you've chosen to own a firearm—and especially if you own it for personal safety and self-protection—you'd better know what you're doing.

After knowing the laws (which sort of goes without saying, don't you think?) it makes sense to understand crime avoidance, and strategies and tactics for armed response in a dire emergency.

These are books for responsible and concerned private citizens. Know your rights and obligations. Help protect yourself and your family from firearms accidents and crime. Order your copies of these classic books today. **Wholesale orders are welcome!**

IN THE GRAVEST EXTREME
by Masaad Ayoob $9.95
Widely recognized as the definitive work on the use of deadly force. This former law enforcement officer describes what you actually face in a lethal confrontation, the criminal mindset, gun-fighting tactics, the judicial system's view on self-defense cases and more. Dispels the myths, truly excellent—a must for any armed household & especially CCW permit holders.

ARMED AND FEMALE
by Paxton Quigley $5.95
Read about the tough decisions of a former activist in the anti-gun movement, who finally chose the victor over victim psychology. Features lessons she learned through extensive study, research and personal experience. Compelling reading, packed with thought-provoking ideas and advice.

GUN-PROOF YOUR CHILDREN
by Masaad Ayoob $4.95
One of the world's leading experts on lethal force issues, this father of two shares his thoughts and very practical ideas on gun safety for kids in a classic short booklet. Includes a good primer on handguns for the novice.

THAT EVERY MAN BE ARMED
by Stephen P. Halbrook, $16.95
Put to rest any questions you have about the intent behind the 2nd Amendment. With 1,300 annotations, Halbrook looks at, reports on, and quotes sheaves of actual original documents of the founding fathers. There may be confusion on this issue in America today, but as you'll see, there wasn't any back then. The title is from a quote by Patrick Henry, "The whole object is that every man be armed. Everyone who is able may have a gun." Henry's peers make similarly unambiguous remarks, removing all doubt.

THE TRUTH ABOUT SELF-PROTECTION
by Masaad Ayoob $7.95
Get the facts on every aspect of personal safety, from evasive driving to planting cactus by your windows. Lifesaving techniques will help keep you, your family and your possessions safe, prepare you for defense if it becomes necessary, and guide you in buying lethal and less-than-lethal goods, from locks to firearms.

STRESSFIRE—Gunfighting Tactics for Police
by Massad Ayoob $9.95
Heavy-duty reading for advanced students and those citizens who want the deepest understanding of lethal confrontations and how to survive in a deadly encounter. Master lethal-force specialist Ayoob pours out the experience and techniques which make him a sought-after world-class expert, in a page-turning style you won't forget. Not for the faint of heart, this book will make you think.

NO SECOND PLACE WINNER
by Bill Jordan $14.95
An absolutely unique discussion of armed response by a man who literally made it his trade. Author Jordan worked the U.S. Border Patrol of the old days, for 30 years, and lived to tell about it. In the process, he became one of the deadliest shots of modern times. In an easy and unassuming way he describes with chilling clarity what it takes to come out on top of gun battles. "Be first or be dead... there are no second place winners." Packed with his personal tips on draw-and-shoot techniques, with wonderful stop-action photos.

The GUN OWNER'S GUIDE Series

THE ARIZONA GUN OWNER'S GUIDE
by Alan Korwin
"Indispensable"
–Arizona Highways Magazine
ISBN: 0-9621958-3-9 , 160 pp., $10.95

THE TEXAS GUN OWNER'S GUIDE
*by Alan Korwin
and Georgene Lockwood*
"Comprehensive and well-researched... bridges the gap between the complex laws and everyday life... your book is excellent." –Texas State Senator Jerry Patterson, Co-author of the Texas Right-To-Carry Law
ISBN: 0-9621958-5-5, 256 pp., $14.95

THE VIRGINIA GUN OWNER'S GUIDE
*by Alan Korwin
and Steve Maniscalco*
ISBN: 0-9621958-7-1
Coming in autumn of 1996, $14.95

THE CALIFORNIA GUN OWNER'S GUIDE
*by Georgene Lockwood
and Alan Korwin*
ISBN: 0-9621958-9-8
Coming in 1996

THE FLORIDA GUN OWNER'S GUIDE
*by Donna Lea Hawley
and Alan Korwin*
1-889632-00-7
Scheduled for early 1997 release

Why take chances when you can have a word-for-word copy of *every* state gun law, along with plain-English descriptions of everything about gun ownership and use—buying, carrying, permits, self-defense, deadly force, weapons laws, fed laws, youth laws, gun safety and more—this is comprehensive coverage of state gun law. Widely acclaimed, takes all the mystery out of bearing arms. You have a right to know what your laws are.

GUN LAWS OF AMERICA

Every federal gun law on the books, with plain-English summaries
*by Alan Korwin
with Attorney Michael P. Anthony*
ISBN: 0-9621958-8-X
368 pp., illus., softcover, $19.95

It's like having an entire gun-law library at your fingertips. Covers the hard-to-find "proper authorities" laws, the National Guard, the Militia, citizens, collectors, manufacturers, importers, global disarmament, explosives, great laws, bad laws, 70 pages of juicy intro material, the lost National Right to Carry; without a doubt *Gun Laws of America* is the fundamental firearm reference book.

"Outstanding" –Bob Corbin, former Arizona Attorney General

Also by Alan Korwin:
WICKENBURG! The ultimate guide to the ultimate western town
Learn all about this amazing American city, spawned by gold, now a visitor's delight.
ISBN: 0-9621958-1-2
176 pp., illus., softcover, $9.95

SCOTTSDALE
by Alan Korwin and William Franklin
Voted America's Most Livable City, visit the world-famous destination resort outside Phoenix in a full-color large format with luscious prose.
(American & World Geographic Publishing)
ISBN: 1-56037-019-X
96 color photos, 104 pp., $15.95

❖

Include $3 S&H for one book, $4 for two, and $5 for three or more. Send your name, address, and a check or money order to:

BLOOMFIELD PRESS
12629 N. Tatum #440
Phoenix, AZ 85032
1-800-707-4020 Visa/MC OK

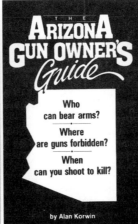

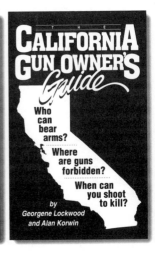

Published by

BLOOMFIELD PRESS

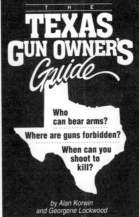

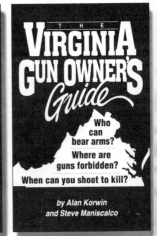